"Not since Leonard Cottrell's *Lady of the Two Lands* (1966) has such an engrossing, well-researched collective study of Egyptian power queens been available. Definitively recommended for anyone with an interest in ancient Egyptian civilization or women's studies." —*Library Journal*

"An accessible spin through the corridors of power in ancient Egypt, corridors that converged on thrones on which women reigned . . . Cooney provides welcome insights into pharaonic politics while bringing numerous little-known Egyptian women to the fore." —*Kirkus Reviews*

"This book shines as an introduction to ancient Egyptian society and beliefs centered around elite women's experiences." —*Booklist*

"Cooney discusses the women's leadership . . . and speculates about what they must have experienced...her stories of these remarkable women . . . will enchant those wishing to imagine what ancient Egyptian court life was like." —*Publishers Weekly*

"*When Women Ruled the World* (or at least the Egyptian part of it) draws the reader into many less known aspects of ancient history with an informal prose and style for the general reader." —*New York Journal of Books*

Christmas 2021

Dear Audrey,

Here's wishing you a
very Merry Christmas.
Hope you enjoy the book.
Love,

Grampy Tony
Grandma Pat

WHEN WOMEN RULED *the* WORLD

SIX QUEENS OF EGYPT

KARA COONEY

NATIONAL
GEOGRAPHIC

Washington, D.C.

Published by National Geographic Partners, LLC
1145 17th Street NW, Washington, DC 20036

First paperback printing 2020

ISBN: 978-1-4262-2088-3
Hardcover ISBN: 978-1-4262-1977-1

Since 1888, the National Geographic Society has funded more than 13,000 research, exploration, and preservation projects around the world. National Geographic Partners distributes a portion of the funds it receives from your purchase to National Geographic Society to support programs including the conservation of animals and their habitats.

Get closer to National Geographic explorers and photographers, and connect with our global community. Join us today at nationalgeographic.com/join.

For rights or permissions inquiries, please contact National Geographic Books Subsidiary Rights: bookrights@natgeo.com.

Interior design: Nicole Miller

Printed in the United States of America

19/VP-PCML/1

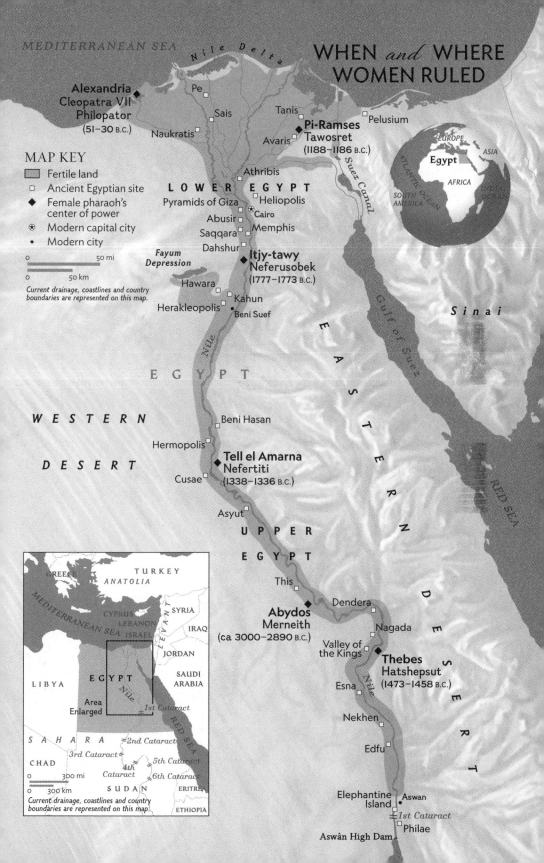

MEDITERRANEAN SEA

Nile Delta

WHEN and WHERE
WOMEN RULED

Alexandria
Cleopatra VII
Philopator
(51–30 B.C.)

Pe

Sais

Naukratis

Tanis

Avaris

Pi-Ramses
Tawosret
(1188–1186 B.C.)

Pelusium

Suez Canal

Athribis

L O W E R   E G Y P T

Pyramids of Giza

Heliopolis

Cairo

Memphis

Abusir

Saqqara

Dahshur

Itjy-tawy
Neferusobek
(1777–1773 B.C.)

Hawara

Kahun

Herakleopolis

Beni Suef

*Fayum
Depression*

MAP KEY

- Fertile land
- □ Ancient Egyptian site
- ◆ Female pharaoh's center of power
- ⊛ Modern capital city
- • Modern city

0 ——— 50 mi
0 ——— 50 km

*Current drainage, coastlines and country
boundaries are represented on this map.*

Globe inset:
EUROPE
ASIA
Egypt
ATLANTIC OCEAN
AFRICA
SOUTH AMERICA
INDIAN OCEAN

S i n a i

Gulf of Suez

E
A
S
T
E
R
N

E G Y P T

W E S T E R N

D E S E R T

Beni Hasan

Hermopolis

Tell el Amarna
Nefertiti
(1338–1336 B.C.)

Cusae

Asyut

U P P E R

E G Y P T

This

Abydos
Merneith
(ca 3000–2890 B.C.)

Dendera

Nagada

Valley of
the Kings

Thebes
Hatshepsut
(1473–1458 B.C.)

Esna

Nekhen

Edfu

D
E
S
E
R
T

RED SEA

Elephantine
Island

Aswan

1st Cataract

Philae

Aswân High Dam

Inset map (lower left):
GREECE
TURKEY
ANATOLIA
CYPRUS
LEBANON
SYRIA
IRAQ
ISRAEL
JORDAN
LEVANT
MEDITERRANEAN SEA
EGYPT
LIBYA
Nile
Area
Enlarged
1st Cataract
SAUDI
ARABIA
RED SEA
S A H A R A
2nd Cataract
CHAD
3rd Cataract
5th Cataract
4th
Cataract
6th Cataract
SUDAN
ERITREA
ETHIOPIA

0 ——— 300 mi
0 ——— 300 km

*Current drainage, coastlines and country
boundaries are represented on this map.*

ANCIENT EGYPT CHRONOLOGY

Year	Reign
ca 3200–3000 B.C.	Nagada III/Dynasty 0
ca 3000–2890 B.C.	Dynasty 1
ca 3000–2890 B.C.	**Merneith**
ca 2890–2686 B.C.	Dynasty 2
2686–2613 B.C.	Dynasty 3
2613–2494 B.C.	Dynasty 4
2494–2345 B.C.	Dynasty 5
2345–2181 B.C.	Dynasty 6
2181–2160 B.C..	Dynasties 7 & 8
2160–2055 B.C.	First Intermediate Period
2055–1985 B.C.	Dynasty 11
1985–1773 B.C.	Dynasty 12
1777–1773 B.C.	**Neferusobek**
1773–1650 B.C.	Dynasties 13 & 14
1650–1550 B.C.	Dynasty 15
1650–1580 B.C.	Dynasty 16
ca 1580–1550 B.C.	Dynasty 17
1550–1295 B.C.	Dynasty 18
1473–1458 B.C.	**Hatshepsut**
1338–1336 B.C.	**Nefertiti**
1295–1186 B.C.	Dynasty 19
1188–1186 B.C.	**Tawosret**
1186-1069 B.C.	Dynasty 20
1069–664 B.C.	Dynasties 21–25
664-343 B.C.	Dynasties 26–30
343–332 B.C.	Second Persian Period
332–305 B.C.	Macedonian Dynasty
305–285 B.C.	Ptolemaic Dynasty
51–0 B.C.	**Cleopatra VII Philopator**
30 B.C.–A.D. 395	Roman Period

CONTENTS

INTRODUCTION

Why Women Don't Rule the World

In the fifth century B.C., thousands of years after her lifetime, the Greek historian Herodotus wrote about a certain Nitocris, a queen whose husband-brother had been murdered by conspirators. The young, beautiful woman claimed her revenge by inviting all the collaborators to a grand banquet in a fancy and newly commissioned underground hall. When the men were all happily eating and drinking, Nitocris ordered the floodgates opened through a secret channel, drowning them all in Nile waters. The rebels thus dispatched, her final act was to throw herself into a fiery pit so that no man could exact his retribution on her. (One wonders whether the fiery pit could have been any better than whatever torture they might have meted out.) Two centuries after Herodotus, the Egyptian priest-historian Manetho, compiler of Egypt's most comprehensive history, included a section on Nitocris, adding that she had light skin and rosy cheeks, reigned alone for 12 years, and had a pyramid built in her honor.

Nitocris's story has everything: political intrigue, incest, fabulous Egyptian booby traps—and, most important of all, a beautiful young queen avenging her husband's murder with cleverness and bravery. Offing herself before they could take (presumably sexual) revenge on her makes her even more appealing. There is only one problem. There is no evidence from that time of Nitocris—no burial location, no statuary, no texts, no monuments, nothing—to prove that she was more than a historian's fantasy. But her narrative fits some extraordinarily familiar patterns for well-documented female rulers of ancient Egypt: She was the last ruler of her family dynasty; she acquired power by marrying her own brother; she acted in fierce protection of her husband, her brother, her patriarchy; she resorted to deceit and trickery to gain power over her enemies; and she was misunderstood by her own people, who would erase her image from monuments around Egypt. Indeed, there is enough to Nitocris's legend to suspect that what might seem like nothing more than a salacious story is actually composed of kernels of truth, embedded in a romanticized cultural memory that has come down to us in fragmented and dramatized form.

In one place on our planet thousands of years ago, against all the odds of the male-dominated system in which they lived, women ruled repeatedly with formal, unadulterated power. Like Nitocris, most of these women ruled as Egyptian god-king incarnate, not as the mere power behind a man on the throne. Ancient Egypt is an anomaly as the only land that consistently called upon the rule of women to keep its regime in working order, safe from discord, and on the surest possible footing—particularly when a crisis was under way.

We might forget that a culture so beautiful—with its golden masks and colossal statues, gods with crocodile heads, and hieroglyphs of whimsical complexity—was also ruthlessly authoritarian. We might also overlook that its tone—overtly masculine, defined by pyramids and god-kings and obelisks—was not just supported but enabled by its female foundation of power.

What about ancient Egypt allowed this kind of political and ideological power among the acknowledged weaker sex, plagued by pregnancy, nursing, monthly hormonal shifts, and menopause? It might seem incongruous for ancient Egypt's authoritarian state to support potential threats to traditional masculine power. Perhaps ancient Egyptian women were made of stronger stuff, gifted with ability and ingenuity greater than women elsewhere. Or maybe the Egyptians were more tolerant and less threatened by female political rule because they had created a social system of gender balance through laws that supported land ownership and social freedoms for both sexes, allowing women decision-making power and access to divorce. Or perhaps the polytheistic Egyptian religion, reliant on the defensive strength of ferocious, bloodthirsty, and mercurial goddesses—Sakhmet and Mut, Bastet and Isis—demanded that its adherents take the political acumen of women into consideration in the real world.

Whether women are too hormonal, grudge-bearing, untrustworthy, self-interested, child-oriented, or simply too softly feminine to hold real power is certainly a topic of discussion still, underscored by the 2016 U.S. presidential election between Hillary Clinton and Donald Trump. But these ancient Egyptian female rulers, though long dead, haunt us across the generations with their forthright presences, their intentions, and their unabashed authority, forcing us to question the reasons for their influence and continued relevance today. They demand we query why our grandmothers, mothers, sisters, and daughters are always swimming upstream, no matter how much they hustle. Why did women achieve such levels of formal power in ancient Egypt when so many others across time—up to today—have tried and failed?[1]

ONCE UPON A TIME, there were women who ruled the world. Six of them—Merneith, Neferusobek, Hatshepsut, Nefertiti, Tawosret, and Cleopatra—climbed the highest and wielded the most significant power: not as manipulators of their menfolk, but as heads of state. Each started as a queen—a mere sexual vessel of their king—but each became the chief decision-maker, and five of them served as king outright. Though each woman must have had the gravitas, skill, intelligence, and intuition to rule, each was also put in power by an Egyptian system that needed her rule.

But this positivist story conceals some darker twists and turns. These Egyptian women were power brokers, to be sure: educated for complex tasks and supreme leadership, ready to hold the highest position, able to see and move the pieces on the board. But viewed through another lens, they were utterly powerless, mere pawns of a patriarchal system over which they had no control and could never hope to alter in the long term.

Allowed into positions of real and formal authority, in the end their power was a short-term illusion each time it occurred. These female kings were mere placeholders for the rightful masculine leaders who were too old or too young to rule—or hadn't been born yet. Often, the men who came after them erased or omitted their names from the formal "king lists" of monarchs created by the royal temple.

In the long run, ancient Egypt was no less cruel and oppressive to women than every other complex society on Earth—but, here, they snatched the gift away after graciously bestowing it. So even ancient Egypt—the only state that consistently allowed female rule—suffered a woman leader only when it had to, expunging her from the eyes of her people as soon as possible.

To understand this strange and contradictory tale of unadulterated female power wielded by poorly remembered women over an extraordinary 3,000-year run of ups and downs, let us turn to the women themselves. If we follow their stories, their decisions, their circumstances—if we attempt to see into their private and public lives—then maybe we can comprehend how they ascended to the highest echelons of political power in the richest and most successful land of the ancient Mediterranean and North African world, only to be harshly judged for taking the power that had been freely given to them.

Merneith, one of the earliest embodiments of female power from ancient Egypt, ruled during Dynasty I (3000–2890 B.C.), at the dawn of the Egyptian nation-state, when kingship was new and brutal. She never took on a formal position, but she appeared in king lists as the person who ruled on behalf of a son thrust into the position of king too young. Eleven dynasties later, **Neferusobek** of Dynasty 12 (1985–1773 B.C.) gave structure to the power Merneith had held only through the men and boys around her. She was the first woman who took the Egyptian kingship as her formal title, ruling alone for about four years. Neferusobek achieved what Merneith could not.

Hatshepsut of Dynasty 18 (1550–1295 B.C.) created the most powerful female kingship Egypt had ever seen. Hers was a reign marked by accomplishment, clever strategizing, empire building, and prosperity. But the next king was not her son; indeed her lack of male offspring was what made her kingship necessary. Without a son to keep her legacy intact, her name was removed from the religious and historical record, her images scratched away, her statues smashed to pieces. Her rule was seen as a threat to the men who came after her—the very men she had personally placed into positions of power.

A century later, **Nefertiti**, also of Dynasty 18, would have heard stories of the audacious Hatshepsut. Nefertiti had to try a different tack to power, one that defended and shielded not only her femininity, but her identity. It is no surprise that Egyptologists still argue about whether Nefertiti achieved the kingship at all. She effectively did it in disguise, setting Egypt on a path to recovery after a period of great turmoil. Nefertiti is remembered to us as a great beauty, a chiseled face of loveliness and sensual desire. But she may have been much more if recent investigations are correct.

During Dynasty 19 (1295–1186 B.C.), another woman— **Tawosret**—found access to power through her husband, an unrelated royal heir, and brutal civil unrest. When she became king, Tawosret took a road neither Hatshepsut nor Nefertiti had dared tread upon. She ascended the throne unprotected by father or husband or son. Tawosret boldly stood alone as sovereign, eschewing secret identities, new names, or masculinization. Her tomb in the Valley of the Kings shows her as a female king, but that sepulcher would be taken over by the very same man who had her violently removed from power.

After Tawosret, female power lay dormant in Egypt for a thousand years. In a land where women had repeatedly risen to the top, achieving ever greater heights, Egypt fell to foreign empires, obstructing the female authority that kept the people of the Nile protected when everything fell apart. Then **Cleopatra VII** entered the scene. She almost doesn't belong on this list of ancient Egyptian queens, being a member of a Macedonian Greek ruling family (the Ptolemaic Dynasty lasted from 305 B.C. to 30 B.C.). But she too ruled Egypt, and likely knew of the great women who had sat on Egypt's throne before her. Her ascent to leadership clarifies Egypt's penchant for feminine rule as a necessary aid to shore up a weakened regime. Her entrée to power was through the men around her—father, husbands, brothers, lovers, sons. Cleopatra was a master tactician who understood how to manipulate her relationships to the benefit of her ambitions and of Egypt. If anyone in our story could have achieved genetic legacy, it would have been Cleopatra, via her children with Julius Caesar and Marc Antony. Her supposed obsession with glamour, greed, wasteful spending, and poor military strategizing have all ensured her place in history as a failure—but she was perhaps Egypt's greatest female ruler.

Egypt's political system allowed these women to rule—in fact, demanded they step into the arena of power—and it is that mystery we will attempt to solve by examining the strategy of each queen.[2]

The Egyptians certainly recognized that men were superior in terms of physical strength and biological economics (reproduction outside of one's body is both handy and efficient). But they also understood that leadership by a woman was always preferable to throwing in one's lot with a warlord. Most of the women in this book achieved power not through violence but through political consensus. As a rule, women recognize that their position is fragile; Egyptian female rulers understood the need to constantly shore up their power, rather than beat their chests and bang the war drums. This rendered them essential in moments of crisis. In calamitous times, women were invited into power instead of allowing violent men to exacerbate the discord. Relying on female leadership replicated the mythologies of ferocious goddesses protecting their dynasties: Isis shielding her son Horus from his homicidal uncle or Hathor protecting her father Re-Horakhty from rebels. Egyptian society elevated its queens, allowing them to rise up to the top precisely *because* a woman doesn't usually resort to military conquest and fractious aggression.

This doesn't presume that Egyptian female rulers were peaceful, however (Hatshepsut ordered brutal crackdowns on Kush; Tawosret probably played a part in the assassination of a chancellor and maybe even a king). But, in general, these female leaders didn't tend to foment war against their own. (Cleopatra is a notable exception, but when she raised an army it was against a brother who was trying to kill her, not against the Egyptians themselves.) But, overall, these women were the cautious choice for a circumspect and prudent Egypt when it seemed that all hope was lost.

The Egyptians were light-years ahead of us in their trust of female power. Indeed, many of us have become cynical, knowing that our society is not post-gender any more than it is post-racial. We can lament that the system is rigged, that there is nothing a woman can do to change society for the better, that all the biases against female power are already encoded into our DNA, that some of the most powerful women in American society have already been completely erased or forgotten because they don't fit traditional feminine values (think Janet Reno or Janet Yellen). We can bemoan the fact that we have demonized the women who demonstrate ambition (think Hillary Clinton), and that our society is unspeakably cruel to women, shaming them for their age, their looks, their weight, their height, their voices, their hair and makeup. We can complain that women are some of the worst critics of other women, that girls willfully denigrate other girls to maintain their social power. We may be a 50/50 society in terms of gender, yet women do not hold 50 percent of the power. We say it's because of the patriarchy, because it was never an even playing field to start with. But when the cynical voices rise, ancient Egypt calls out from the past, reminding us that there was once a society on this planet that valued a woman's calmer, more nuanced political skills.

Why are we so hostile to female rule yesterday and today, so rancorous to female ambition for power? How does that aversion take shape? Because we are not just talking about Cleopatra, Nefertiti, and Tawosret, but also Hillary Clinton, Angela Merkel, Margaret Thatcher, Theresa May, and Elizabeth Warren—all of whom have been discredited as erratic, drama-prone, inconstant, deceitful, opaque, flighty, illogical, even evil, ruled only by hot flashes and full moons.

I have been teaching a class at UCLA called "Women and Power in the Ancient World" for four years. In 2017, for the first time, I didn't have to convince my 200 undergraduate students of gender disparity. I used to document this phenomenon with slide after slide, illustrating the lack of women in leadership positions in Fortune 500 companies and modern government, unequal pay across the board, and the blatant lack of religious leadership by women within Jewish-Christian-Islamic-Mormon traditions in the world (not to mention within global Buddhist or Hindu leadership). But the 2016 U.S. presidential election revealed a visceral opposition toward women in power that did all the explaining for me.

In 2017, the revelations of sexual harassment and sexual assault against women by scores of powerful men in America brought the imbalance of power between the sexes into even starker relief. It's gotten personal. And nasty. Misogyny now has a face, but we avoid looking directly at its smudged, dirty visage as much as possible. New revelations of sexual harassment and assault committed by yet another man in authority appear every day—and yet we want to drop the hot potato of misogyny, desperate to talk about something else. Political scandal. Collusion with the Russians. Trump Hotel profits. Evangelical apologists. Everything and anything so that we don't have to talk about how we feel about females in politics; so we don't have to stand up for women like Angela or Hillary or Elizabeth; so we don't have to openly face how little power women have in our society and why they have such a hard time getting it; so we don't have to pinpoint how the American people took down Hillary Clinton through personal attacks based on phantom suppositions of misdeeds, including pizza parlor child-prostitute rings, rather than evidence. And so our pessimism continues to grow. None of the allegations of Donald Trump's personal flaws in this realm—his womanizing, past and present, a porn star among them, or the possible distributions of hush money to those many women—have swayed his base. Our hostility toward strong and empowered females is everywhere. What is it that we are afraid of?

If we put pictures of Theresa May, Angela Merkel, and Hillary Clinton alongside pictures of Vladimir Putin, Donald Trump, and Barack Obama, what might we notice about our unbidden responses, our own (mis)perceptions of power in men and women? Are they old or young? Are they sexy? (Did that question disturb you?)

Sexual value is social value to human beings, whether we openly admit it or not. A man can breed into his seventies. He essentially remains genetically useful until the end of his life; thus his political power can be rewarded, if he so chooses, with more sexual partners as a social bonus that many leaders still cash in on. By contrast, a woman in her fifties, sixties, or seventies can provide no such sexual value to society through reproductive viability; thus no female leader can take on more sexual partners because of her power. The very idea of an older woman—say, Margaret Thatcher—with a bevy of boyfriends is not only laughable; it is aberrant, perverted. But when Donald Trump bragged to Billy Bush about sexually assaulting women, many dismissed it as "locker room banter"—and yet he is the oldest president the United States has ever had. The older female is a crone—old, useless, discardable. Although we don't want to contemplate women's visages absent of beauty, the faces and bodies of older men in power have been normalized. Donald Trump is still considered deserving of his beautiful wife, many decades younger than he is. And shirtless Vladimir Putin, riding an ATV or working out at the gym, is a man who continues to use his sex appeal for political advantage.

Even if some of us might feel pride when we consider powerful women's achievements and the strength of their convictions, their authority often comes across as scary, angry, shrewish, or aggressive when compared to that of male leaders. Whether we want to admit it or not, voting a woman into office makes most Americans feel uncomfortable, even threatened, because she appears more strident and shrill and bossy than her male counterpart, according to countless sociological studies.[3] And so we come back to the stark reality in which we live: In modern history, few women have ascended to the position of political head of state in countries around the globe; few women find positions of power in the world's military systems; few women manage to become CEOs in economic powerhouses; and a female pope or Dalai Lama is unimaginable.

The end result of this discussion is that most of us—male or female—feel a hell of a lot more comfortable if a man tells us, decisively (even derisively) what to do. We are more likely to feel safe and protected if a man, rather than a woman, is ordering us into a war. And a man will be judged less harshly than a woman for strident speech and powerful arm gestures while firing up a crowd.

Simply put, modern female leaders are far more distrusted than their counterparts were in the ancient Egyptian world. And that is what I would like to examine in these pages: what female power has been in the past and what it can become in the future.

A long time ago, in a land far, far away, women called the shots with a regularity that stuns and confuses historians. Egypt fostered female ambition, knowing it would set its people on a cautious and steady course and save their world for millennia to come. Let's take a look at how these women were able to launch themselves to the pinnacle of their society.

CHAPTER 1

MERNEITH

Queen of Blood

From the very beginning of Egypt's formation as the world's first regional state, female rule was not only permitted, but required. This differentiated Egypt from other parts of the ancient world. A country protected by expansive deserts, stormy seas, and Nile cataracts, it was not threatened by constant invasions and massive changes of population, allowing the same religion, social structure, culture, and language to flourish and develop, in a strange petri-dish experiment, for almost 4,000 years. The result was an extraordinarily risk-averse society with few regicides or coups. Instead of being rewarded for highly competitive warlording, Egyptian elites found more incentive to go along with the pyramidal social structure and the status quo, even to the point of sacrificing their own lives—or those of their children—to see the kingship continue intact. Egypt would always be different from any other state in the Mediterranean, North Africa, or the Near East because its unique geography and topography forged the most perfect and stable divine kingship the world has ever known.

The ancient Egyptian king was unassailable—geographically, culturally, religiously. Even his name identified him as such: *nefer netjer*, "the perfect god." The first kingship had passed from the god Osiris to his son Horus, making each Egyptian king the living manifestation of the falcon god Horus ever after. The king was divine, even in human form, and his lineage was meant to follow from father to son forever. To protect this transfer of power when it was threatened, the female was essential because her emotionality—her perceived violent temper, scheming, magical abilities, motherly love, sexual desire—was the very tool necessary to protect the next king. A mother would be least likely to raise arms to compete with her own son. A wife, sister, or daughter would be closest to the king without acting as a potential political threat. This is why the richest and most fabulous tombs surrounding the king, from the earliest to the last dynasties, were usually of females. Queens were even given pyramids of their own in Dynasties 4 through 6 (2613–2181 B.C.) as well as Dynasty 12 (1985–1773 B.C.). The queen's power didn't compete with the patriarchy but rather supported it, providing it with strong foundations. For the ancient Egyptians, the masculine and the feminine were two sides of the coin of power. Queens were the king's best assets.

This inclusion of the female as an essential part of working government shaped Egyptian mythology and ideology as well. The scattered narrative fragments of Osiris, Horus, and the goddess Isis—from the Pyramid Texts to the Coffin Texts, private prayers, and mythological tales—are ancient, forged when kingship was developing along the Nile, when feminine power played a new and integral role in the running of the state, protecting the king from harm but also allowing the legal and just transfer of power from father to son.

The queen mother was the arbiter and protector of this divine and most delicate transition. Indeed, in the last temples dedicated to the divine feminine, in holy places like Dendera's Temple of Hathor, we see carefully crafted and detailed imagery of Isis helping Osiris to be reborn, in all its sexual glory. We see the god reaching out his hand to his erect member ready to re-create himself through sex with himself—but it is Isis who manufactures the circumstances for this miracle of self-re-creation to happen at all, facilitating and receiving the god's seed to make the next generation of kings, to conceive Horus, the god of kingship himself. It was Isis who bred and bore Egyptian kingship. It was Isis who acted as the magician who pieced her broken husband Osiris back together after his brother Seth had cruelly cut him up into dozens of pieces. She is the alpha and omega of Egyptian kingship.

The Narmer Palette, a flat stone with figured decoration made around 3000 B.C., is one of the earliest documents of Egypt's mighty kingship, and it is surmounted by images of the divine feminine. We see a cow goddess with curved horns. She bears no name on the stone palette; she might represent one of the cow goddesses Bat or Hathor. Whatever her name, it is she who fed, nurtured, and installed King Narmer's power. It is she who looks over him from the heavens and grants her support to his kingship.

The earliest written mythology for the divine feminine is found in the Pyramid Texts, first written down in Dynasty 5

(2494–2345 B.C.), in which the goddess is a mother, lover, daughter, bringer of food, provider of protection, the one who awakens the dead king, and the spark for the resurrection of kingship. Here Horus, as the heir of Osiris, finds his place; the chief actors are male, the system undoubtedly patriarchal, but these kings can succeed only because of the feminine, because of Isis and her kind. Just as the ideology of smiting justified the king's public execution of those viewed as dehumanized enemies, the ideology of Isis raised the status of the royal woman as fierce protector of the king (her husband, brother, or son), as well as purveyor of magic, fertility, and even apotropaic violence that orbited the monarch. But this same ideology must have supported the idea that the king needed female companionship in death, encouraging the sacrifice of hundreds of women, in addition to men, during the earliest dynasty of Egyptian kings. Their integral connection to kingship was, for many individual Egyptian women, also their undoing.

Ironically, then, a female could rule only in the most unequal of social systems, which could demand such human sacrifice: the most totalitarian and authoritarian of governments, in which giant behemoth statues are built and enemies are executed publicly and brutally, splattering the king himself with the blood and brains of his dispatched enemies. A queen existed only to support the patriarchy, to link father to son in an unbroken line of succession. (And that is the dark side of Egyptian queenship; it was not a sisterhood to promote other females or to broaden inclusive participation in government, but a mechanism to buoy up one man, and one man only.) Egyptian royal women helped to ensure the power of an exclusive and elite group—and thus the power of their fathers, husbands, brothers, and sons. They guaranteed prudence, safety, and protection.

In ancient Egypt, female power made a dramatic entrance when kingship was new and the state was in its first glimmers of formation. When the chosen successor to the kingship was too young to rule on his own, presumably after the untimely death of the king, it was decided that the child's mother would rule in his name. When the boy was old enough and mature enough to act on his own, the woman would elegantly, and discreetly, hand over the reins to her son. Allowing the woman to exercise power for a young sovereign was a perfect way to protect the patriarchal order, if only temporarily. Egyptologists call this a *regency* system, and the ruling woman a *regent*. The Egyptians never formalized the position with a title but used it unerringly to maintain dynastic succession without a break in the line or an invitation to conflict between men.

In such circumstances in most other places in the ancient world, rivals backed by armed forces would have swooped in, killed the king's son and close family, and taken over. But Egypt, with its protected borders, rarely experienced invasions from abroad. Military competition was generally not a means of advancing one's place internally, either (particularly during times of prosperity and functioning government). Egypt would develop into a safe and prosperous country, growing grain with little effort from the rich farmland inundated every summer season by the Nile. No more than a handful of kings were murdered over its long history.

It was, in fact, the perfect breeding ground for an invulnerable divine kingship to be forged. Only here, where one was rewarded—richly—for keeping eyes downcast and going along with the status quo, where money grew as easily as stalks of grain, where invading armies were always stymied by the desert sands that surrounded this massive riverine oasis, could such a profound belief in the sanctity of the king's person have developed without political pushback or cynicism. People are happy to do what they're told if there is plenty to go around; Egypt was so prosperous in agricultural and mineral wealth—gold, electrum, granite, turquoise, and carnelian—that armed competition among its people was not commonplace. The prudent and cagey Egyptian elites maintained their divine kingship at all costs over three millennia, more or less, of native rule—even when a king died unexpectedly, leaving a mere boy in charge of this most powerful country.

Even if the Egyptians denigrated the ruling potential of a woman because of her sex (and there is no indication that they ever did), it was in their best interest to allow educated, elite women to rule, if only to protect their prosperous, even easy, lifestyle, which suffered few outside competitors for the throne. If invasion from beyond was not a threat, then all one had to control were potential dangers from within. Thus, it was less perilous to allow the accession of an inexperienced and weak king than to end the dynasty and change the ruling family, which in turn would upend the administration—the thousands of officials, courtiers, and priests who held wealth and power in ancient Egypt. No one wanted to risk losing such easy riches.

By this logic, no one was interested in allowing an uncle to make decisions on behalf of his underage nephew-king. That uncle was a clear inside threat, potentially destabilizing a carefully balanced system of elite families. Egyptians understood that men are the most likely aggressors in human society, and that an uncle's interest would be best served by killing the young monarch and crowning himself in his place. The safest alternative was to allow women related to the young king into power—a tactic the Egyptians employed repeatedly.

In places like Mesopotamia or Syria, it made sense for the ruling elites to support an able-bodied and mature man as the next king—never a little boy, because the city-states of Northwest Asia suffered from constant territorial competition, warlording, and aggression, within a complicated and unstable system of switching allegiances. There were few natural boundaries. Protecting a young king there would have been foolhardy. But in Egypt, where the Nile rose every summer and receded every fall, leaving behind a fertile, rich mud in which to sow wheat, barley, and flax, and where roving bands of marauding troops rarely marched, perfect and divine succession was meant to move from father to son in a seamless and unbroken line.

If the new king was young and vulnerable, as the young god Horus was at the death of his father Osiris in Egypt's mythologies, then his mother should step in as protectress. This is what Isis had done when she took Horus into exile in the marshes, healing his many wounds from snakes and scorpions with her magic, and allowing him to grow strong enough to one day vanquish his father's murder and take his rightful place on the throne. Egyptian queen-regents were the repositories of Isis's protective actions, as again and again the mother would rise up to protect her son's claim to kingship and maintain this delicately balanced system.

MERNEITH WAS A QUEEN in Egypt's very first dynasty (3000–2890 B.C.),[1] who ascended the throne as mother of a king too young to rule on his own. Archaeologists found her name, accompanied by the title "King's Mother," on seals and sealings from her tomb and from her son, King Den's, tomb complex. She was chosen, it seems, as the least risky option to maintain the royal dynastic line. She would have already put an emotional and genetic investment in her boy. As the mother of the divine Horus, she had the gravitas to actually order around what might have been a recalcitrant and entitled child. She would have seen to his training in mind and body as bureaucrat, landlord, and warrior. She would have made sure, eventually, that his harem was full of beautiful young women, ready to bear potential successors. Merneith's agenda was the continuation of her family's dominance, even if her position also granted extraordinary and unprecedented powers to herself.

Finding Queen Merneith in the farthest reaches of history 5,000 years ago is a formidable task. We have only a jumble of architectural funerary evidence, punctuated by hieroglyphic inscriptions, themselves often indecipherable because Egyptian writing was in its earliest stages of development in Dynasty 1. Indeed, most of the women in this book are evidenced by the buildings constructed in their honor, not by descriptions of their characters. We don't know anything about Merneith's personality or her upbringing. We don't know about the obstacles she faced while acting as regent. We don't know how old she was when the responsibility of Egypt's governance was thrust upon her. We don't know if she was terrified at the prospect and questioned at every step or if she was prepared for the challenge and supported by a team of crack advisers. We don't know how she died (her mummy is not preserved to us, and even when a royal corpse is found, cause of death seems endlessly debatable). What we do know of her can only be reconstructed from the rich findings of archaeologists at the royal burial complexes in Abydos and Saqqara—so macabre that we quickly perceive that she faced challenges and grief unthinkable to most of us today.

When Merneith was a young girl, kingship in Egypt was shiny and new. King Djer, probably her father, had been the second ruler of Egypt's very first dynasty, a family lineage that began with her presumed grandfather King Aha. Strongmen had been fighting for the ultimate prize of kingship for some time in Egypt already, consolidating more and more territory along the Nile Valley and within the Nile Delta until the two regions of North and South were fully united. This process extended back in time a thousand years to the early fourth millennium, when stronghold towns existed in places like Nagada and Hierakonpolis in the Nile Valley and at sites like Maadi and Tell el-Farkha in the Nile Delta.

The ancient Egyptians understood their realpolitik as a cosmic conflict between South and North (Upper and Lower Egypt). Upper Egypt proved victorious and claimed the first dynasty. It was the birthplace of kings, easily uniting townships along the Nile River under the leadership of one man who used that foundation to extend his power over a delta that was more scattered and harder to consolidate from within. The predecessors of Dynasty 1 include kings like Scorpion and Narmer, southern men who documented their dominance over all of Egypt with decorated maceheads or stone palettes showing temple processions, brutally dispatched battlefield dead, or violent rituals (which we can assume actually took place) of the king crushing enemy skulls with a stone mace.

Despite a southern origin, when Egypt was unified into the first regional state on this planet, these kings made the city of Memphis, at the juncture of Upper and Lower Egypt, their capital stronghold. This is where the most important marketplaces and urban centers were, where the kings' biggest palaces were located, where the greatest temples were constructed— even where modern-day Cairo is located.

Though lost to us today, the main royal palace at Memphis would have been built of mudbrick, plastered and painted a gleaming white that reflected the sun's brilliance. All along the exterior, the palace walls were built with recessed niching—a nested set of tall rectangles placed one inside the other, the innermost one the shape and size of a door, creating a kind of false entrance, repeated along the walls. Each niche may have been painted with brilliant red and yellow ochres, carbon black, and Egyptian blue and green pigments.

This stunning polychrome palace wall decoration was the most visible part of this new institution of kingship for the vast majority of people who never met or even saw the king. The monarch was protected behind closed doors, ensconced behind high, whitewashed walls. His symbol thus became the niched recessing of the walled palace itself, what we now call the palace facade. The nesting rectangular design was carved onto seals used to close vessels and doors, onto palettes to grind malachite pigment for eye makeup, onto decorated maceheads displayed aloft in the king's or the priest's hand in the temple. The palace facade was the symbol of kingship par excellence in Dynasty I, and the first written name of the Egyptian king was found within such a rectangular enclosure upon which the falcon of kingship stood.

Symbolically, the king *was* the palace and everything it contained—its wealth, its bureaucracy and taxation, its land rolls, its ceremonial activities, its careful ordering of elites in the audience chamber, and its exclusion of those who didn't belong. The king was embodied in the palace's sunlit courtyards, commodity storage rooms, the royal nursery filled with the king's children and nursing mothers, and the harem apartments filled with young women attending to their skin, coiffure, and fragrance.

It was within the protected walls of such a palace that Merneith likely grew up. Surrounded by the hustle and bustle of urban life outside, she lived in a cool and clean mudbrick structure appointed with textiles and cushions, filled with all the luxuries the peasants never saw—cedarwood from Lebanon, fragrant resins from abroad, fine imported wine (the Egyptian climate was better for beer), fluffy breads, fatty beef and duck in excess. She would have been dressed in linen of the highest thread count, made of the youngest flax fibers, soft and gossamer-thin, to drape her body, wearing jewelry made of blood-red carnelian and azure turquoise from the Sinai, twilight-blue lapis lazuli from as far away as Afghanistan, and gold, always an abundance of gold, from Egypt's own eastern deserts and southern Nubian mines. She anointed herself with frankincense and myrrh. She wore crushed malachite of a rich, dark green around her eyes. Her high position later in life as regent to her son testifies that her own status in the palace was high. Her mother must have been one of her father's most favored court wives, of high elite status, likely from a wealthy family, perhaps very beautiful. High status came with a price, however; she likely saw her share of female aggression and maneuvering in the palace nursery and harem.

The death of the king was a time fraught with doubt, worry, and insecurity—especially when kingship itself was in its infancy, and some Egyptian cities and towns still refused to be ruled by it. Having finally secured a unified Egypt in just the last few generations after hundreds of years of violence, with all the concomitant bloodletting still fresh in their cultural memory, these Dynasty 1 kings manifested their power over their subjects with an obvious and unmistakable monumentality. They built huge palaces with white walls many stories high, temple statues of gods three times as tall as a man, and massive tombs bigger than anything seen before. The Dynasty 1 kings also reified their power with an unblinking stare at human sacrifice, murdering the same elites with whom they had shared a cup of wine, sat at the table for a meal, or held in embrace in the dark hours of the night.

Human sacrifice of family members served multiple purposes simultaneously. First and most important, it viciously culled the most dangerous and threatening elements of elite society.[2] Ancient Egyptian institutions were by their very nature cautious, and it seems to have made sense to the first wielders of divine kingship to dispose of all internal threats to the throne once the next king had been chosen.[3] For a few hundred years of Egypt's history, none of the other contenders for power may have been allowed to survive after the chosen one had ascended it and locked in his succession. Indeed, many of the skeletons of sacrificed dead around the tomb of the king have been determined to be young males, creating a circumstantial case for exactly this kind of politically protective behavior.[4]

To create a royal transfer of power from one king to another with no potential hazards demanded many things: a virile king with a productive harem and nursery, many viable sons, a mysterious and thus unquestionable selection of the next king, and, finally, the removal or disappearance of any potential contenders to the throne. In most later time periods, male royal offspring were specifically not given the title "King's Son" to use into their adulthood and were expected to instead melt into society as one of the other elites (even though all the courtiers would have known his royal parentage). But in Dynasty I, the chosen King's Brothers may have been considered so hazardous to the succession that they were killed in a ritualized and sacred setting.

Other sacrificed bodies belong to women. What threats could they possibly have posed to the next king? Many, it seems. If a particular woman's son was not chosen as king, she could, potentially, attempt to overthrow, or kill, her son's brother. Maybe it had happened before. Or maybe the inclusion of females as sacrificial victims to the king can be explained simply and easily: The king needed sexual partners in the afterlife, just as he needed servants and artisans, who were killed to accompany the king in death, too. Many of the sacrificial victims of the Dynasty I kings were organized according to social status—the highest-ranking women often placed closest to the king's body with the vanguard of young men laid close by as fan bearers or bodyguards and the lowest-ranked people farthest away. Dynasty I Egyptians didn't engage in sacrificial burials with evil intent, but because it was believed that such an act secured a safer future for all. However kingship was contrived in ancient Egypt, it was a bloody journey if the sacrifice of a few hundred souls seemed preferable to the potential threat of allowing them to live.

To manage the transition from dead to living monarch, the new king asked for great sacrifice from his people. He called for beloved family members to walk freely into death before their time, joining the afterlife of their dead lord. We don't know the details of selection or the mechanisms of death, a frustrating reality. But it is possible that there was only one king's son left standing at the end of these bloody rites. We must then imagine that this new king knew and loved many of those who were asked to die. They were likely his own brothers and uncles, his own sisters and aunts, maybe even some nieces and nephews, close palace associates, and friends.

The first day of a new kingship in Dynasty I was characterized not by joyous celebration, but by deep grief and loss. This was not a triumph; it was a brutal misery of publicly performed human sacrifice, maybe lasting weeks or even months, taking place in multiple sites around the country, in rituals that surely tested royal composure. Being a member of the first Egyptian Royal Family meant a life ensconced in luxury, to be sure—but also an insecure existence lived on a knife's edge, utterly dependent on the continued life and impending death of the one man at the top of the social pyramid. When the king died, hundreds went with him—most willingly, for all we can see, but some must have fought, if only instinctually, to save their lives. And what did the king promise his elites in return for their precious lives? Nothing less than immortality itself. Given the evidence of a profound belief system, there must have been some level of rejoicing through the tears.

♛

THE LONG-LIVED KING DJER has just died. His courtiers, including his daughter Merneith, find themselves in an uproar of emotion and worry. Steps are immediately taken, if they haven't already been, to determine who will be king next. We know very little about the method of choosing the royal heir in ancient Egypt—not just in Dynasty I but throughout Egypt's history. Indeed, not much from ancient Egypt is more shrouded in secrecy than the royal transfer of power. Did the king simply choose his eldest son, as many historians assume?[5] Did courtiers sit in quiet huddles, trying to make a politic choice, balancing the differing agendas? Or did the Egyptians allow the gods to choose in a veiled, sacred ritual that took the onus of responsibility away from the courtiers and wiped away all vestiges of realpolitik from the written record? Let us allow for a complicated combination of all of the above.

The sacrificial burials surrounding her father's death would be the first of Merneith's lifetime. They would not be her last. At Abydos alone, 587 people were killed for her father, according to the latest archaeological count: 500 more people than had died for his father before him.

The new king, Djet, did not hold back in the preparations for his father. These macabre rituals took place in at least two locations: North and South. There is still scholarly disagreement about where the body of the king was actually interred.[6] Indeed, the kings of Dynasty I seem to have built at least two tombs, one at Abydos in the South, ostensibly their ancestral homeland, and one or more grand mastaba tombs in the North at Saqqara, at the capital. Each location received sacrificial burials, not to mention unimaginable wealth and commodities deposited into underground storage rooms for the king's consumption in the afterlife.

Merneith was not slated for death. She was needed to join the harem of her (possibly half) brother Djet. She had a purpose still to serve. And so she stood on the white sands ritually laid out at the Saqqara killing fields and watched as her beloved kinsmen and -women were taken from her. Her keening would have matched that of the other young women with whom she stood, their arms upraised, their breasts exposed, pulling at their hair, scratching their chests with their fingernails in mourning. Merneith was likely quite young, maybe still a girl, when she experienced the first significant trauma of her life as not just her father, the king, was taken from her, but so many other precious souls.

How much time was given to the courtiers, girls like Merneith, for emotional recovery before the next stop on the journey? Probably not much. With grief and loss fresh in their minds and armed with the deep belief that the sacrifices kept the king, and, by extension, his country, safe from harm, the court would have packed up and made its way upriver, tacking in their sailing barges to make the eight- or nine-day journey south against the current to the royal necropolis of Abydos, where many more of those in the funerary party would soon die.

Egypt existed only because the river Nile cut through this dry expanse of Northeast Africa. Humanity hugged its banks. Along the route, peasants on the river's edge would have witnessed the somber procession of barges, heard the wailing and weeping, seen the women with heads on their knees, hands covering their faces, and immediately known what had happened. The king was dead; long live the king. And then they would have seen the new monarch in the process of empowering himself with blood: crowned, somber, seated on his throne under a small cabin at the rear of a large barge. The biggest and most embellished boat would have held the body of the dead king, prepared for burial perhaps using some early form of mummification or body desiccation, his corpse wrapped in linen like an effigy, probably dressed in jewels and finery and shielded from human eyes in some kind of shrine. The body would be revealed to his courtiers within the sacred confines of the funerary enclosure at Abydos, where the killing would begin all over again.

The funerary enclosure at Abydos was probably two or three stories high, and it was meant to be an exclusionary place, only allowing the 1 percent of society in and keeping the unclean peasantry out. Anything that happened inside could not be seen, only heard, by those outside: screams and wailing, music and chanting.

Killing nearly 600 people can't have been an easy feat, and it was probably not accomplished in a single afternoon or even a day. There were no bullets, no guillotines to speed the process along—just the standard ancient methods of poison or strangulation or stabbing or bloodletting. We don't know how these people died because the bodies show no obvious marks. Most of the skeletons show no struggle, either. However, excavator William Petrie insists there is evidence that some people were buried alive, because hands were found upright, covering the mouth and nose. Only a very few bodies were trussed and tied.[7] Most, it seems, were simply laid in the grave on their sides in a fetal position of sleep and rebirth, a calm repose that would have been difficult to achieve if they had been killed against their will or engaged in a scuffle. Some skulls show evidence of trauma, but too little to be conclusive of death from a blow to the head. Maybe most were dispatched with a cyanide-type poison, so that they could say goodbye to loved ones as they fell into death.[8] However these people were killed, every elite lost a loved one in those bloody days. Merneith may have lost her own mother in these cruel rituals.

After the sacrifice, at least 269 dead were placed in long trenches outside the four walls of Djet's newly built mudbrick enclosure, with at least 318 more in the trenches surrounding the king's tomb.[9] The local laborers compelled to move these bodies would not have forgotten what they had seen that day. Each grave was marked with a small limestone stela—a flat slab of stone with images and writing—with the name of the deceased, and each grave was separated from the others by simple mud-brick walls. Though sacrificed, these dead were honored and accompanied by grave goods, some of them buried with objects associated with the power they had held in life: cylinder seals if they had been important officials, weapons if they had served as warriors, tools if they were skilled craftsmen.[10] Archaeologists found the remains of wooden coffins in many graves, proving that this was an orgy of economic excess as well as sacrifice. Upwards of 600 wooden coffins represented no small expense in a desert land where wood was a scarce commodity and the best varieties were imported.

About 85 percent of the dead surrounding the tomb of Djer— at least of those for whom markers could be read or bodies identified—belonged to women.[11] Two of these women were quite important, with larger graves located closest to the king's burial chamber, identified with what may have been queen's titles. In all likelihood, one of these two burial spots had been prepared for a high-ranking woman, like Merneith's mother. Perhaps Merneith herself helped to bury her mother, sitting in vigil over the body while it was washed and wrapped, lovingly laying the corpse into the resting place provided, making sure that the proper grave goods were put in place. When archaeologists found these women's tombs, they were surprised to see masses of curled human hair, likely from these women's wigs, a macabre detail of their gender identities.

The burials around King Djer's resting place were reserved for his most intimate associates—wives and court entertainers. Two of the limestone stelae identifying the dead show that a pair of dwarves were also interred, and archaeologists found a skeleton that has dwarflike physiognomy.[12] These men were probably favorites of the king—good luck symbols, entertainers.

When the king and his treasures were finally installed in the Abydos tomb, the hole was filled with clean white sand and then capped, probably with some kind of a mound, now long gone. The massive enclosure was also dismantled, ritually taken down to the first few layers of brick, walls pushed in on themselves, most of the bricks probably then taken to build the enclosure of the next king just next door. The new king Djet had the whole enclosure covered with the same clean, white sand, leaving no visible trace of the horrors witnessed over the previous days or weeks: something that only archaeology would reveal 5,000 years later.[13]

Sacrificial burials were a power display fueled by a nascent kingship, clearly seen and consumed by the very people they were meant to control—elite families on the inside of the power structure who could theoretically threaten the king. The practice worked, establishing a deep reverence for authority and maintaining a status quo by show of blood to support a patriarchal system of power. Thus, one finds among those sacrificed no prisoners of war or slaves, but elite women and men—the young, the healthy, the valuable. Why bring the old and infirm into death? How could they serve their ruler? Why kill the least valuable and most dehumanized before an audience if this would produce no authentic sounds of mourning for the beloved leader? No, instead we see young adults and children sacrificed before the eyes of their parents, mothers sacrificed in front of their children, brothers in front of their brothers. The power to waste such precious human life was seared into the memories of all who witnessed it.

Sacrificial burial was abandoned when Dynasty 1 was over and another ruling family took control. When the new kings of Dynasty 2 (2890–2686 B.C.) took power, it was likely a good political move to abandon such rituals in order to become the kind and loving shepherd of the people, rather than the king who fed on the blood of his subjects. The practice was no longer needed in any case. Egypt's divine kingship had been firmly established, and there was no fear of overturning the authoritarian and patriarchal regime any longer. Starting with Dynasty 2, the Egyptians made due with stand-ins, like cattle or other animals, figurines of servants performing tasks, or statuettes of sexy ladies bringing food offerings, all of which could be interred with the dead.

MERNEITH NOW SERVED as one of King Djet's many wives. After the death rituals, she would have returned to the palaces of Memphis and Heliopolis with the sovereign, her lord and god-king master, traveling with the court up and down the Nile as need and pleasure required. We know little about her husband, except that he was the fourth king of Dynasty 1 and his name was that of a cobra, able to strike and kill his enemies, as we see from the well-preserved limestone Abydos stela that bears his name and is now displayed in the Louvre Museum in Paris.[14]

No matter how long Djet's reign, it ended unexpectedly, before any of his sons could grow to adulthood. When he died, he left much unfinished business, including mere boys as potential heirs and many anxious elites to sort out the rest. This was Egypt's first documented succession crisis, and it hit when the regional state was still in its infancy. The son chosen—Den—was much too young to have ruled on his own. Merneith, the boy's mother, was brought forward, it seems, to handle the practical decision-making for him. Merneith became one of the first recorded in a long line of queen-regents who ruled for sons who needed time and protection to grow into their crowns and thrones.

The evidence for Merneith's regency is circumstantial, as it is for every Egyptian queen-regent. The Egyptians, it seems, never wanted to directly state that the king's mother was calling the shots. The best evidence we have that Merneith ruled for the boy is her inclusion in a number of king lists. These include contemporary texts that name her as King's Mother in a lineup of other monarchs and, perhaps, on the great Palermo Stone,[15] a monumental temple inscription naming every Egyptian king from Dynasty 1 to Dynasty 5 (3000–2345 B.C.), now housed in a museum in the Sicilian city of Palermo. How young Den was when chosen as the next king remains, as we must expect, completely veiled from our eyes. But his occupation of the throne thrust Merneith into power. Indeed, Den may have been selected as the lucky candidate specifically because of his high-ranked and presumably educated and strong-willed mother: a woman the elites could all agree on to take the reins of Egypt's leadership, if only temporarily, while Den grew into a man.

Merneith's first responsibility as regent was to bury her husband, King Djet, in another round of sacrifice and economic excess. This would absolutely prove to her people that her young son could sit on his throne unaccosted, safe, and empowered. Her previous experience with sacrifice, probably 10 years earlier, must have haunted her memory. Still, she had no choice but to see the rituals done. For the young King Den and his mother Merneith, it was much more than a brutal establishment of kingly dominance. It was a means of showing everyone that just because the next king was a mere boy, the gods still favored him. Merneith could not hold back and let gentle emotion take over. And so she buried her dead husband with sacrificial numbers second only to his father's, a few hundred souls fewer than the almost 600 people buried with the venerable Djer.[16] Merneith did not shy away from the crueler necessities of this transfer of power.

But Merneith made some key changes in this round of royal retainer sacrifice. She seems to have buried more important and established people, and more men. As Egyptologist Ellen Morris explains ominously, those sacrificed for King Djet "moved from quantity to quality"—fewer, but more important people, as evidenced by the stelae listing their elite titles.[17] It seems likely that Merneith was tasked with personally deciding who would receive the honor of accompanying the great god, King Djet, into death. The practice was not just to show honor, but to feed the power of the newly dead god-king, so that he could help sustain the living monarch here on Earth: her own son. The king's fledgling power had to be fed with blood, it seems. There was no better means of creating a compliant elite during a succession crisis than shock and awe, the promise of a fast track to membership among the favored afterlife court of the god-king, and an indispensable moment to rid a very young son of potential threats to his throne.

Who were the most likely threats to Merneith and her son, now a young king? The boy probably had many brothers whose bloodlines were just as impeccable as his own. Perhaps there were even older Kings' Sons. Let us assume that Merneith was indeed the daughter of a king (Djer) and the sister-wife of another king (Djet). If so, then her son may have had primacy of position when succession was in play because of the high-ranked mother to whom he was born. Other Royal Sons, born to lesser wives, even if they were more mature and able to rule, may have been passed over because of their lower female lineage. Whatever the circumstances, it would suit Merneith well to rid her son of all these threats. At the same time, Merneith may have been viewing other court families with increased suspicion.

A young and immature king provided the perfect opportunity for insurrection, rebellion, coup, and assassination. Better to remove all potential threats at the beginning of this vulnerable kingship, showing each and every elite family who was boss.

It was likely no small thing to Merneith that her son's accession to the throne may have saved her own life. Had another boy been chosen, she might have accompanied her husband into death as his helpmate, protector, and sexual companion. But she still had duties to fulfill for the living Horus on Earth. The King's Mother would have been an essential courtier, even after the king reached maturity, keeping the king's harem full, watching over the nursery of royal children, and keeping a careful eye on the goings-on at court. In Merneith's case, her role as King's Mother was even more integral, for she was making all the practical decisions for a king too young to rule.

The first stop on King Djet's funerary journey into the afterlife was probably Saqqara, where most of the important people lived. As Merneith and her son watched, dozens of courtiers would be sacrificed and buried around a great mudbrick tomb probably belonging to the dead king. This was young King Den's first experience with such gory rituals. We can only imagine how it formed his character or what Merneith may have said or done to protect his tender emotions, or to harden his heart, upon watching friends and family die before his eyes. It seems the new king had to get his hands bloody, too, because in one burial chamber once lined with wood and gold leaf, archaeologists found the skeletons of two young gazelles on a mudbrick platform. The throats of these animals, representative of chaos, were perhaps cut in front of the body of dead king Djet: an act probably performed by the heir to the throne, the very young King Den, maybe even instructed in the task by his mother and regent.

Merneith and Den made sure the tomb was stocked with all the material possessions a king would ever need in the heavenly realm, including a magical wand of ivory, furniture, tools, sandals, golden implements, and, of course, human beings. The subsidiary burials rounded out the king's possessions, and he took at least 62 souls with him in his tomb at Saqqara. Even some of the king's dogs were sacrificed to accompany their master.[18]

Most of these graves are of young adult males, but a disturbing number are females accompanied by a child. What use would it have been to Merneith to sacrifice women who could have later joined her son's harem? No, these were likely rival wives and their sons, Den's brothers, who could have been chosen as king instead. And Merneith and Den must have been hyperaware that this could have been their fate had Den not been marked somehow as monarch. Merneith left her name on the whole bloody affair: Stone vessels with her name and titles on them were found in Djet's Saqqara tomb, some calling her Sma-nebwy Merneith—She Who Is United With the Two Lords, Merneith[19]—perhaps a clear statement that she was the link in the chain between the dead and the living king. At Abydos, even more people were sacrificed under Merneith's supervision: 154 people were placed around King Djet's funerary enclosure, and at least 174 around his tomb, for a total of 328 individuals.[20]

Merneith ordered the deaths of fewer people than had accompanied the previous king, but what was her strategy? What was the pattern? Unlike the sacrifice for her father, the majority of the dead for her husband were male adults. (There were no children sacrificed at Abydos, at least as far as the archaeological reports clarify.) It seems Merneith made the calculated decision to cull the masculine threats to her young son's throne (and from what we know of Dynasty I rites, these men all went to their deaths willingly, probably in a brilliantly whitewashed funerary cult enclosure whose walls mimicked a palace, shielding the sacred rituals from prying eyes). The mourning from this sacrifice would have been mostly of female voices, of mothers mourning their sons, sisters mourning their brothers, daughters mourning their fathers, as Merneith willed these elite men to remove themselves from her (and her son's) sight and accompany the dead king into the afterlife.

Merneith understood power and succession, and these rituals clarified that her son was the next in an unbroken and sacred line of kingship. She may herself have been the great-granddaughter of Narmer, one of the first kings to rule over both Upper and Lower Egypt, and she illuminated her son's place in this lineage when she buried King Djet with an alabaster jar bearing the name of King Narmer, one of the first Abydos kings, an essential ancestor.[21]

If the burial proceedings of her father had traumatized her, those for her husband must have hardened her. Merneith willingly exercised a dark and terrifying power for political control on behalf of her son. Her life in court was pampered and luxurious, to be sure, but she forged her real authority in blood, death, and public sacrifice. We can be sure that she had personally seen Narmer's stone palette housed at the Temple of the Falcon God at the archaic site of Hierakonpolis to the south and understood the images of enemies carved into the stone, publicly dispatched and beheaded, their heads placed between their legs, the dead men arranged in neat rows. She must have seen such skull-crushing rituals against enemy combatants herself, during the reigns of her father and husband. Death—of foreign antagonists or of loved ones—was part of her life. From childhood, she knew that even the members of the royal palace were expendable, exchangeable, and, when given the honor of accompanying their god-king into death, they had no choice. It was up to her to select wisely from among those people who could serve her son's new kingship best.

Merneith probably ruled six to eight years for her young son, until he reached the age of about 16 or 17. We have no idea how old the Egyptians felt a ruler needed to be, but given short life spans in an anxiety-ridden world hit hard by constant epidemics and rife with accidents, parasites, and infection, adulthood in the ancient world would have started early, especially for a king. The Palermo Stone king list mentions King Den and includes the achievements year by year of his reign, including strange and vaguely understood events like "The First Time for Counting Gold" in Year 4 and "Second Census of the Cattle Count" in Year 5, both of which were formal displays of the king's riches and must have happened under his mother's rule.[22] Merneith was shoring up her land's economic foundation, knowing that with more wealth came political power. The Palermo Stone does not record how many years she lived, but we can assume that she continued into the sole reign of her son, influencing him and more gently directing his rule until she died.

♛

MERNEITH'S OWN TOMB was initially thought to belong to a king when it was discovered by British archaeologist W. M. Flinders Petrie in 1900. She was buried at the royal necropolis of Abydos, in the same lineup of great monarchs of Dynasties 1 and 2, in a tomb of the same approximate dimensions and of the same building technique and materials as the men before and after her. It wasn't until more attention was paid to the funerary stela found at her tomb that archaeologists began to think there might be more to the tomb's inhabitant than met the eye. The stela was inscribed simply with the name Merneith, Beloved of the Goddess Neith, carved in raised relief on its surface.[23] The archaeologists who discovered the tomb wondered why the name Merneith was not accompanied by a hawk hieroglyph at the top, as this denoted the god Horus and divine kingship incarnate, a necessary accompaniment to any king's name on such a stela. It was only with the discovery of a short list of kings from an adjacent tomb that archaeologists realized that Merneith was female, probably a queen. On a short king list made just after her death, Merneith's name is written between that of King Djet and King Den, accompanied by the title King's Mother. But why would a King's Mother have been buried like a king? Merneith must have acted as regent for King Den, archaeologists realized: her power so palpable that her son had thought she deserved the kingly honor.

Her tomb was well built. The subterranean burial chamber was dug into the sands of southern Egypt and lined with mud-bricks, creating walls that were plastered and whitewashed. No trace of her body survives, but it must have been carefully prepared and laid at the central chamber of her tomb, lined entirely with precious imported wooden planks. The mudbrick chambers around her body were filled with grave goods, some of which were found exactly as they had been deposited by the undertakers 5,000 years before, in pottery vessels once filled with beer, wine, olive oils, perfumed unguents, honey, and other foodstuffs. Many of the items found in her tomb do not bear her name, but that of her son, because it was he who allowed her this honor of burial in the royal necropolis.

Merneith's tomb contained horrors as well as treasures. Surrounding it were grisly trenches filled with the dead, canals in the sand lined with mudbricks and separated by single brick walls so that each sacrificial victim would have a room of his own in the next life. Who were these people? It's hard to know for certain. Most do not have preserved names and titles. Perhaps some were women who served as domestic servants or men who toiled in scribal duty, taking down tax rolls and writing diplomatic correspondences or historical records. Some may have been young warriors who acted as guards and servants of the dining hall or gamekeepers of hippo and crocodile hunting in the marshes. Forty-one skeletons were uncovered at Merneith's burial site, surrounding and protecting their lady's body. Another 79 souls were deposited around her funerary enclosure,[24] the massive, once brilliantly whitewashed structure where her funeral likely took place under the watchful and nervous eyes of assembled elites.

Such a tomb is a testament to Merneith's value to her people—to her son, King Den, and to her courtiers, elites with military power enough to overthrow her and her young son if they had wanted to. How old was her son when she was buried? Maybe in his thirties or forties, if he ruled for fortysomething years from around the age of 10. How old was Merneith at her death? Maybe 50, certainly mature by ancient standards. What were Den's feelings toward his mother? Respect, certainly. Love and tenderness, maybe. Bitterness, perhaps. She had been the queen-regent acting as placeholder for her young son, lacking any formal position of power. The Egyptians nonetheless honored her with a king's burial.

Presumably, Merneith herself was part of the planning for her own tomb preparations. The Egyptians started such things early. Construction of her grand and kingly tomb may have begun during her regency with her personal input, and then later with her son's explicit support and permission. A regency must have been a tricky thing, even for the Egyptians who relied on it so often: If you never take power formally, it can never be formally taken away. Merneith probably stepped back from the real decision-making as her son came of age, but likely he would always have been in awe of her, deferring to his mother's wishes and opinions. As long as she was alive, the co-reign between herself and her young son probably persisted, no matter what Den may have thought privately on the matter. And we see that, even into death, this woman had the authority to order the ultimate extravagance for herself, this tomb—a display of power so great that it was reserved only for god-kings, confounding the archaeologists who found it 5,000 years later.

♛

SINCE THE HISTORY OF MERNEITH is very much an accounting of death, we can let the dead communicate the relative importance of their masters. Merneith's other tomb, at Saqqara,[25] contained just a few dozen sacrificial graves, but here she also received a solar boat burial, to ferry her along the Milky Way to the Northern Imperishable Stars, where the kings dwelled, or to join the circuit of the sun on his East-West route—no small honor for a queen-regent and almost certainly provided by her son, King Den, placing her on par with every male ruler in the necropolis. At Abydos, 120 sacrificial victims accompanied her body: not a massive number in comparison to what had come before.[26] Why so few? That she was a woman was immaterial. Less blood was shed for her because her death did not bring with it the vulnerability of royal succession. There was no need to cull the ranks of young men who could threaten a new kingship at her death; her son lived on as king. Her burial would not have necessitated the same ritual sacrifice to protect a vulnerable power transfer as for her father, her husband, or her son—all of whom had many more victims than she did—because they required them to secure the throne.

Merneith also possessed no harem to accompany her into death, no wives to bring with her. And, likewise, there were no boys in the nursery whose continued existence could harm her offspring's nascent kingship. Therefore, the individuals sacrificed for Merneith may show a lower status with no real hierarchy because she just brought her household servants with her. As it happened, Merneith's end did not require a selection, or any kind of political statement. Thus, fewer people in total, particularly fewer young and valuable members of society, were asked to die. Not only did a woman's rule protect Egypt's royal lineage at a vulnerable point; it also lessened the brutal impact of sacrificial burial on its people.

Merneith was likely not even the first Egyptian matriarch to rule on behalf of her son. In the earliest years of Dynasty I, a few generations before Merneith was born, at the royal city of Nagada, a queen by the name of Neithhotep probably ruled as regent after the death of another great king of which history is uncertain, either King Narmer or King Aha. She acted as regent for the young king's son, waiting for him to grow into his own authority.[27] Queen Neithhotep's name was even contained within the palace facade in one inscription, an honor generally reserved for kings.[28] Merneith was the only other queen known to have been given this honor. When Neithhotep's tomb was found at the site of Nagada, it was also thought by the discovering archaeologists to belong to a king.

Merneith must have known of this great queen who blazed her path. They even shared a name with the Goddess Neith, one of the oldest and fiercest of Egyptian female divinities: the symbol of the Red Crown of the North, a bloody reminder of the darker side of female power, the huntress, the vicious protector of kingship and the defender of the royal line, the one whose bloodlust had to be slaked with intoxicants. Both of these queens were well-named, given the actions they had to perpetrate to protect their royal lineage.

Just as Neithhotep seems to have been the matriarch of Egypt's very first dynasty, Merneith set up her son King Den to act at the dynasty's apex. Den was her greatest legacy. He grew into his reign with grace and skill. He was the first to use the title King of Upper and Lower Egypt, something every king after him would copy. His tomb preserves imagery of him defeating enemies of western Asia, probably on a campaign in the Levant, labeled as "The First Smiting of the East"[29]—an action Egypt's later warrior-kings, like Thutmose III, another young king empowered by a female regent, would mimic.

Den also left inscriptions in the Sinai peninsula—the first Egyptian king to do so—where he led campaigns to get the Bedouin population there under his control.[30] His reign is believed to have been 42 years in length, including Merneith's regency: an astonishing amount of time to establish his control over the farthest reaches beyond Egypt, extending the borders farther than any previous king. The Palermo Stone includes extraordinary detail about his reign, giving notable events year by year, including "The Making of a Statue for Weret-Wadjyt" in Year 18 and "The Smiting of the Setjet People" in Year 19.[31] There was much smiting of different peoples and much building of divine statues and holy places during Den's time as king. He was both a warrior and a pious chief priest, reigning during prosperous times.

The Egyptians understood that to make a fine god-king, to fashion a foundation of power safe from warlording and competition, they had to invite a woman into the key role as decision-maker. Only a woman could put a susceptible and weakened country on better footing.

In the end, what was Merneith's legacy? Do we remember her? Or, more important, did the Egyptians? The answer may be the expected and deflating no. Memory of her would be short-lived, as patriarchy demanded, even if it was her cautious, feminine rule that saved Egypt's kingship. She does appear on a king list found in the tomb of her son—but just a few reigns later, on inscriptions from the last part of Dynasty I from the tomb of Qa'a, one of Den's successors, there is no longer any mention of Merneith.[32] Neither is she included in any of the lists of kings from later times—those inscriptions or papyri that name who begat whom in an unbroken line of royal succession. Thousands of years later, when the Ramesside kings documented their power, attempting to connect to the archaic kings of old, they didn't include Merneith, the woman who kept the patriarchal line of Dynasty I alive, paving the way for their own kingship millennia later. Like so many Egyptian royal women who stepped into decision-making power, Merneith was used when she was expedient, because her agenda as Royal Daughter, Wife, and Mother demanded prudent behavior and not risky action. She was asked to lead the country and its people and was then discarded from the annals of history. But she ruled, nonetheless.

Once power had been formalized and a status quo created in the blood of their relatives, the next queens would see their power reified. No more informal status markers. The next queens of Egypt would take the title of King.

CHAPTER 2

NEFERUSOBEK

The Last Woman Standing

Merneith was Egypt's trailblazer. But other women soon picked up the mantle of sovereignty, some influencing the king behind the throne as queen-mother, as in Dynasties 4 and 5, others calling the shots on behalf of their young kingly son, as happened often in Dynasty 6. There is even the story of Nitocris, mentioned in the Introduction, who supposedly took the 6th Dynasty kingship into her own hands after avenging the murder of her brother-husband. Since the only evidence we have for this account comes from Greek sources almost two millennia after her probable lifetime, Nitrocris's story is sadly relegated to mythology rather than history.[1]

But in Dynasty 12, another Egyptian woman would rise, and for her we have unshakable evidence—of her person, her life, and her radically different means of attaining and keeping power. This woman would—stunningly—act as head of state without any male accompaniment. She would serve as the last monarch of her withered family, of her dead father and husband, of her deceased brothers, of her soon-to-be-defunct dynasty.

There is no feminism to speak of at this point in history: no preserved understanding on the part of any of these women that their rule could potentially change the patriarchal system going forward. There was also no sense that saving a family dynasty based on masculine succession meant acting against women's own future interests in political power. How could there have been such socially radical ideas in ancient Egypt, one of the most unequal societies on the planet, where control was concentrated among a few dozen wealthy families, dependent on pure linear succession? Still, that very same authoritarian regime might occasionally allow women to rule alone and close out a dynasty for the very reason that women often govern differently from men: tamping down competition and veering toward protectionist decisions, avoiding scorched-earth policies, and building consensus. Female rule kept power within the family unit. It was a further means of protective consolidation for a society that would rather suffer a woman ruler than allow an unrelated warlord to step into power, potentially triggering generations of brutal conflict thereafter.

Such lone-wolf women were generally in charge of Egypt for just one to five years. They ruled without a living male companion, lover, or co-ruler (or at least none are preserved in our documentation). Such women had already failed to produce a son; otherwise, they wouldn't have been in this position. Strangely, none of them could save her dynasty in the end, each serving as the last gasp of a family line. With the deaths of most of them came a new ruling family. This was a pattern that would repeat itself as ancient Egyptian civilization matured: Nitocris of Dynasty 6 (if later sources are to be believed), Neferusobek of Dynasty 12, and Tawosret of Dynasty 19. All closed out their dynasties; all ruled alone; none was able to put one of her children on the throne after her.

It's for this very reason that these women are shrouded in mystery. Indeed, few new dynasties celebrate the preceding ruling family. Nitocris's history was well erased by those who came after. We may be perplexed that these women were allowed to rule at all. But their sovereignty provided time to reset the board for another game, a few years of peace and safety, even if everyone understood that this female king was only delaying the inevitable.

But there's another piece to this puzzle of female rule in ancient Egypt. This wasn't just a question of strategy and logic; it was also a question of fervent religious beliefs. In many ways, allowing a female king in this Northeast African land was the inevitable result of a deep and abiding faith that a king was actually divine in body and soul. Thus, there is every indication that the daughters of such a godly monarch deserved the same respect and social elevation as his chosen male heir. There was, it seems, a religious need among the pious Egyptians to allow the royal line to expire to its very last gasp precisely because it was imbued with the supernatural. Whether that ultimate breath came from a male or female ruler didn't seem to matter. That was how much they revered their god-kings.

This is not to say that there was no realpolitik at play. The practice of female rule at the end of a dynasty allowed the Egyptian elite families time to gather their political and economic forces, to shore up their support for their own push for the throne. Time and again, in Dynasties 12, 18, and 19, we see royal women—daughters or wives of the king—stepping into the breach to contain a succession crisis, to allay the fears of the elite families, and to keep Egypt functioning. But each time the Egyptians allowed such a woman to rule—old maybe, unpartnered certainly, without progeny of her own—it was only a short-term solution, putting off the inevitable battle (military or political) for the throne. In a way, the most astounding part is that the ancient Egyptians would so often choose the path of the female king at all, instead of picking a capable man in some way related to the Royal Family: a man who could sire sons, rather than a barren older woman.[2] But the Egyptians opted for prudence and caution, favoring direct linear relations of the king, repeatedly choosing King's Daughters as their rulers, even if they could not continue the royal line themselves. Ancient Egypt is probably the only state on Earth at that time that would willingly choose a non-procreating individual to head up a hereditary monarchy. It's a strange decision.

How an Egyptian dynasty could even fall into the crisis of having no male heir is perplexing. The harem provided one man with multiple women, sometimes in multiple places, in order to produce as many children as possible. There must have been dozens of women populating the harem in Dynasty 1, hundreds of wives in Dynasties 6 through 12, and in later dynasties perhaps even a thousand brought in to sexually excite, service, and reproduce for the god-king of Egypt.[3]

Where was the harem located? What did it look like? We hardly know. Only a few locations have been identified.[4] As need would have it, they were often attached to royal palaces—mud-brick structures with whitewashed walls, polychrome decoration, and embellished floors. Courtyards would have been open to the sun, probably shaded by date palms and fig trees, populated by birds, monkeys, and fish in pools. Each harem would have an accompanying nursery to raise and educate the king's off-spring. The harem was staffed by male officials who administered the lands connected to it, making sure enough income was received from those lands in the form of grain (money in the ancient world), flax, and other commodities. They even made sure the royal women were working at the harem crafts, some of them producing linen fabric of the highest quality on a loom. Having sex with the king and bearing his children was only one of many responsibilities for these women; it seems the Egyptian harem was meant to be economically self-sufficient.[5]

The harem's very purpose was to intensify the sexual repro-duction of one man—the Golden Horus, the Lord of the Thrones of the Two Lands, He of the Sedge and the Bee, the Bull of Egypt. One of his main duties as king was to visit the harem as often as possible, to impregnate as many women as possible and thereby maintain Egypt's future. This was not just practical political strategy; it was sacred duty. The King's Sons were as important to Egypt's continued success as the flooding of the Nile or sowing wheat and barley in the fields. Given all the advantages of palace, wealth, and an overabundance of fertile women, what could go wrong?

A number of things, it turns out. We can imagine that at least a few of the kings in Egypt's history had little interest in women and wanted to sleep with men instead. Even in such a situation (always unwritten, mind you), we can imagine the monarch would at least make some effort to reproduce. His family's future depended on it; he wouldn't have been the first man with homosexual tendencies to fit within the strictures of patriarchal society. If the king were unable to perform sexually, his condition was probably no secret; we can be sure that the harem women would have been charged with doing their best to excite, entice, and procreate—maybe with helpful advice from the King's Mother or some other official.

But even if everything worked right in terms of interest and bodily function, the king's seed might be infertile. Most monarchs were chosen for the throne as functional young adults, and thus a gossipy court would have been cognizant of the king's physical appearance and defects, including his sexual preferences, deviance, and past ability to sire children. But sometimes, the new king was chosen as a child, unable to be sexually active or produce children when crowned. Such a young king, divine though he was, would have constituted a giant question mark to his people until he could start visiting the harem to reveal the extent of his sexual abilities, and courtiers could see with their own eyes the fruit of those sojourns. Until then, there would be nothing but whispers in palace corridors and talk of possible magical or medical prescriptions (there was little difference in the ancient world between doctors and magicians) or other political solutions. The lack of a male heir was nothing less than a risk to national security itself.

The Egyptian royal harem, for all its advantages, introduced another problem to the Royal Family line: incest. It is well known that relations between father and daughter or brother and sister will result in less viable, less attractive, less healthy offspring. The taboos against incest take on religious, moral, and economic dimensions for almost all cultures and peoples. Biologists have proven natural aversions to incest even in animal species.[6]

If, however, you happen to be monarch of all Egypt—the most powerful kingdom in the Mediterranean, the ancient Near East, and Africa—well, then, incest might be viewed differently. The Egyptian king might copy the sacred relationship of godly brother-sister pair Osiris and Isis, whose incestuous union nonetheless produced Horus, that falcon god representative of omniscient kingship on Earth. Isis and Osiris had sexual relations because, according to legend, the world was new and the only beings populating the Earth were the four children of the Earth god Geb and the sky goddess Nut: Seth, Nephthys, Isis, and Osiris. Did the Egyptian Royal Family practice incest because of this mythology? Of course not. The mythology was undoubtedly formed by the social necessity and human behavior that preceded it.

In the human realm, the political and economic reasons for the practice of incest were compelling, allowing wealth and power to remain within one close-knit kinship group. If a powerful and wealthy man has a daughter, he will look for a young man from a nearby influential family as a prospective husband for her. Then, he must provide his daughter with a dowry—

lands, furniture, and clothing that she can take with her to her new home. Not only that, the father must now welcome his new in-laws into his family in some capacity, giving a share of his wealth to them, giving them a measure of decision-making authority over his daughter and her offspring. Biological health can come with economic and social costs, not to mention a loss of political control.

As a result, Egyptian kings often took a different tack. Having a highborn princess marry her own brother when he became king, instead of another elite man outside the family, kept the wealth and influence safe within the household. There were no pesky sons-in-law to wrangle and cajole. There was no question as to who controlled the upbringing of the children born to King's Daughters when they were also a product of the King's Son. Therefore, many Egyptian princesses stayed in the palace, never leaving to form a household of their own.

This practice of self-protection and power-hoarding created a special place for the Royal Daughters of ancient Egypt, many of whom were elevated to the position of Great Royal Wife—the highest-ranked queen—when marrying a (half) brother who became king. Many such Royal Daughters also held important priestly positions as a power extension of their living father or brother, serving at his pleasure and at his side in complicated rituals within Egypt's sacred temples. Highly designated women—Royal Daughters and Sisters especially, but also Royal Mothers—were the most visible and viable members of the Egyptian king's court; their names and images were often published in the reliefs carved into temple limestone and sandstone because they, as women, were little threat to him. They acted for Egypt's masculine divine kingship, for the protection of their own dynastic line. These women were the very foundation of a king's power.

So how often was the offspring of an incestuous union chosen as king? Often enough. It was a smart strategy to choose the product of an inbred royal union—not just to enrich the king's close family, but to maintain the balance of power among elites and courtiers as well. Such a choice avoided any asymmetrical relationships between the elite families. An outside family whose daughter bore the next king could suddenly rise dramatically in stature and wealth in relation to all the others, thus destabilizing a carefully calibrated system.

Choosing the offspring of an incestuous coupling, however, risked a different kind of problem of which the Egyptians must have been well aware: poor health and the potential sterility of the next king. So, generation after generation, the Egyptian Royal Family was faced with an extraordinarily difficult choice. They could pick the son whose parentage would keep regicide and warlording at bay, maintaining all the elites in their current positions of power and wealth, preserving the status quo for the next 10 to 20 years. Or they could look further into the future, erring on the side of healthy biological offspring, and select the heir produced by a nonroyal woman from a powerful provincial family—cognizant that the woman's father (and the new king's grandfather) would want an important position at court and a significant increase in income. The girl's brothers (the new king's uncles) could also be counted on to throw their weight around in the palace, expecting revenues and influence of their own—to say nothing of all the cousins and distant relations who would hope to profit from the union.

If we accept that human nature hasn't changed much in the last 4,000 years—that people in power like to keep it that way—we can expect the ancient Egyptians to have opted most often for the course of action with immediate benefits: incest. Not every time, of course, but whenever it was expedient. Taking into account the very short life spans of these ancient people in comparison to our own—25 to 30 years was average, according to most demographers; 50 years of age was practically ancient[7]— it might have seemed a useful decision for everyone involved. We modern humans, with our life spans of 80 or 90 years, might look on institutionalized incest as self-sabotage. But we do not have the ancient Egyptians' cautious political perspective, nor their anxious, short-term outlook on life.

We do, however, share the same difficulty with long-term thinking. Even when our own shorelines are disappearing, when flooding and radically high temperatures are palpable in our cities, when droughts make water scarce and increase tensions, when mass migrations begin from war-torn regions with ever scarcer environmental resources, we still put off the decision-making that would change course on human-induced climate change. Such farsighted decisions demand community agreement and continuity of action over genera-tions—something that is tricky to manage politically because such course changes destabilize us economically, geographi-cally, militarily, even religiously.

And thus, for 3,000 years, the ancient Egyptians clung to royal inbreeding as a lifeline, quite literally, resorting to it again and again, even if it meant a succession crisis in a decade or two when sterility inevitably set in. Indeed, many courtiers must have seen the impending disaster coming from miles away. Not only did these educated elites know their history, being well aware of how past dynasties had ended, but they saw with their own eyes the health and appearance of these children as they grew up in the palace. Some royal offspring, particularly those of the King's Sisters, would have had weak hearts, cleft palates, strangely shaped faces, vast overbites or underbites, overly large heads, malformations of limbs, or clubfeet, as well as intellectual deficiencies. The courtiers also noticed that the king preferred the beautiful and symmetrical products of nonincestuous coupling when he visited his harem. They saw which women were more fruitful and which couldn't conceive. Yet, in the end, when it came time for a choice between a beautiful and fierce son produced by the daughter of a strong governor and landowner from Upper Egypt who had access to armed men and great resources of his own, or that strangely shaped and somewhat dim offspring of the King's Sister whose interests were fully bound up with the palace and who had no family to introduce potential upheaval—well, too often, it seemed the collective choice was the unhealthy one.

Dynasty 6 may have ended, in part, because of incest. So, too, probably Dynasty 12. And Dynasty 18, if Tutankhamun, with his own clubfoot and DNA showing incestuous origins, represents such systemic choices. The two stillborn fetuses found in Tutankhamun's tomb are evidence of what happens by look-ing inward toward anemic political protection, rather than outward to vigor and strength. The dynasty of Tutankhamun started off with a full brother-sister marriage and almost saw its demise right out of the gate when Amenhotep I—the product of that sibling union—could produce no children of his own. Even with a course correction after Hatshepsut, Dynasty 18 returned to its incestuous ways and probably met its end owing, in part, to the taboo.[8]

This means, of course, that female power in ancient Egypt would have been at its height when royal incest was also most prevalent, when Royal Daughters and Sisters married their king and became influential queens. The more inbreeding, the more influence the royal women exerted—an uncomfortable alliance for everyone involved. One might have thought that inbreeding would somehow have been legally or morally disallowed in the ancient Egyptian Royal Family at some point, given the obvious hazards. But incest was the go-to strategy even for the Mace-donian Greek kings who began their native rule in Egypt in the fourth century B.C. Indeed, the Ptolemies practiced brother-sister inbreeding with a documented and alarming consistency never seen under the Egyptian kings of old.

♛

QUEEN NEFERUSOBEK enters our story at the end of her dynasty, when the full effects of her family's inbreeding would have been most pronounced. The queen's forefathers of

Dynasty 12 had moved their capital city to a new and virgin location near the Fayum, a verdant and rich offshoot of the Nile, south of Memphis. This was a land of intensified agriculture and great wealth: an oasis of beauty and calm, close enough to Memphis to connect with its old moneyed elites, but far enough away to create a base of power separate from them. The Fayum was the calling card of the Dynasty 12 sovereigns, tucked away, isolated. It was also the realm of the god Sobek, the fierce and virile crocodile deity of the Nile, after whom Neferusobek herself would be named. This new capital city was situated at the entrance to the Fayum oasis, and it was called Itjy-tawy—"The One Who Seized the Two Lands"— established by Neferusobek's great-great-grandfather, Amenemhat I, the first king of Dynasty 12, when the family line was fresh and new.

Amenemhat I seems to have started out as a mere vizier, serving the Dynasty 11 kings in Thebes. The method of his power grab is unknown, as the Egyptians were typically silent about such unsavory historical details that marred their perfected kingship. Whatever way Amenemhat may have seized the throne, it was he who moved the capital city to the Fayum, only to be killed not long into his sovereignty by a trusted, but unnamed, person in his new palace. This act of unexpected regicide and sabotage by a courtier threw the Egyptian authoritarian regime into disarray and panic. No one knew whom to trust. People named names. Others went into hiding. There are veiled references in the literature of this period about what happened after the king was assassinated. The family of

Amenemhat I began interrogations; other elites took flight; men and families went into exile. Everyone in Egypt was busy deciding whose side they were on.

These were the tendentious beginnings of Dynasty 12, when it was open to threat and exposed. Queen Neferusobek found her place at the dynasty's bitter end, some 200 years later, when the Royal Family turned to one another to keep safe. By the time Neferusobek appeared on the Egyptian scene, the Dynasty 1 tombs of Merneith at Abydos and Saqqara were already a thousand years old, and the cultural knowledge of the sacrificial burials that took place in those archaic burial grounds had faded to a distant and forgotten murmur. Whether or not Neferusobek was aware of what Merneith had achieved so long ago, she only had to look a few miles north to the grand tombs of the many powerful queens of Dynasties 4, 5, and 6 for inspiration. She would need it.

Crisis was coming. If other Egyptian dynasties had gone out with a whimper of slow dissolution, degradation, and decadence, then Dynasty 12 went out with a bang of sudden and surprising dysfunction. Up to this point, Dynasty 12 had been characterized by extraordinarily strong kingship, but it was about to experience a sudden, inexplicable, and unforeseen vacuum of power. The turn of events necessitating Neferusobek's rise must have been a shock to every Egyptian elite who had a stake in the political game, including her. It was an abrupt fall after reaching the loftiest heights of authoritarian control.

Neferusobek's grandfather, King Senwosret III, had taken on Egypt's powerful provincial landowners and won. He had expanded Egypt's foreign borders to its farthest extent: into the Levant to the north and into Sudan to the south. Egypt's territories were as vast as they had ever been. He made this Nile stronghold—and, in particular, its royal treasuries—richer than it had been for generations. Senwosret III's foreign campaigns were legendary and brutal. Egyptian intellectuals wrote poems about their king's ferocity, inventing creative and beautiful new ways to communicate how their lord had vanquished his vile foe, leaving nothing but a bloody and dismembered pulp.

Senwosret's son and Neferusobek's father, Amenemhat III, thus inherited in the year 1860 B.C. an Egypt that was safe, consolidated, and fabulously wealthy, practically drowning in gold and precious stones. The king had reset the balance of power over his elites, pulling more of their agricultural resources into his own vaults. Huge sources of income were being exploited as never before. The mines in the Sinai, with turquoise, copper, and amethyst, were running at full tilt, as were the gold mines in the eastern deserts and Nubia. Grain production was also going strong. Once the provincial landowners were vanquished and their private armies seized, much of their income could be funneled directly to the palace to distribute to elites and temples as the king saw fit. Amenemhat III would rule for an astonishing 45 years—a reign characterized by plenty, by unshakable control of his people, and by an astoundingly secure Egypt. But nothing destabilizes royal succession better than a king who hangs on to life too long, nor the undocumented and unmentioned products of family incest who likely populated the royal nursery.

Neferusobek was likely born toward the later end of her father's 45-year reign. She had an older sister, named Neferuptah (Beauty of Ptah), who would marry her own long-lived father, thereafter elevated to the position of a King's Wife. Neferusobek learned young that the King's Daughters were often reserved to marry the king themselves. If their lord was blessed with long life, as their father Amenemhat III was, then those girls might join their father in his bed when they were old enough. Indeed, Neferusobek may have been anticipating the day she herself would marry her father and be elevated to the title of King's Wife, as her older sister had been.

Neferusobek was born into the greatest of excess. She was the product of the royal harem and nursery, a King's Daughter. She was ostensibly born to a mother who was one of hundreds of other women who sexually served king Amenemhat III; if her mother had been a King's Daughter, too, there is no record of it. Neferusobek would have understood in her bones the scheming ways of women to whom much is given in terms of material goods and luxury but scarcely anything noteworthy in terms of purpose and activity. She would have learned the destructive boredom of the women in the harem. She would have witnessed firsthand their political machinations, as each tried to seduce the king better than the next woman, so that she could produce the next royal heir and become the next King's Mother, thus winning the golden ticket to running the entire royal harem—if not Egypt itself through her son.

Neferusobek would have seen girls brought in from all over Egypt to marry her father, to excite him and draw out his seed.

She would have seen some pregnancies thrive and others fail. She would have heard the screams of women dying in child-birth, the groans of those in the final pushes of successful labor, or the wailing of women who held a dead son in their arms, maybe succumbing to the latest intestinal scourge to hit the palace. As a girl, Neferusobek must have felt the sting of a slap if she said something inappropriate or went someplace forbid-den. She saw the difference in the treatment of royal boys and girls: upbringing, breastfeeding, training, thread count of their clothes, education, all of it. In the harem, the birth of a girl was greeted with disappointment and an attempt to conceive again as soon as possible. The birth of a boy was met with rejoicing and the input of all the mother's bodily resources to ensure that the boy thrived and survived. Neferusobek would have known that her aunts served her father in the harem, too, and observed that the children of these unions were less healthy than the others—misshapen or slow—but favored nonetheless because of their royal blood.

The story of how Neferusobek accumulated and consolidated her royal power is woefully incomplete—but it most likely found its source in the harem, an institution created to keep royal succession as seamless and unchallenged as possible, but which also favored the power of King's Daughters, like herself. Most members of the harem did not receive any mention in official documentation, like temple reliefs or even bureaucratic papyri. There would have been no reason to mention a mere harem wife in any sort of formal text until she produced a son who was also chosen as the king's heir: a slim chance to be sure.

The other way to be recognized would be if that King's Wife was serving in some kind of ideological capacity as priestess in one of the great temples, unlikely for all but the highest-ranked royal women.

While the harem was a method of controlling females and ensuring that their bodies were available at the king's request, it was also a place where a tiny minority of women could find power by means of their offspring from the king. Such highly placed women made the rules in the harem and could likely lessen the chances of a beautiful provincial girl influencing the king directly or indirectly; they could possibly even use their sway over the king to divert income from certain officials connected to a certain girl; and they could use access to priests and magicians to hex or curse enemies. They could even, though documentation for this is sparse, engage in outright murder if the situation demanded, maybe using poison or some other quiet means of dispatching a rival.

It's as if the harem were created to give all the royal women—the King's Mothers, Sisters, and Daughters—the home-court advantage. We can only imagine the anxiety the mother and father of a new provincial harem girl felt once they realized she had somehow made an enemy of a powerful princess. A royal woman's wrath could impact the provincial girl's entire family—maybe even the entire province from which she came. Little of this activity would ever have made it onto the historian's page, because the harem was always veiled in secrecy, safe from prying and profane eyes. We receive glimpses of the potential drama only when, in the rarest of circumstances, evidence of a trial is found, in which one of the harem members was accused of conspiracy or murder—true for Dynasties 6 and 20, at the very least.

One of the most puzzling parts of the Egyptian royal harem was its lack of eunuchs. Given the high stakes, the secrecy, and the intimate activities engaged in within its walls, it's surprising that it was not monitored by men whose sexuality was contained and eliminated so that they were no threat to the king.[9] Other harems throughout history, including those of ancient China and Ottoman Turkey, have been administered and guarded by these gelded men, but there is no evidence of human castration ever having occurred in ancient Egypt. Why do we see no proof of such protective practices in an authoritarian regime as hierarchical as this one? Probably because ancient Egypt was such a closed society territorially and culturally. A multitude of institutions already kept competition between Egyptian elites minimized, perhaps lessening the need to de-sexualize the men around the harem.

♛

NEFERUSOBEK'S WORLD WAS ostensibly one of privilege, loneliness, scheming, and waiting. She was a princess called The Beauty of Sobek, named for a fierce god of the Nile inundation, a deity of aggressive sexuality and violent fecundity. It was quite a name for a princess who seems to have waited many years for a life's purpose, anticipating the day when she would marry her aged father or when he would die and she would be linked to her brother, the next king, as a great Royal Wife of the highest bloodline and most direct of royal lineages. She never did join her father in sexual congress, for reasons that remain hidden—and by the time he finally died, all her brothers had long since grown up and left the nursery, attaching themselves to families of their own. Many had certainly already died themselves as their father's 45-year reign finally ground to its end. A strange problem in ancient Egypt: to live so long that all your heirs die before you. (Remember that historians have the ever vexing problem that the Egyptians of this time did not publish the existence of Royal Sons until they were marked as heir, so we don't know how many predeceased their father.)

Because of a lack of documentation about King's Sons, there is fervent disagreement among Egyptologists about who the next king—Amenemhat IV—was. He calls Amenemhat III his father in preserved texts, but his mother Hetepti is never called King's Wife in her titles. Therefore, some historians think she was never a member of the harem at all, that Amenemhat IV was not really a King's Son as he claims, but from outside the Royal Family, only to marry Neferusobek and use *her* as the linchpin to the Dynasty 12 family line.[10]

Assuming, however, that Amenemhat IV was a true King's Son, he married his full or half sister Neferusobek upon his accession, thus raising her status in measurable ways and channeling more power to the female elements of his family. Royal women in Egypt always had titles connected to the king in some fashion—King's Daughter, King's Wife, King's Sister, King's Mother. Some titles were more powerful and useful than others at certain times. Indeed, most Egyptian harem women must have known that an unassailable path to power was as daughter or mother—positions perceived as supporting the patriarchy—rather than as wife or sister, relationships level with the king that could undermine hierarchical authority. Neferusobek was now queen, and the chief one at that, but a King's Daughter to boot.

Using her husband as a pathway to power could incur distrust and dissent—in ancient Egypt as much as in any other patriarchal society. Claiming descent through the bloodline of the father, the king, however, was seen as a purer and nobler means to gain authority. A daughter would have treated her father, as the elder, with deference and respect; the sister or wife perhaps less so.

We have a modern case study of this circumstance in the great distrust of Hillary Clinton when she was First Lady, the "overreaching" wife of President Bill Clinton. People asked who she thought she was, what she was trying to gain, by ruling behind the throne, so to speak: having an office of her own, an agenda of her own, trying to reorganize health care in the United States without the elected position from which to do it. But the same people—especially Trump supporters—did not show nearly the same level of distrust when a daughter, Ivanka Trump, received high-level interim security clearance and attended important policy meetings, because she was supporting her patriarch in a subservient position. First Lady Melania Trump, by the same token, has less justification for power, and seems well aware of it, spending her time on fashion, White House decor, and a purported anti-bullying social media platform, keeping her office and staff far away from the halls of power.

Authoritarian regimes thrive on placement of family members in positions of power, but each person's familial connection to the ruler needs to demonstrate that person's support, not challenge of the regime. This is probably why there is so little pushback among Trump's base about Howard Stern radio interviews in which Trump openly discusses the sexual attractiveness of his own daughter and how he would have dated her if she weren't his kin. It fits with the same patriarchal, not to mention narcissistic, model. Neferusobek understood the power dynamics of authoritarianism, too; she didn't attempt any recognizable power grabs as queen. She must have known that the timing was not yet right.

Indeed, when Amenemhat IV was crowned and married his sister Neferusobek, we can imagine the Egyptian nobility heaving a great sigh of relief, knowing that their status quo would be upheld for another few decades at least and that new heirs would soon enter the royal palace. The linkage with his (half?) sister Neferusobek would have only strengthened the situation in their eyes. Egypt was strong and prosperous. The provincial elites had stopped warlording. The borders were stretched from Syria in the north to Sudan in the south, and income from abroad was plentiful. What could possibly go wrong?

Everything. After nine years of rule, Amenemhat IV died with no viable heirs. Not one prince of the royal pair makes it into our historical documentation. Let's assume that Neferusobek and Amenemhat IV were indeed brother and sister. At this point in the dynasty, we can infer the inbreeding was already prevalent enough to make procreation a problem for these two siblings. But what about other women in the royal harem, all those lesser wives? Some of them must have been able to produce offspring for the new king. But we see no evidence of harem sons, either. It is possible that incest—the same adaptation that protected the Royal Family, that kept outside threats at bay, that consolidated wealth and power in one central unit—produced a sterile king, thus bringing the Royal Family to its knees.

With the death of their sovereign after a comparatively short reign, all the courtiers looked to the royal, not to mention divine, family to solve the situation: to maintain the balance of power among the elites, to keep the wealth and income pouring in. But the highest-ranked family member left was a woman. Dynasty 12 found itself in a succession crisis of the highest order. Neferusobek could be regent to no boy. And so she stepped forward as nothing less than king, using her descent from the great King Amenemhat III to justify her rule. For the first time in human history, we see a royal woman claim the highest office in the land—the kingship itself—for the simple reason that there was no royal man to take it. How extraordinary that in ancient Egypt women were chosen to rule even if they couldn't reproduce, even if they couldn't populate a royal nursery with heirs to the throne. In ancient Egypt, continuing the family dynasty was about much more than prolonging a divine father-to-son lineage; it was about continuing a balance between elites;

continuing the economy of trade, mining, and agricultural checks and balances; continuing the pact between the gods and men; continuing the divine kingship itself. A woman could never have stepped into power with only her ambition, without a collective agreement; Neferusobek's kingship was based on the needs of her people, on consensus.

Even a powerful and growing elite likely wanted the monarchy to remain strong and centralized, protected from outside influences; they also benefited from that balance, limiting the need to battle one another and to raise private armies that invaded other provincial elites' territories. Strong kingship kept Egypt prosperous—something that just about every wealthy landowner desired (not to mention the million or so peasants who had no political voice). Egyptian kingship was still the linchpin of its authoritarian, patriarchal society, worthy of preservation by a population that avoided danger at all costs. If the royal dynasty failed, the entire game was up, for the landowners, too. Royal monopolies would then close, including the gold mines in the eastern desert; the mineral mines for granite, quartzite, turquoise, carnelian, and natron, too. Trade with the Levant, Syria, and the northern Mediterranean would stop; the exploitation of Nubia, ground zero for gold and electrum, would cease. As long as they were enriched by it, Egyptian elites seemed to go along with anything to see the dynasty continue peacefully, including looking the other way when incest was endangering the King's Family and even allowing the rule of a woman before seeing their beloved Nile Valley descend into anarchy.

Neferusobek's father had died at 55 or 60 years of age, maybe even older, probably leaving her to wait beyond her own prime childbearing years until she married her brother, who died after nine years of rule. So let's guess that Neferusobek was in her thirties when she was crowned king, suggesting a mature and steady person, if not one biologically suited to continue her family lineage. She may not have produced an heir for her husband, but neither had any other woman in the harem. She seems to have posed no threat to the elites around her; to the contrary, the kingship became hers with no evidence of conflict or friction. The first documented female kingship in ancient Egypt was given to an experienced and worldly woman who had education and understanding. Neferusobek had nothing long term to gain from assuming the throne, no son to whom she could give her energies and acumen, no husband from whom to derive her power, just a means of keeping Egypt safe while everyone figured out their next move.

THERE ARE TIMES IN HUMAN HISTORY no one wants to live through. The Bronze Age Collapse of the 13th century B.C. The Assyrian sack of Thebes in 663 B.C. The fall of the Roman Empire in the fifth century. The Black Plague of the 14th century. We read about such times and wonder how we would react if faced with such adversity. Did Neferusobek have second thoughts as she entered this new phase of her life? Because Egypt's prospects would soon plummet, the entire land poised to enter a new phase of uncertainty and panic, its strength about to be cruelly tested. The signs were already there on the horizon. There had been a series of low Nile inundations, resulting in poor harvests during the last years of her father's reign, a trend that only continued into her brother's time as king. Famine and drought caused widespread destabilization and misery, much worse than an overly long reign coupled with inbreeding could ever produce.

Whatever her thinking on her new situation, Neferusobek became Egypt's first female king. For the Egyptians who went all-in with her, there must have been a collective decision among the highest courtiers to formalize this unprecedented instance of female power, to have Neferusobek go through the weeks of temple activities, initiations, meditations, and ceremonies that invested her with the divine power of sovereignty (which, everyone now solemnly agreed, she had possessed, unrecognized, since the time of her birth). For her countrymen, there was no longer any point in referring to her as "queen." That title was only used for women subservient to their sovereign. Now that Amenemhat IV was dead, leaving no male heir, it was up to Neferusobek to protect the family dynasty as (S)he of the Sedge Plant and the Bee, Mistress of the Two Lands, and Daughter of Re: kingly titles that were feminized specifically for her in Egyptian hieroglyphic inscriptions. She was king. Nothing else.

Stepping into her new role, Neferusobek got busy. She had her images placed in temples all around Egypt; three statues were found at Tell el-Da'ba in association with Dynasty 12 temple installations.[11] Frustratingly, none of her named statues have her face preserved. One of these sits in the Louvre today. Unfortunately headless, it depicts her wearing the Nemes headdress falling over her shoulders, the very same striped headcloth that Tutankhamun would wear much later in his golden funerary mask. This headdress was a marker of kingship, to be sure, even though we can see that this statue represented a woman in a dress with shoulder straps. Neferusobek, it seems, was openly admitting her feminine gender in her new representations, but combining it with traditionally masculine kingship. She is wearing a queen's dress, but she has tied on the kilt of kingship over her feminine garb, knotted much higher than a masculine king's kilt would have been: above her navel and just below her breasts. Around her neck she wears the same pierced heart amulet worn by her grandfather and her father, a sign of Dynasty 12 strength and of her direct linear descent from those great kings. She did not lie to her people or to her gods about her gender; her femininity was there for all to see. And yet she layered the masculinity of her new office over her feminine self.[12]

Some of us may wonder why women need to embrace masculine clothing and mannerisms in order to display power. When we think of the array of fashion choices available to the modern woman and the simultaneous strictures imposed on those who dare to occupy positions of power, the options narrow considerably. The power suit is one alternative for the ambitious woman, but does one wear trousers or a skirt? Does one include something as masculine as a tie? Usually not, as it implies a certain sexual identity. Can cleavage be shown? Doubtful, but it depends on a woman's age. High heels finish out the look, allowing a woman to be perceived as taller, approaching the heights of the men around her, but heels too high are viewed as slutty. Still, the woman in power must masculinize more than her dress. She must change her voice, too, forcing it to be modulated and lower. A quick perusal of YouTube videos of Hillary Clinton from her first presidential run in 2008 and her later bid in 2016 indicates she also got the message to de-feminize her speaking style. These contortions to which women must commit are in no way new to humankind, as the example of Neferusobek demonstrates.

Neferusobek also seems to have masculinized her own face. If a statue fragment in the Egyptian Museum in Berlin (it was destroyed in Allied bombing runs) belonged to Neferusobek, then her visage was fearsome, awe-inspiring, even terrifying to behold. Copying the intimidating statuary of her grandfather, Senwosret III, and her father, Amenemhat III, this statue shows a formidable woman with high cheekbones, a face carved with worry and attention, deep-set eyes that could spy on even the sneakiest of officials, and giant ears that could hear even the barest whisper of a future traitor. Her forehead was high, her brow ridge low and intent, her mouth absolutely unsmiling: not just fierce, but dour. This statue remains unmarked and uninscribed, but there is compelling evidence that it could be Neferusobek as queen or king.[13]

The gender ambiguity was not to stop there. When she ascended the throne, five royal names were bestowed upon

Neferusobek. Each reflected the unexpected, novel, and (we should assume) anxious situation of a female taking the throne in the absence of a male heir. Hers is the first full titulary (all five names) that we have for a female king of ancient Egypt, and it seems she worked with her priests to make some clever adaptations to convey femininity of person with masculinity of activity.

First off, her Horus name was written as a feminized version of a Horus bird: *Heret*, not *Her*—a female falcon, Horusette, if you like. We have come far from Dynasty 1, when Merneith could take no claim to the kingship, earning a stela with her name and a tomb in a necropolis reserved for kings—but bare of title with no Horus falcon to adorn her tomb marker. Neferusobek was allowed to become not only a Horus king but a female version of that hawk, representing the same far-seeing omniscience. Her Horus name was *Meryt-Re*, "Beloved of Re," similar to Dynasty 12 priestess titles and thus granting the expected religious aspect to her rule. With this name, Neferusobek and her supporters seem to be claiming both that she was beloved of the sun god himself and that one of her foundations of power was her priestly affiliation before she took the kingship.

Neferusobek's next name, her Two Ladies appellation, linked her kingship directly to her father, Amenemhat III, with the phrase The Daughter of the Powerful One Is (Now) Mistress of the Two Lands[14]—a name without doubt meant to assuage skittish officials worried about the prospect of a female king. The point is clear: She is making her claim to power through her lineage to her father. The daughter of one of Egypt's most successful kings was stepping in to seal the breach; in other words, you can all relax now.

Neferusobek's Golden Horus name was "The One Stable of Appearances," a bit arcane and unclear. Intriguingly, the name links her to Osiris himself, because Osiris is connected to stability, but it is feminized, as if Neferusobek were claiming to be a female version of Osirianized rebirth that would enable Egyptian kingship to rise again in strength and glory. Her fourth name, her throne name, was enclosed in an oval cartouche as Ra-Ka-Sobek and translates as The Life-Force of Sobek Is Re: an indication that her own personal connection to the crocodile god Sobek through name and temple activity enabled nothing less than the rising and setting of the sun itself. And her last name, the birth name and the only part of this name she had owned before her coronation, was, of course, Neferusobek, meaning "The Beauty of Sobek [of the Fayum]," a link to the economic and political stronghold of her Dynasty 12 family.[15]

Now that she was invested with the weight of masculine kingship and its fivefold titulary, Neferusobek felt the need to communicate that this authority served not her alone, but all of Egypt. She was not taking on power in a selfish manner, but only to uphold her father's dynasty, as a good daughter would. What better way to prove this point materially than to finish her father's temple complex at Hawara, a wondrous and innovative place that classical authors would later call the Labyrinth? It would legitimize her kingship for all her elites to see because

Hawara was located right next to their capital city of Itjy-tawy. When she finished her father's pyramid complex, she made sure to mark the place with her own name as well. In fact, on one preserved column we see an evocative image of the transfer of power from father to daughter: The Horus falcon accompanying the name of her father hands the scepter of kingship over to the Horus connected to her own name.[16] What seems like a selfless act of filial piety was actually a necessary ploy to legitimize her reign.

As Neferusobek ordered the pyramid complex finished, she also took an unprecedented step and ordered her father deified within his temple spaces. All kings were considered divine, to be sure, and all dead kings had a greater divinity among the company of ancestor kings, yes, but Neferusobek created special cult spaces for the worship of her father as a god at his temple at Hawara. In deifying him, she set aside extensive lands whose income of grain and flax and livestock would support an ongoing cult, paying priests an annual salary to regularly make offerings to the statues of the dead king, all in order to justify her own female kingship as ordained by the gods. Neferusobek would thus act as her own father's chief priest(ess) in his temple cult: a brilliant ideological power move.

We might ask why Neferusobek's husband, Amenemhat IV, did not finish the pyramid complex of his father himself during his own kingship. Was there some kind of drama during his reign that took his attention elsewhere, some lack of interest in supporting his father? What could have been more important than finishing your father's funerary installation and thus legitimizing your own reign as his extension in a perennial kingship? The easy answer to this question is: Amenemhat IV didn't need to. He was a son of his father, a man, the expected heir. He would have ordered work on his own funerary complex instead, not wasting valuable building materials and precious time on his father's glorification.

Neferusobek, on the other hand, was a woman who desperately needed to advertise her political connection with this dead king. Note that she didn't choose to finish the burial complex of the previous king, her dead husband-brother; at least we have no evidence of that. A political connection to a dead husband was far more tenuous and of far less worth to a female ruler.[17] Being the sister-wife of a short-lived, dead king was a nonstarter politically. Being the daughter of a great and long-lived ancestor, the sovereign, however, was a brilliant way to legitimize her pioneering, feminine reign.

In fact, archaeologists who dug at Hawara found Neferusobek's name preserved at her father's pyramid complex nearly as often as Amenemhat III's.[18] This points to some real strategic thinking on the part of Neferusobek, as she made the link from father to daughter and cut her husband-brother out of the picture entirely. Indeed, she highlighted the narrative that not only had her father wanted her to rule alongside him during his lifetime a decade before, but that he'd wanted her rule to immediately follow his kingship, instead of her brother's. Her propaganda was so convincing that historians used to think she ruled alongside her father first as co-regent, only to be followed by her husband-brother.

It should come as no surprise that women need to work doubly hard to prove their right to power. They have to look to the menfolk around them who can support their claim, rather than detract from it—to their fathers and patriarchs, not to their husbands and lovers. They must clarify to a suspicious public that they are not greedy and conniving, power-hungry for their own sakes, but concerned for the success of a broad swath of society. How does one do that except by somehow downplaying her own ambition, or subsuming her power to that of a male associate, or allowing herself to be interrupted in important meetings, or apologizing more than her male counterparts, or appearing more tentative in her decision-making, or not applying for positions and promotions she might think she isn't qualified for? A woman is rarely congratulated for grasping for more, for reaching higher. Women know exactly how their ambition is perceived by the public, and they must veil their power grabs in a warm and cuddly swath of nonaggression and nonthreatening verbiage, dazzling smiles, colored hair, and a calm and steady gaze, maternal even, without holding their head too high, but not too low, either. Is it any surprise that today's women don't even apply for political positions of authority if they have to walk through a gauntlet of abuse dissecting their appearance, demeanor, age, weight, and sexual past while simultaneously walking a tightrope of unspoken demands for masculinization?

At some point in Neferusobek's story, her elder sister Neferuptah died. When and how she succumbed to death is unclear, but this King's Daughter was buried in her own small pyramid at Hawara,[19] at her father's royal pyramid complex. King Neferusobek would honor her sister by endowing their father's temple with a cult for her, too—which is the only reason we know the woman existed at all, and is a testament to some of the tender human emotions Egyptian history usually lacks. With the loss of her sister, Neferusobek must have felt that she really was the last one standing of her Dynasty 12 family.

There was no time for rest. Neferusobek remained quite active all over the Fayum, setting up temples and statues for the god Sobek especially and connecting her kingship to the town of Shedty, a site in the Fayum with a vibrant temple to the crocodile god.[20] It was a fitting task for her, since her name, The Beauty of Sobek, was directly associated with the Fayum area, where the capital city, Itjy-tawy, and the pyramid complexes of her ancestors were built. This was ground zero for Egypt's newest concentrations of wealth: All the highest elites were based here, and all the rest of Egypt's mineral and imperial income was funneled here. Neferusobek left monuments to her divine crocodile namesake throughout the Fayum, forever linking her royal person with Sobek's creative power[21] and probably making a material statement to her courtiers that Egypt's strength would indeed rebound. Just as Sobek's inundation of the Nile brought new life, Egypt would find its virility again.

It is ironic that there was so much building under way to a god of masculine reproductive strength just as Egypt's most powerful dynasty had failed to produce even one male heir in its great harems and as a female king ostensibly beyond reproductive age was chief ruler of the land. But in ancient Egypt, as new life comes from death in the manner of Osiris's rebirth, Neferusobek was calming the fears of all the Egyptian elites, using divinities like Sobek and Ra, gods of cyclical re-creation and strength, Nile and sun, respectively, to physically demonstrate that Egypt would find its strength again. She inhabited her place as a sort of mother-king over all of Egypt, ruling differently than the men of her dynasty, investing less in warfare and social control; working toward consensus, rather than force; creating acceptance of her rule, rather than demanding it outright. Her legacy would ideally be Egypt's rebirth after her reign was over. She knew, as did every elite around her, that with her death, the kingship would move to a new family.

While they waited for that eventuality, Neferusobek had work to do running the country. Inscriptions in Nubia show that she was active to the south of Egypt, suggesting that the gold mines and trade routes were still functioning. However, inscriptions also reveal that evil forces were now at work; a very low Nile flood was recorded in her third year:[22] evidence that Egypt was on the brink of falling into decline from a significant series of insufficient inundations that, if they continued, would result in failed crops, famine, starvation, and collapse for her people and maybe even militarized competition among provincial landowners as scarcity set in. Neferusobek must have felt it was her responsibility to get Egypt back on course.

THE NILE WAS ANCIENT EGYPT'S life-force, and usually this great beast of a river made things extraordinarily easy for its people. Egypt looked first and always to this water source—not to the Red Sea, not to the Mediterranean. Every winter the monsoons would start over South-Central Asia and then sweep over to the Ethiopian highlands, pelting the lands with heavy rains. Those waters would drain into channels that merged into the Blue Nile, flowing northwest until they united with the White Nile in Khartoum in modern-day Sudan. The flooding would start in Egypt in late spring, reaching full inundation in high summer. For most people, the floods constituted a period of heat, lack of work, living off stored food, hunger, flies, lots of napping and, presumably, sex. It was a waiting game: waiting for the waters to recede; waiting for the rich, black, silty mud that would be left behind; waiting for the earth to dry out enough for the furrows to be plowed and planted. The results were usually fast and glorious: tall, ripe stalks of grain, filled with fat, juicy kernels.

Except sometimes this entire magical livelihood failed and failed colossally. The gods could indeed abandon their people, receding into chaos along with their great powers, causing low inundations, failed crops, famine, and disease. If the monsoon rains didn't come to Ethiopia and Eritrea, Egypt would not receive the necessary water. If the monsoon rains were too heavy, not only would Egypt's floodwaters be too fierce, wiping away homes and villages, but the inundation would lay upon the fields too long, leaving no time for the crops to flourish, cutting growing seasons back to nothing, resulting in the same devastating losses of wealth and life.

It was not Neferusobek's fate to be blessed with an easy kingship. She was only on the throne because of her dynasty's inability to produce a male heir, but she now had to deal with intolerable famine as well. We can assume that she tapped her rich grain stores, opening state-controlled bins to feed hungry Egyptians by using the great wealth amassed from the years of plenty. Neferusobek, a learned woman, would have known the poems of suffering in the absence of strong government, and now she herself was to live through what she had read about as a child—the grief, famine, low Nile, infighting, anxiety.

Meanwhile, everyone likely talked and schemed about the inevitable change in dynasty. Everyone knew Neferusobek was the last of her family. Maybe she had lovers. Maybe she was still, just barely, of childbearing years. Perhaps she was trying to produce an heir herself. If so, she never marked her sexual partners in her temples with inscriptions as a male king might with his queens, and we see no evidence of any son or daughter who could keep her dynasty going. This is the part of Neferusobek's rule that is invisible to us—the messy, human, personal interactions between ruler and ruled, of her own soul searching in the darkest hours of the night, of her own desperate and failed strategies, of shifting alliances and power grabs as courtiers and provincial landowners devised ways to keep their power positions while Egypt descended further into disorder.

And then it happened, much sooner than expected. After only three years, 10 months, and 24 days, according to the Turin king list, Neferusobek's reign came to an abrupt conclusion. Her death meant the end of one of Egypt's greatest ruling families.

How Neferusobek died remains an open question. Some Egyptologists—including renowned figures like Alan Gardiner and Nicolas Grimal—postulated that she met an untimely end, murdered for taking the kingship that didn't rightfully belong to a woman.[23] But the fact that she took the sovereignty and ruled unopposed for years, finishing the temple of her father, suggests otherwise. Egypt needed her—a woman—in their darkest hour.

She even had the time to begin her own funerary complex, probably at Mazghuna, close to Dahshur and her father's complex at Hawara.[24] Two unfinished pyramids have been found there with similar architecture to Amenemhat's temple at Hawara, and some archaeologists have assigned the southern unfinished pyramid to Amenemhat IV and the northern one to Neferusobek. But the site has still produced no definitive proof that these structures belonged to them.

Was Neferusobek interred here? If so, no evidence of a grave site has yet been found.[25] In some ways, it doesn't even matter because, most intriguingly, a stela found at the site proves ritual activity for Neferusobek, indicating that people were worshipping her here as a divinity after her death, just as they had her father.[26] Furthermore, a papyrus from Harageh mentions a place called Sekhem Neferu, meaning something like "The Power of Beauty," probably the name of Neferusobek's unfinished pyramid complex.[27] It is certainly scanty evidence, but it seems this female king was buried with respect, not murdered or pushed aside. Indeed, even with all the instability and chaos into which Egypt was descending, Neferusobek had created enough goodwill among her people to earn a cult that fed and cared for her afterlife existence, that gave thanks for her service to her country.

What, if anything, had her short kingship accomplished? On the surface, it doesn't seem like much. After her death, and with no sign or record of armed conflict, the throne was transferred to the next dynasty, the 13th. Amazingly, there's little evidence of fighting between most dynastic shifts in Egypt—and there isn't any for this transition, either. Dynasty 13 would consist of a series of short-lived, somewhat impoverished kings, none lasting more than a year or two, all impacted by the agricultural devastation now ravaging Egypt. Their burial places were sad heaps of stone, built not by the masses of laborers who hauled giant blocks and carved wall after wall of inscriptions with delicate hieroglyphs, but by a motley and poorly trained crew using reused stones and recycled funerary materials.

Should we put the onus for the dynasty's failure on this woman's shoulders? Or was she just the last, best representative of her family standing in an acute crisis of dynastic failure? We could, as so many historians have done to countless women, blame this downward slide of ancient Egyptian society on a woman, arguing that with a female calling the shots, the elites took their chances and exploited her weak position, demanding payment for their cooperation. Or we could see the larger threats and challenges over which Neferusobek had no control. Still, this essential question haunts our narrative: Was the female leader the reason for the crisis, or was she allowed into power only when catastrophe was under way?

Indeed, if it weren't for climactic events at the end of Dynasty 12, Egypt may have continued its kingship in some sort of centralized fashion, even with a shift in ruling family. As it was, the rule of the Dynasty 13 kings was feeble and territorially truncated. Famine ripped Egypt into multiple sections of rule, the Delta split into different factions, the Nile Valley as well. Migrations of foreigners from across the Sinai destabilized Egypt. Dynasty 13 would prove to be strange, its like never seen before or after in Egyptian history, characterized by shared power and shared wealth and an almost regularized swap of kings. But Dynasty 13's extension of peace against all odds was, it may be, Neferusobek's true legacy, although no historian has ever granted her that credit. She was no usurper of power that didn't belong to her. She was allowed to rule by her elites, even if only for a few years, thus affording them time and space to figure Egypt's next, best move. Neferusobek embraced that cautious and prudent Egyptian way of doing things, knowing that the end of the family was inevitable, but maybe also understanding that if the transfer of power could be put off, even for a little while, then the fallout would perhaps not be so great.

Even if she could produce no sons, Neferusobek was the mechanism by which the elites could fashion a solution to their power vacuum—because a woman rules differently from a man. And the Egyptians, in their way, thanked Neferusobek for what she had done for them: She was preserved in most of the king lists. She wasn't considered heretical or undeserving because of her sex. No, she protected her land in a time of distress, and for that she was honored.

CHAPTER 3

HATSHEPSUT

Queen of Public Relations

Hatshepsut broke all the rules. She gained her power during Dynasty 18 (1550–1295 B.C.), as Egypt was on the upswing, not as it was descending into a crisis of anarchy, economic devastation, and civil war. Hatshepsut's reign is the exception to the rule. She remains, arguably, the only woman to have ever taken power as king in ancient Egypt during a time of prosperity and expansion—and thus many historians have interpreted her kingship as an ambitious and immoral power grab. (Remember that Merneith and Neferusobek selflessly took up authority only to mitigate disaster.) Hatshepsut broke yet another rule: She acted as regent for a boy who was not her son. And then, to keep up her rule-breaking streak, she extended her power over Egypt for more than two decades: the longest tenure of any female leader of ancient Egypt.

Despite all her rule-breaking, Hatshepsut was somehow able to do everything right—securing and expanding borders, enriching the elites, building houses of stone for the gods throughout the land, engaging in risky trade ventures with faraway lands—and left Egypt better off than she'd found it. She did what the gods would have expected of a male king and more. None of the queens who came before or after her managed to transcend the crisis they had inherited and leave Egypt in better shape after their rule. Indeed, it seems we are interested in these women rulers precisely because of their association with failure. They are our cautionary tales: the stories historians enjoy dramatizing, the opportunity to show that female leadership is a dangerous thing.

But as Hatshepsut would discover, success can be tricky. If performed traditionally, as the gods would expect, good rule is abstract, something another leader could easily take credit for as his own. Indeed, Hatshepsut's own nephew and co-king would later erase her figures and texts and reassign credit to his father or grandfather for much of what she had done.

Hatshepsut represents the most powerful of all the Egyptian queens, yet few today can even pronounce her name (*Hat-shep-suit* is the best way to go for the English speaker). She presents the historian with a different challenge: This woman has had to be excavated and revivified by Egyptologists, saved from the void and judgment imposed on her by men who came after her.

♛

EVERY FEMALE KING IN OUR STORY stands on the shoulders of the formidable queens who came before her. One hundred years after Neferusobek's reign, the tattered remnants of

Dynasty 13 had slunk down to Thebes to regroup, leaving their Fayum city of Itjy-tawy behind. Egypt's southern Nile Valley was well-suited to reboot native Egyptian rule, and Thebes would eventually birth a new ruling family—Dynasty 17. Tetisheri was a formidable queen of the dynasty who ended up much more famous than her little-known husband, a certain Senakhtenre. Not only was she long-lived, but she kicked off her royal lineage on divine footing. Tetisheri was a slight, cheerful, and beautiful woman, if a British Museum statue of hers is to be believed, who bore many children, including a son who would become King Seqenenre Tao and a daughter, Ahhotep, who would be paired to her brother as Great Royal Wife.

The new dynasty considered itself vulnerable, it seems, so much so that sibling marriage became an expedient means of consolidating power within the family. It worked for a time. When Seqenenre Tao engaged in battle against a Levantine-Nubian coalition, Ahhotep was trusted implicitly to rule Thebes in his absence, looking after her soldiers, expelling rebels in the vicinity, punishing fugitives, and generally ruling the Theban region with such formidable authority that she would be long remembered for her political and military abilities. But this was a time of deep uncertainty; King Seqenenre Tao soon ended up dead (his mummy shows a gaping ax-shaped hole in his skull, making the cause of death pretty clear to all who visit the Egyptian Museum in Cairo), but not before the siblings were able to produce yet another brother-sister pair who would eventually rule over Egypt: King Ahmose and his sister-queen Ahmes-Nefertari.[1]

This new royal lineage, Dynasty 17, clearly viewed itself in opposition to a dynasty of foreign, so-called Hyksos, kings in the north (comprising Dynasties 15 and 16, concurrently) as well as Nubian kings to the south now allied with the Hyksos. A nativist movement was born in Thebes, a kind of Make Egypt Great Again upwelling of anti-foreigner sentiment; this Dynasty 17 of Thebes strived to take both the Nile Valley and the Delta back under centralized Egyptian control and expel the Hyksos from their lands. The long war for the control of a united Egypt was under way.

Alongside this strife rose a new age of female rule. When these Dynasty 17 warlords rode off to battle against their Levantine rivals, they trusted their women to maintain power in Thebes and elsewhere in Upper Egypt: women like Tetisheri, matriarch of her dynasty, and her daughter Ahhotep, in whose coffin was found a gilded battle ax and a necklace made of golden flies to celebrate the dead enemy upon whom the insects feasted.[2] As we might expect, when there was crisis—in this case, a war of expulsion and reunification—the Egyptians demanded that their women take power to support the patriarchal hereditary kingship. None of these women of the 17th or early 18th Dynasties became kings themselves; there was apparently no need, with so many strong warrior-sons to take the place of a father when he fell. But these Theban women were a harbinger of great female kings to come.

The transfer of the kingship from King Kamose (who ruled after his father Seqenenre Tao was killed on the battlefield) to his brother Ahmose seems to have been enough for later historians to start a new dynasty, the 18th, which started off as the 17th had ended—on an incestuous and protective note. Dynasty 18 began with a sibling marriage between King Ahmose and his full sister–bride Ahmes-Nefertari. The new family lineage was also grounded upon strong female authority. When Ahmose died precipitously and Crown Prince Amenhotep I was much too young to rule, his mother Ahmes-Nefertari acted as regent, making all the decisions on behalf of palace, temple, and state. The New Kingdom began with real and unadulterated female power in every sphere of government.

Queen Ahmes-Nefertari shielded her son from his immaturity, training him into his sacred post. But she couldn't protect him from his sterility, a condition almost certainly brought about by her sexual union with her brother. The ancient Egyptians never touch upon this sore spot directly, but Amenhotep I never had any children we can find in the historical or archaeological record. Put simply, there was no heir. One would think this made him the subject of derision and hostility in later historical records and temple documents. But the young king was considered quite special—even an extension of his mother's kind guidance and power. Indeed, the mother-son pair were depicted together for centuries after their deaths, deified as the patron divinities of Thebes, working not for the extension of their family lineage but for Egypt's betterment.

There was still a profound problem, however. The country, so recently rid of its foreign overlords and reunited into Upper and Lower Egypt, lacked a crown prince. How it was decided to invite a grown man named Thutmose into the palace as the next king, we will never know—but we can be sure that Ahmes-Nefertari had something to do with it.

Thutmose was Theban, just like the Royal Family. He had likely served as a general in the wars against the Hyksos kings and was probably related to the family in some way, maybe as a son of the dead king's brother or sister. If he was surprised that the kingship came to him, we have no record of it. He accepted the throne and became Thutmose I to later Egyptology: the first of many kings to bear this name, meaning "Born of the God Thoth." To consolidate his position within the Theban Dynasty 18 family, he married a princess named Ahmes: a woman probably related to the family of the dead king, Amenhotep I, and Ahmes-Nefertari.

The crisis of succession had been resolved—and not by making the last woman standing the king, as had happened in Dynasty 12. Egypt instead rescued itself from its own infertility by choosing a strong and virile man. There is no proof of bloodshed or civil war; somehow, courtiers, priests, and provincial landholders agreed that a grown man could take over a dynasty not his own. Or at least, there is absolutely no proof of dissent surrounding his elevation to the kingship. Maybe the Egyptians had finally learned some hard lessons from all the recent royal inbreeding, having just been through two generations of full brother-sister marriage. Perhaps it was only when the last stakeholder, the great queen Ahmes-Nefertari, stepped aside from the kingship herself, a role that she could have easily taken according to past custom, that the Egyptians anointed this non-royal Thutmose as king over them. However it came to pass, their choice of new king was brilliant. Thutmose I was a born warrior, extending Egypt's borders farther into the Levant than had the Dynasty 17 kings of Thebes. He crushed the gold-producing provinces of Nubia and Kush, ensuring more mineral income than Egypt had seen in some time. And he produced many children in his harem—sons and daughters with few markers of incest, we can guess, as his new blood would have strengthened the royal line.

His eldest daughter was Hatshepsut, descended from his most highly placed wife and thus connected to the old Dynasty 18 line: a venerable bloodline for a princess who would be named Egypt's highest priestess (and probably at a very young age, too). Hatshepsut learned the incantations and engaged in sacred and secret rituals, supposedly with the god Amun himself, the nature of which we can only guess. Whatever her actual responsibilities in the temple shrines, she saw firsthand how influential Egypt's priesthood was, and how an ideological base of power could make or break a ruler. In the years to come, she would use this experience and knowledge to launch her own power bid.

With her new position as high priestess, Hatshepsut gained all the material wealth that came with an institutional household as well. She was now God's Wife of Amun,[3] a powerful holy woman in control of her own palace, income-producing lands, treasury storerooms, and hundreds of personnel from priests to bookkeepers to farmers tilling her fields. She was trained to conduct rituals that maintained the workings of the universe by helping the god Amun remake himself sexually every morning.[4]

She understood her cosmic importance, but she was also a young woman of worldly power and influence.[5] She had it all: She was educated, trained in decision-making, rich in palaces and estates, and thrown into close contact with the most powerful priests in Egypt—not to mention the king himself, her father, Thutmose I. She would have grown up knowing her value to her king, her gods, and her people.

For all her later path breaking and glass-ceiling busting, it seems Hatshepsut was a dutiful daughter who supported Egypt's patriarchal system. She represented her family in Thebes while her father was active in the urban elite centers of Memphis or Heliopolis, or out on summer campaigns to the Levant, Libya, or Nubia. In this way, Hatshepsut acted as an extension of her father's authority within Thebes, Egypt's most powerful religious center and the birthplace of kings. Her femininity and bloodline made her the perfect choice for such a position: an infiltrator in a hierarchy of priests in one of Egypt's richest temple institutions and a woman who could pose no political threat to the king's own power. It was in her best interest to protect her father's agenda. And untethered to any man, Hatshepsut had yet to produce any children to fight for, whose suits she would promote as the next heir to the throne. To place such a daughter in a temple position radiated power back to the king, without the worry that she would take any for herself.

But there were storm clouds on the horizon. Word would have come to Hatshepsut that one or more of her brothers had died unexpectedly: brothers who were the best-suited heirs to the throne. This loss must have been quite a blow, because the king actually memorialized the boys in temple stone, an almost unprecedented signal of mourning.[6] The palace was most likely thrown into upheaval with the death of these highly placed princes, knowing that every mother of a Royal Son, along with their own families and entourages, were all pushing their boys forward as the next best candidate for the kingship. No crown prince was chosen as heir in the days to follow, though; at least there is no record of it. Then, Thutmose I himself died after 10 years of rule—probably a natural death as a mature man. And everything changed for Hatshepsut.

After her father's death, she was no longer King's Daughter in anything but title. She would have to link herself to one of her brothers as wife, as queen; it had likely been planned for her all along. One such brother was chosen, whom historians call Thutmose II, an unready and unhealthy boy, it seems, based on what anthropologists have noted from examination of his preserved mummy's enlarged heart and pockmarked skin.[7] Regardless, he was now called upon to fulfill his duty as the next Horus, the golden falcon, bearer of the crook and flail. His Great Royal Wife? It was never a question. It would be Hatshepsut, the highest priestess in the land, highest-born daughter of Thutmose I. If the position of God's Wife of Amun extended temple power to her father, now it was needed for her new husband and half brother, King Thutmose II. She was probably quite a bit older than her new husband, too.

Thutmose II would not have expected this sudden shift in his circumstances. He was probably third or fourth son, not second or first. To suddenly be called upon as king of the most powerful and richest land in the world was too much to ask. He left little mark on the landscape with his short kingship. Scholars debate the length of his reign, as they do all things that happened 3,500 years ago; he ruled either three, nine, or 10 years.[8] If it was nine or 10, then he was a sad excuse for an Egyptian king—hardly any temples with his name on them, no campaigns, no mortuary complex of any worth. Let us cut Thutmose II some slack, then, and agree with most of the king lists and with the extant archaeological evidence that he ruled only three years. It would fit better with the small amount of material left behind and allow us to understand why Hatshepsut was able to gain so much power when he died.

Thutmose II left behind a daughter, Nefrure, born to Hatshepsut, and a nursery full of two-year-olds, toddlers walking around unsteadily, princes and princesses who were still breastfeeding and, given their station, would nurse for many years to come (either from their mothers or from wet nurses if their mothers had been favorites of the king). How could any of these small children possibly serve as king?

Dynasty 18 was off to a rocky start; all of Thutmose I's sons were dying untimely deaths. However, the stars were aligned for a resurgence of authoritarian strength, now that healthy Nile inundations over many generations resulted in regular and fruitful crop seasons, now that income was flowing in from productive mines and quarries, now that Egypt was finally able to launch successful military campaigns that created streams of tribute, and now that the trade routes were once again open from Lebanon in the north to Kush in the south. This was no time to be rudderless. It was time to capitalize on all the blessings heading Egypt's way.

WHAT DO YOU DO when you find yourself on the board of a fabulously wealthy corporation with a two-year-old CEO, whom you are contractually obligated to employ? You invite a leader to work with that boy, someone who will appear as no threat to the rest of the board members or shareholders. The boy's mother would have been a perfect choice to act as regent because his agenda would be her agenda. She would train him well; she would be proud when he succeeded; she wouldn't try to shift him aside to suit her ambitions; she'd want him to be a better version of himself—until he came of age and she could step back into the shadows. But, strangely, when the next king was chosen, the child's mother did not act as his regent. A rule was being broken. The Theban family that had so long consolidated its power to the point of incestuous infertility would not allow anyone else to rule on behalf of their future king. It would be Hatshepsut or nobody, female offspring of both the old family of King Ahmose and the new lineage of King Thutmose, who was allowed to govern for the unready child. Hatshepsut had made her first move on her path to kingship.

We know by now that the choice of the next Egyptian king was one of the most secret of Egyptian rituals, the most unseeable of political transitions. But the naming of Thutmose III to the throne surprisingly provides a bit more information to us. In the preserved texts, we read that an oracle was used to choose the next king among the gaggle of princes. In every oracle proceeding, the statue of the god Amun was brought out of his shrine and placed into a barque carried aloft by his high priests, who then manipulated the god's movements to answer questions or give directions about future choices.

The actual mechanism of how the oracle worked is veiled: Did the priests carrying the god decide in advance what to do? Or might they have taken some sort of psychedelic substance to let their own agendas go and enable them to channel the wishes of their god? We don't know, but Thutmose III would claim in the preserved texts that Amun himself picked him to be king.[9] Recorded in temples built by the kings, such stories are always colored with a propagandistic tinge, but apparently, all the young princes—*nestlings*, they were called—were gathered into a great hall of the sacred space, and the god Amun himself was brought forth as oracle to choose the king among them. The god moved about, circling the boys, apparently mulling his decision, and then decided upon the young Thutmose. The intent of writing down this story later during the king's reign is crystal clear: The god chose Thutmose III. No mortal was ever given the credit (or the blame) for this course-altering decision. Indeed, the oracle was a means of removing such determinations from human hands: a useful tool for the ancient Egyptians who shied away from open political discussion and responsibility. It would also be a useful way for Thutmose III to later claim that Hatshepsut had nothing to do with his ascent to the throne; this was the gods' doing and no one else's.

The palace line was that the king had been handpicked as the son of the god himself. But the way such a decision was reached was certainly more complicated, ostensibly requiring input from a variety of wealthy landed aristocrats, or through closed-room discussions of high-level courtiers, complicated by whispers of mothers in the harem, each of whom had a horse in the race. There must have been ongoing formal and informal discussions on this most important of topics for at least a few days while plans were put into action to embalm and bury the young king who had just died. The momentous decision was influenced by a number of factors, including the health of the child, but perhaps more important, the mother of the boy: her outside connections, how influential they were and could become (not to mention the identity and lineage of the priests holding the oracle aloft and thus making the decision on behalf of the god).

For whatever reason, an outside and uninfluential woman's son was chosen by the oracle of Amun, the priestly bearers apparently directed to the boy by the hand of the god. Why? Maybe some of the other sons were the product of incestuous unions, none of them viable candidates (especially with the memory of Amenhotep I's sexual failure still fresh in everyone's mind). Whoever Thutmose's maternal family was and wherever in Egypt they came from, the choice for their boy would have invited the in-laws into the palace, bringing all the issues that come with those who suddenly see new potential for acquiring power. As Hatshepsut had borne no son to her brother, the decision was made for everyone to serve the genetic health of a continued dynasty, not the ultra-protectionist stance of an inbred Royal Family. Except that, by picking this particular boy, they simultaneously allowed a member of the old Royal Family—Hatshepsut—to pull all the strings. It was a stroke of brilliance.

This was a very sensitive point in Egypt's history; its continued prosperity and peace balanced on a knife's edge. Now was the time for consensus, not for a choice in which few believed or one that acted against the economic and political interests of powerful landholders and courtiers. Now was the time for a peace builder, a representative of continued affluence, a prudent and cautious thinker, not a hotheaded risktaker. Consensus landed on a two-year-old named Thutmose, but he was just a cipher. His choice was the tool that allowed Hatshepsut to lead Egypt with careful and clear direction.

The new king, Thutmose III to Egyptologists, was named in his coronation *Menkheperre Thutmose*, a throne name meaning "The Manifestation of Re Endures." Sun god or not, he was probably hard to corral during the lengthy and complicated coronation ceremonies that happened in multiple locations throughout Egypt—at Thebes, Memphis, Heliopolis, and almost certainly elsewhere. The boy's first introduction to his new life was of being told what to do, where to stand, what to hold, what to say, and how to act, and not being allowed to run around outside in play. It was probably torture for a young boy, and an experience that would have taught him self-restraint at an early age. For Hatshepsut as Egypt's high priestess and regent, it was more of what she was already trained to do: more arcane rituals, chanting, secret initiations, sleepless nights spent fasting and waiting, discussions with elites and priests. She was the one prepared for this; she was the one ready to lead Egypt through this rite of passage.

There was no bloodshed or contest in the transfer of power from one king to the next, but anxiety lasted nonetheless—because their new king was a mere infant. All the stakeholders involved had families and children of their own. Indeed, each of them had probably lost half of their own children, most before the age of five. In a place where child mortality was as high as 50 percent, this was just a reality of life.[10] Malaria, intestinal diseases, parasites, accidents—there were more than enough ways for a child to die. It was ludicrous to expect that this precious two-year-old, upon whom so many had pinned their hopes for continued enrichment and stability, could make it to 10 or 12 or 15 and finally to a manhood that produced viable sons of his own. Yet they had been left with a nursery of living King's Sons, so the circumspect and pious Egyptians had no choice but to back this baby-king. The living son must continue the steps of his father.

Only in ancient Egypt was there so much ideological certainty in their god-king that everyone nonetheless bet everything on less than half a chance that the boy would live long enough to procreate. If he died, all their schemes and hopes would be quashed as a new representative of the Royal Family was found, bringing on all the messy politicking and maybe even armed conflict among warring factions. If any other place in the ancient world had tried to install a toddler as king—in the Levant, in Mesopotamia, in Greece, or in Rome—the young King's Son would have been dead before the week was out (after which a mature warlord, still holding the bloody knife, would have been installed in his place while his minions slaughtered the young king's surviving family members). Even in Egypt, we might expect power brokers to back a grown male relative of the Royal Family instead—not one in direct lineage, but close. There must have been other sons of Thutmose I alive when Thutmose II died who could have served on the throne of their dead brother. Many other hereditary monarchies would have followed this course instead. But not the ancient Egyptians.

The Egyptians had already created a complicated set of mythologies to grapple with exactly this kind of succession problem. You will remember that Osiris, king of Egypt, was murdered by his brother Seth before his time. His young son Horus was not mature enough to take control of Egypt on his own. The dead king's brother Seth made his claim to the throne, while Isis, the boy's mother, retreated with Horus into the marshes, protecting him from the many assassination attempts launched against him. Finally, when Horus was able, he began his contention for the throne, fighting his uncle Seth in a series of epic battles, on the one hand, and formally submitting his legal case to the tribunal of gods on the other. The ruling of the divine tribunal was very clear in deciding that the son, not the brother, should always rule after the father, no matter how young he may have been at his accession.[11] Therefore, choosing the brother of the dead king, instead of the son, was asking for civil war. In a system able to produce dozens, if not hundreds of Royal Sons, brother would fight brother, in ever changing alliances and shifting loyalties, seemingly forever.

In ancient Egypt, divine patriarchal bloodlines were more than respected; they were revered. This was a place for which historians have clear evidence of collective cohesion among courtiers, of social contracts among elite landowners and institutional stakeholders in which almost everyone looked to the seamless transition of the crown from one generation to the next to secure their incomes. Here, warlording paid no dividends. Coups and secret alliances only harmed; the potential reward for the risktaker was infinitesimal, the potential for painful discord and destruction certain. Therefore, people consistently chose strategies of rule that rewarded a linear progression of power, even if that solution wasn't particularly cautious (like choosing a small child to rule the largest regional state in the known world). In ancient Egypt, everyone was expected to know his or her place. Unless you were king, humility was the order of the day. Now it was the time to be humble to a two-year-old.

But the real power behind the throne was the highest priestess in the land, Hatshepsut. It seems that everyone who was anyone trusted her to be Egypt's decision-maker. She was the God's Wife of Amun with whom many elites had already worked and thrived. And here is the material point about an Egyptian realpolitik cloaked in religious mystery: The choice of Hatshepsut as regent must have steered the decision of which prince was selected (by Amun, of course) as the next king. Choosing Hatshepsut meant the rejection of any child with a strong and influential mother—and, by extension, a strong elite family lineage—and thus demanded a boy whose mother was poorly educated or inappropriate for rule herself, or both. We should never forget that it was actually the regency of Hatshepsut, whose leadership everyone seemed to desire, that shaped the selection of the next king, not the other way around.

Imagine that you're a highly placed Theban priest with powerful extended family connections in the area. You know Hatshepsut is the aunt of this child Thutmose, this new king. You also recognize that she is ready to do the job of regent. In fact, you have seen her do her job as God's Wife of Amun very well because she served with you as high priestess in one of Egypt's most powerful temple complexes. Not only that, her husband-brother was younger and less experienced when she became his queen, and you saw that Hatshepsut had been the decision-maker. In the midst of this succession crisis, she would likely be your choice to lead Egypt into the future. She could help build a bridge between the last regime and the next, ruling with caution and solidarity.

High officials, like the courtier Ineni, were happy enough to record their loyalty to the high priestess in their own tomb chapels, openly calling attention to their regent, if not formally naming her as such. Loyalist autobiographies like these demonstrate not only that Hatshepsut had the support of her elites, but that she was a functional leader, immediately able to step into the breach, to make orders and see those commands followed. She was likely quite young—maybe only 16, although Egyptologists continue to debate her age—when invited, or even cajoled, into the position of regent. In the hieroglyphic tomb text, Ineni tells us:

> He [Thutmose II] went up to heaven, and he united with the gods. His son was raised in his place as king of the Two Lands. He ruled upon the throne of the one who begat him. His sister, the God's Wife (of Amun) Hatshepsut, fulfilled the needs of the land, the Two Lands following her counsels. She was served; Egypt was obedient. The divine granaries were efficient and overflowing. The prow rope of Upper Egypt was moored in the south. The stem rope was the beneficence of Lower Egypt. A mistress of decrees and words, effective were her counsels. The two banks were content with her speech. Her majesty praised me and she loved me. She knew my excellence in the palace. She provided me with things, and she made me great.[12]

In reading this translation, it's straightforward that praise for Hatshepsut was not only clearly formulated but also obviously self-serving. Ineni states that Hatshepsut was good at her job—skilled in deciding what to do and in telling people how to do it. He also maintained that all the elites were thrilled to have her in charge, that she wasn't throwing her weight around or being difficult in any way. And then we come to the crux of the matter: Hatshepsut not only recognized the quality of an excellent official, but she rewarded Ineni with "things," making him "great." What's not to like in this female regency for a toddler king if everyone benefited materially?

And this is the point. This vulnerable kingship was an opportunity to become richer than ever before. Everyone had a price, apparently, and some officials were able to gain financial reward for their cooperation with the palace.

The evidence is everywhere. Egyptologists have to study a great deal of material culture during their careers, committing to memory temples, tombs, statues, stone blocks, and fragments scattered about the Egyptian landscape and the world's museums. The task can be overwhelming for the best of us. But Hatshepsut's regency made the task of memorizing all that stuff that much more difficult. Before she took power, there was just not that much material production in Dynasty 18, not that many statues and stelae for Egyptologists to commit to memory because Egyptian elites had neither the material wealth nor the political power to commission such things. But Egyptologists also know that after the reign of Thutmose III began, there was a veritable explosion of monumental production by elites—tomb chapels, statuary, reliefs, luxury goods.[13] Apparently, they had been given a newfound income and the allowance to produce "things" with a grandeur not seen since Dynasty 12.

The amount of production is astounding. It was a testament to Egypt's growing wealth and power, to be sure. The crown was erecting more monuments than ever before, but analysis of the changing proportion of it all suggests that there was more to it than just an improved economy. The explosion in nonroyal monument creation speaks to that changing balance between king and elite—and what was now so striking was the upward trajectory of those elites serving under Hatshepsut as regent. During the previous reigns of Amenhotep I and Thutmose I, elites didn't and couldn't produce as many tombs and statues. Once the reign of Thutmose III started, however, with Hatshepsut firmly ensconced at the helm of the ship,[14] the balance of influence shifted, allowing us to conclude that it was actually the elites who were running the show, making sure to communicate, politely, that if they were going to have this girl rule over them, then they had better benefit handsomely.

Now that we have pulled aside a few veils, we can see the means of Hatshepsut's rise to power more clearly: It was elite influence and avarice that called upon her to lead them. They chose someone of direct royal lineage, someone they thought they could easily influence, someone equal to the task; and it was their choice of Hatshepsut that, in turn, called for a boy disconnected from the most highly placed families to be king. The patrician Egyptian families were running the show; they were the ones who vaulted Hatshepsut into this unprecedented position. Was Hatshepsut just a tool? Leaders have often been used as fronts for power held by others—from George W. Bush acting as the unaware leader for a veiled and insidious agenda actually carried out by Dick Cheney et al., to Aung San Suu Kyi of Myanmar, who vaulted her party into power in recent elections, only to be used as a kind of cipher prime minister when the slaughter of Rohingya minority people continued unabated.

And, of course, there are the queens representing a variety of countries in a fragmented Europe: Elizabeth I of England, Mary Queen of Scots, Catherine the Great of Russia, Maria Theresa of the Austro-Hungarian Empire, and Isabella I of Castile—each of whom was, arguably, politically placed by power brokers, queen-makers if you will, as pawns in a larger game, until they were able to master the rules of the chessboard as queen in their own right.

HERE WE ARRIVE AT A THEME that haunts Hatshepsut's rule within Egyptology: the notion that she took power because her ambition demanded it. This kind of thinking comes from what we might call the Great Man hypothesis (in this case, the Great Woman Hypothesis), based on the belief that one person could step into a place and time and seize authority, even if others didn't want to grant it. It implies that one person could lead a nation into ruin or war, without influential people serving under him or her having much of a say in the matter. Such historical perspective is not only outdated but also erroneous, casting too much of the blame for humankind's woes on the ambitions and whims of single individuals. How many of us can go out into the world and just get what we want, when we want? None of us. Not Donald Trump. Not Barack Obama. Not Hillary Clinton, certainly. Not even the political mastermind and ex-KGB operative Vladimir Putin. We must all work with the social system given to us, balancing power with the people who support us, so that we can have military might, economic institutions that work, and ideological support in temples and places of worship.

So how much credit, or blame, can we give to Hatshepsut on her path from regency to kingship? All? Likely not. Some? Yes, certainly. She was there, ready to create a balance of power among the elites, and she held the gravitas of pure royal blood. But Ineni's inscription clarifies (and the Egyptian material record confirms) that Egypt's patrician families were supporting her power while simultaneously taking more wealth and influence for themselves, exploiting this delicate situation for their own advantage and forever after destabilizing the balance of power between elite and king.[15]

How much was Hatshepsut pushed around by these same elites—subtly and with decorum, of course—as she learned her new role before the age of 20, and how much was she able to push them back, in turn, despite her inexperience? She likely had to give up much more during the negotiations of her junior years, pulling in more influence as her worldliness grew; as she had more cards with which to bargain; as she built alliances and collected social debts; as she gained more institutional knowledge; and as she opened up new sources of income that only she could control. Only with time and hard work would she have been able to hold more sway over all those courtiers and priests and landed aristocrats.

Tides can turn, but Hatshepsut was likely starting her rule from a disadvantage, a bit of a pawn, as the elites around her took more than they gave back. Whatever the reality of the situation, there is no evidence that she pushed back too hard. She was a traditionalist, after all. She supported the status quo. It was her job to see Egypt continue in strength, to see her nephew grow into his kingship, and to see her family dynasty thrive.

And so Hatshepsut found herself in an interesting and unexpected place—unprecedented even, a traditionalist in the most nontraditional of situations. When she had served her father, Thutmose I, as God's Wife of Amun, she had been the King's Daughter. When she had served her husband, Thutmose II, in the same post, she had been the King's Sister. But now that she was serving as high priestess under the new king Thutmose III, she was only an aunt—a full two steps removed from his lineage. This new king was not her son, and, arguably, as time went on, his agenda would not necessarily align with her own to-do list. Did the courtiers worry about Hatshepsut's relationship with her nephew in this way? Did they think in such a strategic or long-term fashion? Or did they just want to continue the authoritarian regime so they could survive and thrive during the transition from one king to another, a rare opportunity in a succession crisis? It was only as the reign of the young king entered its second and third years that the problems began to emerge.

The new king likely had no clue as to what was going on. And he wouldn't have much of an idea how political power was balanced and manipulated for some 10 years more. Thutmose III ruled only because Hatshepsut had been there to secure his reign. She probably reminded him of that fact from time to time as he grew up. Hatshepsut, for her part, only ruled because Thutmose III was so young, and because the Egyptian system needed a female regent already on the inside to balance competing interests from outside the palace. We can wonder if an adolescent Thutmose III ever reminded Hatshepsut of this reality as she grew older herself. As for Thutmose III's mother, incongruously named Isis, we hear nothing of her during the king's boyhood. If she enjoyed political support to serve as the king's regent, instead of Hatshepsut, it was utterly silenced by the faction favoring Hatshepsut.

Hatshepsut was provided with excellent training for the tough spot in which she now found herself. She would have had knowledge from her own studies, perhaps, of Merneith of Dynasty 1, certainly of Neferusobek of Dynasty 12, and firsthand training from the women of her own family. Ahmes-Nefertari may have even been a beloved matriarch who trained her in her priestess duties as a girl—and she had already observed her own mother, Ahmes, rule on behalf of her young husband-brother Thutmose II. She had learned how to wield political power (as a woman, no less) from the best, and she continued along that line, doing nothing unusual or out of bounds, keeping everyone as happy as she could.

But maybe Hatshepsut also bided her time, knowing that she would be able to go further in her political career than her mother—because as God's Wife of Amun, she had a foundation of ideological, political, economic, and priestly support that her mother never had. As an erstwhile King's Daughter, she held unbreakable links to palace, temple, and army officials. She enjoyed connections to influential men of the treasury. And the boy she ruled for was so young that her influence would be felt for much longer than a few measly years. Hatshepsut knew she would make her mark for a good decade, at the very least.

She seems to have realized early on that it was all about human resources. If she could just figure out how to work elites in her favor, or against one another, then she could take more control of the game. Indeed, her modus operandi was to pick those officials to work closest with her when their ambitions could serve her own interests—and only her interests. Likewise, if she couldn't control a well-connected elite, then she could place him in competition with other such officials by assigning him particular posts. She set up Senenmut, a man with no connections to the patrician families, in the treasury, putting him in charge of her most important schemes. But she also named Ahmose-Pennekhbet, a man from an established patrician family, to the same treasury post. The two men even bore the same titles, ostensibly holding the same positions in some kind of competitive fashion. Perhaps Hatshepsut had realized that if elites were going to exploit her anyway, taking more than their due, she had to figure out how to get them to compete with one another for her favor.

Hatshepsut's other avenue to further her influence were the gods themselves. She was a master at cloaking her political ambitions in a veil of ideology, taking the onus of any power grabs off herself and calling her actions simply the will of the gods—a duty, she informs us, she was divinely commanded to shoulder. Thus she showed herself in temple scenes—in Nubia, in Elephantine, in Thebes—interacting directly with the gods as no regent or God's Wife of Amun ever had before.[16] Egyptian elites had never before seen the God's Wife of Amun depicted so large, so close to the gods, performing rituals that normally only the king had the power to perform.

Hatshepsut relied on this religious display. She also relied on showing off her piety. She set up statues of her dead husband, Thutmose II, in the Temple of Khnum at Elephantine, putting in the accompanying inscription that they were "for her brother," making an explicit justification for more power for herself because she was a pious supporter of this king who had died too young. She also commissioned reliefs of Thutmose II for Karnak Temple in Thebes.[17] She likely did the same all over Egypt's most prominent temples, showing her elites that her ticket to power as regent was through her relationship to her husband, the previous king and father of the current monarch. Keeping his son safe on the throne was proof of her piety, like Isis watching after Horus. Her continued rule meant the boy's ongoing development—and, by extension, everyone's steady advancement. It was a religious-political-economic statement that displayed her as a kind of divine mother to the boy-king, even though everyone knew she wasn't his legitimate birth mother.

This was a difficult game and one she would soon have to shift. Hatshepsut was acting as God's Wife, a role that, by rights, she needed to relinquish to a direct relative of the king—to a mother, sister, wife, or daughter of Thutmose III, as tradition and prudence demanded. Maybe Hatshepsut still worried that the king's birth mother, Isis, would somehow seize the role of God's Wife of Amun with help from Hatshepsut's political adversaries, thus diminishing Hatshepsut's claim to the regency. The King's Mother, Isis, was the most entitled to the priestess position, in terms of genealogy, not to mention tradition, and everyone at court must have known it. But Hatshepsut had a card up her sleeve: her own daughter—Nefrure, Thutmose III's half sister—who was the ideal candidate for the priestess post—but she was still too young at only three to five years of age at the beginning of Hatshepsut's regency. Hatshepsut was the current inhabitant of the position and the best trained for the job, so she just kept it, and everyone who was anyone allowed her to do so.

Essentially, Hatshepsut was fulfilling the roles for two children of the next generation—acting as the head of state for Thutmose III, but also acting as God's Wife of Amun for her daughter Nefrure. Practically speaking, at this point in her career, she was nothing more than a placeholder waiting for these royal offspring to grow up—and she and her closest supporters in her entourage must have known it. To keep all of their positions and income, they must have realized that what was required was a real, and legitimate, source of power for their mistress.

How Hatshepsut felt about this strange balancing act, this waiting game, we will never know. As a woman, she must have recognized that she was expected to give it all up when Thutmose III reached his majority. But we have no insights into the minds of Egyptian leaders. Ancient Egypt was not like the competitive systems of ancient Greece or ancient Rome, in which decentralization demanded personal and political take-downs in a public forum; in those cases, we can learn about the personalities, desires, or thoughts of individual leaders, however twisted these stories became through the agendas of their story-tellers. In an authoritarian regime like ancient Egypt, disclosures and gossipy behavior got you imprisoned or killed, or both. Therefore, such human foibles and pharaonic realities were simply not published; instead, they were verbally expressed, every leader cast as perfect in the material record. And so we only have the idealized story of Egyptian kingship from which we have to remove veil after veil. But the truth is there, some-where, underneath what the Egyptians chose to tell us.

If we look carefully, we can actually see Hatshepsut and her advisers inexorably and systematically working to make her position permanent. In the first five years of Thutmose III's reign, she sent her most trusted official, Senenmut, down to Aswan to have two giant 10-story obelisks cut from the red granite quarries, ostensibly for her young charge. There Senen-mut carved into the cataract rocks in the Nile River an image, a billboard of the ancient world to any well-connected elite who might sail by, showing Hatshepsut wearing the double-plumed headdress as God's Wife of Amun. In the accompanying text, he told his audience how his mistress had entrusted him alone with this mission (a clever official will always use his service to acquire greater power). Senenmut then claims that the obelisks were ordered "through the power of her majesty," a bold state-ment that anticipated Hatshepsut's future kingship. Senenmut then overtly refers to Hatshepsut as "the one to whom Ra has actually given the kingship."[18] He couldn't call her king, not yet, but he could remind everyone who headed through the Aswan cataract that this woman was already doing the job of king and that they'd best not forget it. It's as if Hatshepsut had ordered a lawyer to start laying the groundwork for her future power grabs, step by step along the path.

In this Aswan graffito, we get that rare insight into Hatshepsut's and her supporters' minds: They were clearly planning her next bold move to the kingship years in advance, and they were strategically publishing her justifications for this inevitable power all around Egypt. Maybe they were even testing the waters by putting such images in different public locations where elites were sure to see them—Hatshepsut performing sacred rites that typically only a king would perform, Hatshepsut standing directly in front of one of the divinities in a temple, Hatshepsut wearing kingly headgear—saving the most brazen claims for the accompanying captions, which only elites could read. Hatshepsut was careful, forthrightly publishing her intentions to formally take on Egypt's highest power before she actually made the jump. With such a lead-up, maybe no one was surprised when the famous oracle of Amun revealed the selection of her as his chosen leader, marking her for kingship before all her people in one of the most public religious festivals at Thebes.

She may even have received her throne name—Maatkara, The Soul of Ra Is Truth, the kind of name reserved for a king—before she actually became king, suggesting that Egypt's priests were more invested in her future pharaonic power than any

other part of society. This name was written in a second cartouche oval exclusive to kings, and it was probably obtained
only after Hatshepsut's lengthy initiation in the temples of the
great gods.

Hatshepsut was clever in creating her pathway to power. So
perhaps it came as no surprise to the assembled courtiers in
Thebes when those two obelisks, which as regent she had
ordered cut for her nephew, Thutmose III, were instead carved
with her own images and names as king. Other early Karnak
blocks show that she commissioned carved temple structures
in preparation for her eventual coronation as monarch.[19]
Maybe the artisans knew her plans before some of Egypt's
wealthiest families.

When she first showed herself as Egypt's sovereign, it was in
female form. Like Neferusobek, there would be no subterfuge,
no disingenuous claim to be a male king. Why should there be?
The Egyptian textual sources show that the words of kingly
power were easily feminized grammatically. Even the Horus
bird—a hieroglyphic symbol in the shape of a hawk—could be
made into a divine female falcon by adding a simple -t. Hatshepsut would manipulate an Egyptian language that was gender
flexible, that could account for a female kingship. What other
written language could do such a thing, using pictures of falcons
and insects and maceheads?

In this first depiction of her power on a Karnak block, Hatshepsut wore a tight-fitting dress, showing her feminine hips
and thighs, but on her head she wore a masculine short wig and
two tall ostrich plumes sitting atop ram's horns. There isn't a

more masculine headdress than one with ram's horns. Like Neferusobek, she layered her masculine kingship onto a feminine person. And, eventually she would take on the titles of kingship itself, calling herself the One of the Sedge and the Bee, King of Upper and Lower Egypt, Maatkara, Hatshepsut.

Women in power have learned that they sometimes have no choice but to layer manly elements onto their feminine selves—like female army officers who wear unisex uniforms, hair neatly tied back, or the female judge wearing not only the black robes of a jurist but also the white wig, the female professional basketball player wearing the same jersey, more or less, as her NBA counterpart, not to mention her coach on the sidelines in an androgynous suit, or the female Anglican minister in the masculine garb of a holy man. There is no feminine alternative for some positions with specific dress. Hatshepsut knew that, just as we do.

This early block showing Hatshepsut as a female king comes from Karnak, in ancient Thebes, the base of Hatshepsut's power as God's Wife of Amun. This was the god Amun's home, where his temples were situated, where his consort, the goddess Mut, and his son, a moon god named Khonsu, were ensconced as well. Thebes was also the birthplace of generations of kings—the Dynasty 17 kings who claimed to have expelled the Hyksos and started the New Kingdom, and the Dynasty 11 kings who had saved Egypt from civil wars and discord. It seemed that Thebes would catapult the world's first great female king into power as well.

Once she had consolidated the southern regions of Egypt, Hatshepsut would expand her authority. As king, she needed to illustrate her power to the elites far north in the Delta, in the urban strongholds of Memphis and Heliopolis, down south at the entrance to the rich gold mines, at Aswan, and farther south in Nubia itself, the source of Egypt's mineral wealth. All along the Nile, Hatshepsut displayed her new position.[20]

She was crowned at or before Year 7 of Thutmose III. The scholarly disagreement about this point is fierce:[21] Some say she moved into the kingship as early as Year 2, others say Year 4 or 5. The actual date of coronation is immaterial because it was the gradual rise in power that was the key part of her strategy. In the end, Hatshepsut used her regency to manufacture a female kingship over time, culminating in months of celebrations at temples throughout Egypt. In Thebes, she set up those two monoliths of stone, mighty obelisks 10 stories high, carved with her name and images as king. She had ordered these towers of stone five or six years earlier; their erection was a miracle to the Egyptian people, a return to Egypt's heyday of engineering marvels that set the king up as god incarnate. To celebrate this acceleration in power, she almost certainly communed with the oracles at each state temple, so that her elites could observe with their own eyes that she possessed the support of the gods in heaven and on Earth, and that they were reinforcing a pious mistress.

We should not underestimate the extent of Hatshepsut's acumen in the workings of ideological power. Because archaeologists have so much preserved from Thebes, we know about the oracle of Amun from her inscriptions at Karnak Temple, how he chose her, how he put the crown on her head with his own hand. We learn that when she revealed herself as a female king to her people, "They saw the enduring king, and what the Lord-of-All himself had done. They placed themselves on their bellies. After this, their hearts recovered."[22]

We should assume that similar rites occurred with other oracles in other temples in other Egyptian cities. In Thebes, Hatshepsut did not hold back in the description of her newfound divinity, telling her assembled elites, "I am beneficent king, lawgiver who judges deeds. . . . I am the wild horned bull coming from heaven that he might see her form. I am the falcon who glides over the lands, landing and dividing his borders. I am the jackal who swiftly circles the land in an instant. I am excellent of heart, one who glorifies her father, attentive of deeds to render justice to him."[23]

In later texts, Hatshepsut baldly, and perhaps somewhat defensively, states that she was taking on this power only because her godly father, Amun, asked her to do so. She tells us that her human father, Thutmose I, introduced her as king to his elites before his death. She tells us that everyone wanted her to be king at such occasions.[24] Hatshepsut knew that a woman's openly declared ambition was perceived with hostility. And so she avoided naming her own ambition at all costs, just as Queen Elizabeth I of England stated upon her accession: "The burden that is fallen upon me makes me amazed, and yet, considering I am God's creature, ordained to obey His appointment, I will thereto yield, desiring from the bottom of my heart that I may have assistance of His grace to be the minister of His heavenly will in this office now committed to me."[25] Or as Pakistani politician Benazir Bhutto claimed that she was only continuing the agenda of her father: "Whatever my aims and agendas were, I never asked for power."[26]

And maybe Hillary Clinton should have more directly disavowed power and personal ambition, in the politic manner of these women. Instead, she took a more nuanced tone: "Whether I am meant to or not, I challenge assumptions about women. I do make some people uncomfortable, which I'm well aware of, but that's just part of coming to grips with what I believe is still one of the most important pieces of unfinished business in human history—empowering women to be able to stand up for themselves."[27]

Hatshepsut would have agreed with Hillary, it seems, but the Egyptian queen would have been much more canny in her public repudiation of personal ambition. In the texts from her second pair of obelisks, we get a more layered understanding of her agenda: "He who hears it will not say, 'It is a lie,' what I have said. Rather say, 'How like her it is; she is devoted to her father!' The god knew it in me. Amun, Lord of the Thrones of the Two Lands, he caused that I rule the Black and Red Lands as reward. No one rebels against me in all lands."[28]

Hatshepsut was king only because the gods put that spark of kingship in her from the beginning. Indeed, she told her people that she could see into the very minds of the gods: "I have not been forgetful of any project he [Amun] has decreed. For my majesty knows he is divine, and I have done it by his command. He is the one who guides me. I could not have imagined the work without his acting: he is the one who gives the directions."

She wrote for the elites of Thebes to read: "My heart is percep-tive on behalf of my father, and I have access to his mind's knowledge."[29]

Ultimately, Hatshepsut's rise to the kingship was irrevocable. How did one say no when every temple, every priest, every oracle, indeed every divinity, was on board with continuing this queen's power? This was a woman who knew in her bones how to construct and maintain religious authority. Once she had access to that most irrefutable and righteous justification, no one could turn her away from the kingship without appearing godless or heretical.

But what was the realpolitik behind Hatshepsut's claim to the throne? Lest we forget—and her single-minded and religiously grounded rise to power can make us overlook this quite easily—when she took the throne, there was already a nine- or 10-year-old boy sitting upon it. This was, again, unprecedented in Egyptian history. Neferusobek of Dynasty 12 ostensibly ruled because there was no one else left to rule, and it would be the same with Tawosret of Dynasty 19. But here in Dynasty 18, in the midst of prosperity and plenty, Hatshepsut was taking the divine kingship she had protected for her family lineage, claim-ing part of a throne already occupied by child-king Menkheperre Thutmose—a monarch whose rule her own political influence had enabled.

But why did she formally become king? We will never know if the boy was suffering from a series of malarial fevers, or if he had just broken his leg in a chariot accident, or if there was a faction of elites behind a strong man with some kind of claim to the throne. Or perhaps we should be looking for a simpler and more obvious explanation. Perhaps Hatshepsut and her entourage worried about the day when Thutmose III and *his* entourage, presumably growing in power as the king got older no matter how little entitled to the kingship he may have been when first enthroned, would push them aside. If such a cabal were growing behind Thutmose III and thus against Hatshepsut's own protectors, then she had to strike immediately, before the king got any older than nine or 10 and she'd have to do it with the strength of the priesthood behind her. Because no one, not even a woman, abdicates from god-kingship itself.

How did the oft-forgotten King Thutmose III react to this change occurring all around him? The woman who had previously sat on a regent's throne, making all the decisions, was now crowned, anointed, endowed, and initiated next to him—indeed with precedence of place, probably on a throne just a bit higher than his own. He himself had been reinvested, his kingship now placed on a weaker foundation. Even his throne name had been changed when Hatshepsut became king—from Menkheperre Thutmose to Menkheper*kare* Thutmose,[30] an implied demotion to everyone but the nine-year-old boy too immature to understand what had just happened. No longer did the Manifestation of the Sun God Endure in him; now only the Manifestation of the *Spirit* of the Sun God Endured in him.

Thutmose III was not the king he once was with Hatshepsut holding the crook and flail alongside him. And yet, what can we expect a child-king to have done about it, especially if the boy was specifically chosen from an unimportant mother from an

uninfluential family? To this boy, plucked from the palace nursery and thrown into the rites of kingship as a toddler, Hatshepsut
had always been the most powerful person he had ever known.
She made all the decisions for him and about him; she always
had. And now it seemed she always would, with impunity.

To MAINTAIN HER POWER in her new role as king, Hatshepsut
worked with her priests to create some radical new manifestations of divine will. Indeed, whenever she made a big power
move, her priests covered her with a volley of public oracular
displays and godly revelations. No Egyptian king before her had
so baldly shown the gods' will to her expectant elites, even pulling the veils from some of the mysteries of divinity by publishing
the moment when the god Amun made his decisions known to
the people who mattered most in ancient Egyptian society.
Hatshepsut had invented a clever marketing tool—the mechanism of political-divine revelation—something to be used by
later rulers such as Akhenaten of Egypt, Alexander the Great,
Caesar Augustus of Rome, Constantine of the eastern Roman
Empire, and on and on to the Ayatollah Khomeini of Iran and
Adolf Hitler of Nazi Germany. When god(s) appear before the
people and anoint their chosen ruler, there is little any dissenter
can do to dissuade the righteous. An ideology fervently believed
is an unassailable social power. Hatshepsut's key to authority
was her ability to wield this robust ideology and to control the
men who administered it.

On a political level, Hatshepsut understood patriarchy and how it worked. She knew her place in traditional Egyptian society and how masculine-derived lineage functioned, even as she transcended those very systems. She thus used her connection to her dead husband, Thutmose II, for a few years, immediately after his death, to prop up his son and her regency. But as soon as his body was cold, she had to look instead to her linear descent from her father. She knew, or quickly figured out, that the Egyptians trusted the longitudinal movement of power from father to son more than the lateral shift from brother to sister.

Hatshepsut recognized, as she subtly moved her nephew, Thutmose III, to a position of less importance, that her capacity to be king now had to come from her own ancestral lineage. She thus had to proclaim loud and clear that she was the eldest daughter of Thutmose I, a title she used in temples all over Egypt, just as she made her bid for the kingship. When Hatshepsut claimed that her father had chosen her and crowned her publicly before all his courtiers, she was indeed using the memory of Thutmose I to legitimize her own reign, but she was probably also looking to Neferusobek's model of justification. Centuries before, Neferusobek had finished her father's pyramid temple at Hawara, that great Labyrinth of Greek legend, carving her name all over the complex for political reasons. The name of Amenemhat IV, her husband and brother, was nowhere to be seen in that complex or anywhere else that mattered to Neferusobek. Now, hundreds of years later, Hatshepsut did the same, putting her father, Thutmose I, everywhere on her monuments, divinizing him, leaving her husband and brother, Thutmose II, out of the game entirely.

More shockingly, even her nephew and co-king was ignored when Hatshepsut first ascended to the throne. Not only, it seems, did she shy away from reminding her people that she ruled alongside a boy-king, but she wanted to obliterate that aunt-nephew relationship entirely. There was no reason to jog the memory of the Egyptian people that this was no traditional co-regency of father and son in a linear patriarchal relationship, that it was actually some strange, upside-down royal partnership between a boy and his aunt. Reliefs that Hatshepsut had started with the boy-king's images show traces of having been removed, presumably at her command.[31] Hatshepsut, it seems, had ordered his depiction erased because her justification for sitting on the throne of Egypt was upended by his occupation of the same throne.

Ironically, it was probably the very lack of linear relationship that got Hatshepsut to the kingship in the first place. If she had borne a son, her regency for that boy would have had a different flavor. Had the king been her child, there would have been no faction of influences from another mother's family members, no entourages, no erasures. *She* would have been the leader of the new king's entourage. Without the competition from and enrichment of another family, Hatshepsut's long-term leadership as king would not have been necessary.

In many ways, we owe Hatshepsut's kingship to that complicated aunt-nephew relationship. Even if she had really *wanted* the kingship, or felt it was her due, given all she had done, if she had been Thutmose III's birth mother, such a political move would not have been even remotely necessary within royal society. A mother would have been able to rule as dowager-queen—wife of the previous and now dead king—from behind the throne quite effectively anyway. Countless Egyptian women had already wielded such influence, Ahmes-Nefertari among them, as formidable King's Mothers. Hatshepsut's ascension to the kingship actually exposes to historians that there were real problems afoot. Hatshepsut, it seems, was having trouble ruling over her nephew (and likely his entourage). We can assume that the in-laws were becoming troublesome. And so she took the kingship outright and formally, with support from dozens of high elites and courtiers, not to mention priests from temples throughout Egypt.

If there were competitive factions in the palace, Hatshepsut's occupation of the throne seems to have forged a balance among Egypt's elites. There is no evidence of bloodshed within the palace walls or outside of them. Thutmose III was allowed to grow up and, indeed, thrive as king. And Egypt settled into one of its most unorthodox co-regencies ever. (Nefertiti would soon eclipse even Hatshepsut with another bizarre instance of shared rule.) It was weird, really: an adolescent boy and a woman entering her thirties, the boy growing older and stronger day by the day, the woman relinquishing her ability to procreate, losing her bloom.

Hatshepsut never ruled alone, but she also had set herself up with quite a challenge: to rule next to a vibrant young king who was quickly gaining more social capital with his nurses and tutors and was making strong friendships with elites' sons in military and academic training. If she had indeed chosen a boy from an uninfluential family as king, then that family was becoming more established with more supporters by the day. And we can imagine Hatshepsut growing ever more defensive and paranoid about Thutmose III's expanding sphere of influence, so that by the time she had her own Temple of Millions of Years built, she included the text: "He who will praise her, he will live. He who will speak an evil thing, ignoring her majesty, he will die."[32]

Things started well for Hatshepsut, on the upswing, moving from princess to God's Wife of Amun, to queen, to regent, to king. Egypt was rich; there was more than enough to go around, to be sure. But now that she was king, her fortunes could only descend as her co-king's virility, acumen, and leadership skills developed and were recognized by everyone in the palace.

And what of her personal life during all this Sturm und Drang? Did she ever fall in love? If she had, there would have been no place for her to record such an occurrence in the ideologically driven record in Egypt's temples. Many Egyptologists have identified the official Senenmut as Hatshepsut's best opportunity for a sexual conquest, even claiming that it was he, her lover, who engineered each of her power moves.[33] But they forget that this woman was the most powerful person—man or woman—in the ancient known world. She didn't need, as would Cleopatra after her, a strong warlord to prop up her reign. She didn't require some official to sexually entice and manipulate because she, as king, could tell any man what to do. If Hatshepsut had sexual affairs, if she fell in love, if she felt she had a life partner—

and all these things are possible—we will never know. There was
no place in Egypt's formal documentation to encode such personal information, no appropriate place for a woman who could
not impregnate any harem to discuss her love interests, no place
for any political competitors to disseminate human details to
discredit her.

Thus, as Hatshepsut climbed higher in her race to power, she
would always have to share it. Even if she had wanted to, assas-
sinating her co-king would have meant a sudden end to her own
power as well—something she may have carefully thought
through. And this is probably why she audaciously tried to utilize
a radically different linear succession, from mother to daughter,
to secure her ongoing legacy after her own death. It had never
been tried before, but Hatshepsut was game. She now looked
to her daughter Nefrure, born to her from her half brother
Thutmose II, to continue her legacy.

Hatshepsut had long since given up her office as God's Wife
of Amun, having transferred that position to Nefrure probably
some years before taking on the kingship. The girl was well-
trained and young, following in the footsteps of her mother.
When she started her menstrual cycle, she likely became one of
Thutmose III's wives, if not his Chief Royal Wife. Nefrure had
pure royal lineage on both sides of her family, unlike Thutmose
III. Hatshepsut probably wanted Nefrure as Great Royal Wife
in the palace to influence a king who was younger and more
inexperienced than herself. And, indeed, the office of God's
Wife could provide the political and ideological foundation for
future rule by the girl. Hatshepsut had seen it done before.

Indeed, she herself had probably wielded power over her own brother-husband, Thutmose II. Hatshepsut may have relied on her daughter Nefrure not only to contain Thutmose III but also to provide both herself and her nephew with a linear connection to the high priestess. Nefrure, as the God's Wife of Amun, was directly related to *both* living kings—as daughter to one and as sister to the other.

We have very little information about Nefrure serving as God's Wife of Amun, but all the monuments and texts point to the girl having taken on this role before her mother assumed the kingship. No direct evidence points to Nefrure joining Thutmose III's harem, but that's only because it was all erased later. Indeed, every circumstantial detail we know about Dynasty 18 royal females suggests that Nefrure married her half brother. The girl would have seen Hatshepsut as her own role model of female power and must have emulated her, collecting more religious and economic authority as she grew older, and prepared for her own role as Great Royal Wife alongside her younger half brother, Thutmose III. Yet we observe no pair statues of Thutmose III and Nefrure, no side-by-side depictions of the brother-sister pair as husband and wife preserved on any stelae or rock inscriptions.[34]

We do, however, note instances where Nefrure appears alone on monuments, calling herself very important and unprecedented names for a Royal Wife or temple priestess. Some of these depictions have been found in the Sinai,[35] far from the elites and power brokers, thus perhaps allowing her to break molds of expectation. But other such grand representations of

Nefrure were set up in Thebes, in Hatshepsut's Temple of Millions of Years—what the Egyptians called the funerary temple of every Dynasty 18 king, celebrating the king's godlike qualities during life and after death. Hatshepsut put massive energy into this temple during her lifetime. Did people talk in fervent whispers of shock when they heard that Hatshepsut had commissioned Nefrure depicted in monumental scale as a future leader? Did Thutmose III roll his eyes at his queen or at his aunt's presumption? We will never know. Because by the time historians had found traces of the evidence, Nefrure's images were already obliterated from the temple: a destruction so complete that we can't even talk with certainty about the woman having been a part of the scene.

Whether she had been included in such monumental images or not, Nefrure seems to have lived far into the reign of her mother and even beyond. When she made steps toward gaining political power, her images were removed, leaving only traces of an erased name for Egyptologists to debate ad nauseam. Nefrure is actually the hardest person in Hatshepsut's story to discuss, so carefully and thoroughly has the evidence of her been eliminated. The very act of her erasure from the Dynasty 18 record is enough to raise our eyebrows, to make us realize that the girl's presence upset some balance of patriarchal power in some fundamental way. There would clearly be a price to pay for so much female ambition; Hatshepsut may have tried to push herself and her daughter's suits too high, until they both were shoved off the cliff together.

Hatshepsut also ran into problems with her own depiction: an issue that was bound to crop up as no other female king before her had occupied the throne this long. Hatshepsut may have looked first and foremost to Neferusobek in the Fayum for models of female kingship. She may have even copied the earlier woman's statuary—showing herself wearing the markers of kingship on a slender female seated body, or kneeling with arms extended, holding round pots. She mimicked the way Neferu- sobek linked herself to her father in a public relations campaign as his choice for rule. Without Neferusobek, Hatshepsut's two- decades-long rule would have been unthinkable. She stood on the shoulders of the woman who had come before.[36]

But, at a certain point, even the powerful Hatshepsut hit a snag with her own feminine depiction. As Thutmose III reached his majority, Hatshepsut entered an in-between land, presenting herself with an androgyny that she had never approached before. One statue of hers, broken into fragments after her rule had ended but glued back together by Metropol- itan Museum of Art conservators, shows her as a female/male king. She looks at her people with a delicate, feminine face, heart-shaped and sweet; with wide-open eyes; a straight, small nose; and a pert smile on her face. Her shoulders are graceful, her legs long and lean. But her upper body is naked. She has slight breasts but no nipples. The statue was a strange compro- mise, an attempt by Hatshepsut to puzzle out an unsolvable problem: to be a mature female king while there was a young man on the throne alongside her.

In her next and most numerous series of statues, Hatshepsut gave in, showing herself as fully masculine—with buff biceps and pectoral muscles—with a wide chest and strong legs, even a square jaw and a masculine face. Yet the texts describing these statues, naming the depicted king, indicate that this was a woman: there are -t's after the *sa* or "son of Re" signs. She could be honest in her textual depiction, but not, it seems, in her figural one.

Hatshepsut's (aging) femininity had become a liability, an unwinnable campaign. And so, in the majority of figural sculptures and reliefs produced during Hatshepsut's reign, she made herself look like a man. This has caused generations of Egyptologists and enthusiasts to question her gender choices and even her sexual identity, asking if she really looked or dressed like this in person, often injecting modern transgender issues into a kingship that was already thousands of years old.

But gender confusion was not Hatshepsut's problem—that she was really a woman who wanted to be a man, or a cross-dresser, or a masculinizing woman, or a lesbian—all of which we recognize today as real identities that do not necessarily overlap and that need to be validated with respect. No, Hatshepsut's problem was that she was trying to inhabit a masculine role within a patriarchal system on a long-term basis while there was a male king already occupying the throne. She simply couldn't compete, no matter how many statues in androgynous guise she created. The people demanded their Bull of Egypt. And so she gave it to them.

With all these obstacles, how did Hatshepsut maintain power? Because she always took precedence over her nephew, Thutmose III, in depicted processions and religious rituals, and thus we would assume it was the same in the throne rooms of Egypt. During her nephew's extreme youth, Hatshepsut was likely able to conduct most of her reign unimpeded by him personally. He was perhaps 14 years old when she began construction on her Temple of Millions of Years. As a youth who still had a great deal of military and political training to undergo, he was probably still controllable, possibly even located somewhere far from her presence on the borderlands or in military encampments.

There is no evidence whatsoever that Hatshepsut ever looked to her nephew to maintain her power; she relied on Egypt's officials and elites to make her mark instead. She depended on men without ties to old patrician families, men like Senenmut, to see her ventures succeed. But she also demanded the support of the old elite families, too, families like that of Ahmose-Pennekhbet from el-Kab; their interests would have been intertwined with hers just as profoundly. Indeed, if there were rival family factions destabilizing the court, joining Thutmose III's entourage of more ambitious elites, they were likely related to the king via his mother's side, that little-known woman named Isis. Thutmose III's maternal in-laws were likely unconnected to Egypt's most powerful families; it's unclear what their agendas may have been or what methods they used to achieve their goals. None of these alliances are clearly visible in the textual record.

Instead, we see other clues that Hatshepsut was not as powerful as she claims to have been, including the fact that she created a tremendous number of new jobs for elites. It was a time of extraordinary professionalization, to be sure: in the military wing, in the priestly ranks, in treasury positions.[37] In other words, it was a time of rebalancing the court, with the king essentially selling posts for influence and support. Bit by bit, this female monarch lost economic and political influence in the long term in order to keep it in the short term.

And what does this tell us about the requirements of female power? If we have evidence for anything, it is of a female king who had to give away more than she kept, who had to allow her elites to take more from the palace and temple treasuries than any other Dynasty 18 king had previously found acceptable. Hatshepsut was blessed with an Egypt rich enough to afford the payoffs demanded to keep her influence going strong at court. This is likely why she made sure she had control of the money, the all-important treasuries, through close and trusted officials—at the palace and at the great state temples. But she also gave those same elites free rein to spend more wealth than ever before on their own statues and tombs, more publicly and visibly than ever before. The days of the pyramids were long gone, allowing a succession crisis and a female king to usher in a new age of hereditary professionalism, when elites could ask for more wealth from their king, get it, and then hand that foundation of power down to their own sons in their own mini-dynasties. Hatshepsut's age was one of enrichment for her officials. But she was so wealthy herself, leaving behind so many grand structures, that it has been difficult for historians to recognize that she was in any way impoverished.

Everyone needed Hatshepsut's pyramid scheme to continue, but it was expensive. She had many temples all around Egypt to update with stone reliefs, new obelisks to commission, new colossal statues to erect, and her own Temple of Millions of Years to build on the Theban West Bank: all job opportunities, all biddable contracts to win. To many treasurers, all of this spending likely seemed unsustainable in the long term, and they may have told Hatshepsut so privately. The best way to bring more wealth into state coffers? A good campaign or two. A little war.

The fact that Hatshepsut was a woman didn't make her any more of a pacifist, it seems, not with legions of new officials on the payroll. And so she brought her army south and terrorized Nubia and Kush more than once, ensuring that new spoils of war flowed into Egypt and that gold mines churned at full capacity. It probably didn't hurt that foreign kings to the north of Egypt, in the Levant, heard about these successful campaigns and felt cowed enough to keep some tribute payments coming into Egypt.

This was Hatshepsut's kingship: a delicately balanced political achievement for a woman dependent upon her nobility's cooperation and co-option. Only great wealth could have allowed such unusual governing schemes. Hatshepsut excelled at spending Egypt's lavish earnings. But it seems she still needed to make a big splash with her elites to maintain her authority, to continually prove that she was the chosen monarch of Egypt. This chip on her shoulder demanded that she organize a trading expedition to the land of Punt, a semimythical place so far away that the prospects must have excited her elites in the same way that Napoleon's expedition to Egypt had energized Paris in the 19th century. When men returned successfully from the sub-Saharan land, probably somewhere near modern-day Eritrea along the Red Sea coast, replete with incense like frankincense and myrrh, the Egyptian people rejoiced. Stories about the fat and misshapen queen of Punt were published and distributed for elite consumption, along with images of the strange flora and fauna recorded by the Egyptians along the journey: visual proof that the trip really had taken place. Hatshepsut was rewarded with the respect of her people for pulling off one of the most daring feats an Egyptian king could perform—a return voyage from the legendary land of priceless aromas and ebony hardwood trees. Hatshepsut even commissioned the expedition with the blessing of the Amun oracle, setting it up as a fait accompli of preordained success. She must have been relieved when the ships actually arrived back in port, laden with goods.

Her political success notwithstanding, Hatshepsut's most enduring achievement may be an architectural one—the construction of a traditional, yet nontraditional, structure in the desert on the West Bank of the Nile, nestled into a great half-moon bay of cliffs sacred to the goddess Hathor. The selection of the site smacked of great confidence or extraordinary insecurity, or both. Hatshepsut picked the most visible, the most sacred, the most beautiful place in southern Egypt for her Temple of Millions of Years, a space where her elite could congregate and consume the achievements she had created during her kingship.

More important, the site was built so that her people could offer gifts to her once she had died and become a great god in the heavens herself. Here, she published in detail her chosen biographical tales. The first story: how her mother was visited by the god Amun, who impregnated the queen Ahmes with his sacred essence, producing the miracle baby Hatshepsut, who against all odds would go on to become female king. To the

Egyptologists who first translated it, the text smacked of self-doubt, a need to excuse her female authority. But Hatshepsut was just following her Dynasty 12 ancestors, putting up a traditional text-image tableau of her own divine origins. Her second contribution to this temple was an account of her father, Thutmose I, introducing her to his courtiers as his heir, his eldest daughter. In her third story, she published accounts of the obelisk pairs she had erected in the Temple of Amun, just across the river on Thebes's East Bank. And for her fourth display, she showed off details of each part of her famous Punt expedition: the men setting off in their ships with Amun's blessing while Egyptians said their farewells from the shores, the land of Punt heavy with the scent of incense balls so plentiful that the Egyptians could scoop them up by the hundreds into baskets, and Punt's odd ruling couple: a giantess of a misshapen queen accompanied by her little husband-king. Even the sea fish were represented in all their intricate differentiation, as if Hatshepsut needed to say, "Look. It really happened."

Hatshepsut continued to show her piety, building temples throughout the land, like that of the goddess Pakhet, She Who Scratches, or that of Mut, the mother goddess for whom she built a porch of drunkenness to celebrate and contain the divine feminine's alter egos of viciousness and softness. She busied herself building in the heart of Amun's sacred temple at Karnak. Here she set up an extraordinary structure that was meant to hold the portable and gilded cedar barque of Amun himself, the method of bringing the god's image to the people in oracular processions.

Hatshepsut knew that she owed her own power to the god's publicly made choice, and she repaid her divine father with a priceless reddish-pink quartzite chapel to house the barque carried aloft by oracle priests. On the walls of this Red Chapel, as the structure is now called, she recorded details of her coronation, of the oracles that befell her, first, when she was a young princess picked out of the crowd by the god for the first time, and, second, during a festival of Sakhmet, when she was finally marked for the kingship by the god. In the Red Chapel reliefs she showed herself not as a girl, but as a full-grown man, crowned in the company of the gods of Egypt. And it was on this building, constructed around Year 16, that she also introduced the image of Thutmose III back into her kingship: the first time she showed herself with her nephew and co-king side by side.[38]

Hatshepsut even celebrated a jubilee—something that Egyptian kings were not meant to have, it seems, unless they reached 30 years of kingship. Perhaps she required more and bigger moments to rejigger her authority, like a junkie constantly looking for the next powerful drug with the sharper high. Thutmose III had come of age. Hatshepsut was now expected to invite her nephew into the official running of the state as a true co-king, not just in name, but also in power. And so she hit upon the idea of an age-old and revered Egyptian celebration that would simultaneously allow her to maintain dominance over her newly empowered co-king: a sed festival. In many ways, it wasn't hard to do. She cleverly made it a jubilee of her family's years of kingship—11 years of Thutmose I's rule; three years of Thutmose II's rule, and 16 years of her joint rule with Thutmose III as regent and co-king, totaling 30 years, the ideal and accepted number. The jubilee would renew their joint kingship, while singling out Hatshepsut as the pair's true leader. Hatshepsut continuously innovated, adding a spin to an archaic ritual in order to find a face-saving way of inviting the up-to-then rather invisible boy-king to take his place on the throne as a man. Thutmose III was now probably 18 years old. There was no way she could have kept him in the shadows any longer, no matter how hard she may have tried.

And so, as her Red Chapel rose in the very beating heart of Karnak's sacred temple, she had the two sovereigns depicted performing rituals together—like the Opet Festival, a celebration of Amun's renewal that took place every year in Thebes between Karnak and Luxor Temples. Both kings are shown walking together on the festival circuit, and in these depictions, Thutmose III always follows Hatshepsut. In some images, they appear as twins—same height, same face, same crown. Other depictions show differentiation only in the headgear and kilts. Their portraiture was indistinguishable; only the text captions with names and epithets help us sort out who is who. She was depicted more often than her nephew, of course—but he was a legitimate and real part of her reign now, presumably with significant military and political training under his belt, able to step up as a real partner in kingship, a general in training, a leader of armies. At this point, Hatshepsut was approaching her forties: old by the standards of the day. It was the perfect time to establish Thutmose III in the context of long-lasting kingship that would continue forever.

Thutmose III, it seems, did all that Hatshepsut wanted in these last years of her kingship. There are no traces that he ever dissented from his aunt or that she was unhappy with him. We need to remember that Thutmose's highest-ranked queen may have been none other than Hatshepsut's daughter Nefrure, linking their agendas quite closely, not to mention sharing information.

There are, however, clues that Hatshepsut was slapped down for overreaching—not on her own behalf, but on Nefrure's. One Egyptologist who documented and excavated her Temple of Millions of Years notes a massive relief of a woman on the third terrace, which he believes to have originally been a depiction of Nefrure.[39] The size and posture showed a female ruler of such large scale that it apparently pushed beyond the traditional bounds of queenship. This relief was modified at some point to remove not only the name of Nefrure but also her elements and postures of power, changing her instead into a modest, if still strangely massive, image of Hatshepsut's long-dead mother Ahmes. What is behind this alteration?

If Nefrure had married the younger monarch Thutmose III, as fits with everything we know of Dynasty 18 royal families and court behavior, then their sons—assuming that she was able to get pregnant by her half brother some three to five years after she took the throne—might have been around 12 or younger when Hatshepsut entered the last year of her kingship. In a way, Hatshepsut had timed it all perfectly—but only if she had been a sole king and a man, that is, ready to pass on her sovereignty to her son. In such an alternative history, one of these sons would likely have attained the throne at Hatshepsut's death, and Nefrure would have been the perfect queen-regent, extending her mother's female domination of the royal palace and temple into another generation.

But Hatshepsut wasn't the sole king. And she wasn't a man. There was a king still living, Thutmose III, who would rule another 30 years after the death of his aunt, making those sons of Nefrure, if they existed, very old—40 or 50 or dead—by the time Thutmose III himself passed on: older and established men who did not need a queen-regent mother to guide them. For Hatshepsut and Nefrure, the timing was actually a catastrophe.

As it turns out, we have absolutely no mention of any sons of Nefrure in the histories preserved to us. Incest could have meant sterility, so maybe there were none. But if Nefrure had produced sons for her brother-husband, and if her authority toward the end of Hatshepsut's joint reign with Thutmose III was real, as the evidence suggests, then Nefrure and her progeny were in for a massive fall. Indeed, Nefrure's images were cruelly assailed and erased all over Egypt. The position of God's Wife of Amun was transferred to one of Thutmose III's wives from nonroyal origins instead of to one of his Royal Sisters or Daughters. And the son chosen to be Thutmose III's heir and crown prince 30 years later was a boy so young that he required a co-regency with his father. Thutmose III had apparently skipped over any older sons of pure royal blood, opting instead for new blood, untainted by the royal female influence of the palace.

WHEN HATSHEPSUT DIED, she was buried in state and with the full respect her station demanded, according to all archaeological discoveries in the Valley of the Kings.[40] At Karnak, Thutmose III even finished some of her buildings and reliefs on her behalf, piously completing her Red Chapel in the sacred center of Amun's Temple and carefully adding his own name to the upper dark-gray stone borders. But in the more visible parts of Karnak Temple, Thutmose III began a very different campaign, one that focused on rewriting his past and on the removal of his aunt. He started by reassigning some of Hatshepsut's colossal statuary to his father Thutmose II and his grandfather Thutmose I.[41] He left Hatshepsut's Temple of Millions of Years untouched during the early parts of his reign, although there isn't any evidence that he lifted a finger to finish the structure, either. It seems Hatshepsut had that task well in hand by the time she succumbed to death.[42]

Thutmose III went on to live a long life, and had a splendid kingship, punctuated by more than a dozen successful military campaigns, exotic trading ventures, pathbreaking architectural wonders, and obelisks of his own—and, unlike anything that Hatshepsut or Nefrure could ever achieve, a harem full of sons. He suffered his own insecurity complexes, it seems, continuously reminding his people that the gods really had anointed him with the kingship, well and truly. It was when Thutmose III picked the young prince Amenhotep, whom we call King Amenhotep II, about 25 years into his sole reign, that he began the more brutal removal of his aunt from her monuments: He smashed her statues to bits, chiseled away the reliefs of the

Punt expedition, and reassigned kingly images to her husband or father. If Hatshepsut had injected her daughter Nefrure into the palace and the harem, likely as a means of influencing her nephew Thutmose III, then that game was now completely up. If Nefrure had borne him any sons while serving as Egypt's chief priestess, then Thutmose III had now reached a stage in his life and a level of power that allowed him to circumnavigate those grown men and their mother's complicated lineage.

By choosing Amenhotep II as the next king, Thutmose was actually taking a page from kings of the Old Kingdom—in particular Pepi I of Dynasty 6, a king who himself had more than enough powerful sisters and daughters with whom to contend. When Thutmose III chose Amenhotep II as his heir, he may have simultaneously ordered the erasure of Nefrure from monuments around Egypt, effectively taking the King's Daughters and Sisters out of power, and elevating instead nonroyal women, women who weren't his sisters. When he chose his young heir, he was sending a message to those same royal women who had constantly told him what to do his whole life: where to stand during this or that ceremony, how to wield a ritual instrument, how to act in court, whom to take as a wife, whom to name as God's Wife of Amun, whom to name as the next king. His last great act as king was to elevate the children of nonroyal women as his legacy because the King's Sister-wives, like Nefrure, had become too powerful. What actually happened to Nefrure, we will never know. From all we can see, Hatshepsut died a natural death and was treated with respect for decades thereafter; we can guess that Nefrure—King's Daughter, King's Sister, King's Wife, God's Wife—was afforded the same honor. Thutmose III was canny; he could wait for his pushback against female power. And when he pulled the trigger to destroy all those monuments, he taught his son to fear royal women in power, too.

Thutmose III's death marked a momentous shift away from royal female power that had been so strong just a few years before. Thutmose III and his son Amenhotep II—not to mention the next kings, Thutmose IV and Amenhotep III—knew *not* to name any King's Daughters or Sisters to the post of God's Wife of Amun. Indeed, they placed nonroyal wives in the post, or sometimes their own mothers, as a way of keeping palace influence in the temple under their own control, not allowing another competing female lineage of power to be created. Thutmose III effectively hamstrung the office of the God's Wife of Amun for generations to come. Lest we forget, every time a minority gains power, those who feel the most threatened are prone to push back—as the men's rights movement is currently reacting to feminism, as evangelical Christians are to secular humanism and atheists, as American white nationalism is to Black Lives Matter and the Obama presidency, as European nationalist populism is to the European Union and its multiculturalism. Thutmose III's Egypt seems to have been undergoing its own threatened reaction to an upswing in female political power, cracking down hard on it and forging a culture that would almost disallow its continuance in their traditional society.

In the end, Hatshepsut may have done everything right. She was a conservative, doing what kings were supposed to do. But her methods of taking power were more than innovative; they were aberrant. She was the traditional nontraditionalist, traces of whose memory were eventually eradicated, because success can easily be claimed by someone else. If you do what the king is supposed to do and set up a colossal three-dimensional statue of yourself as a masculinized female king before a massive temple pylon showing your divinity and unassailability, think how easy it would be to reassign that perfected image to someone else. No need to destroy it; just change the name to her father or husband. Success in Egypt was an abstract for which others could easily take credit, leaving the real person responsible for some actions or monuments unknowable for generations, lost to cultural memory, making Hatshepsut's name more unpronounceable as the generations crept by. Doing everything right ensured Hatshepsut's lost legacy.

Many women already know that their greatest successes and their best ideas are the ones most easily co-opted and claimed by the men around them—in the workplace, in the home, in politics. James Watson and Francis Crick hid the credit for their discovery of DNA's double helix in a brief footnote mention in their *Nature* article; it was British biophysicist Rosalind Franklin who came up with the idea first (and whose photo was shared without her knowledge or consent). When Watson finally admitted it almost half a century later, the pair had already won the Nobel Prize and Franklin was dead. Ada Lovelace, daughter of Lord Byron, was a mid-19th-century math aficionado who helped Charles Babbage, according to his own account, invent the world's first computer with her complex mathematical programming—a fact historians have discounted until recently.[43] The track record of men taking credit for female successes is unbearably long. Hatshepsut was certainly not history's first victim, and she would not be the last.

Indeed, most people don't have any inkling of just how successful our next queen really was—because her accomplishments have, until quite recently, been totally co-opted by the men and boys who followed her.

CHAPTER 4

NEFERTITI

More Than Just a Pretty Face

Nefertiti of Dynasty 18 (1550 to 1295 B.C.) has been immortalized for her beauty. Her limestone bust, now in the Berlin Egyptian Museum, shows a regal and mature woman with a proud gaze, high cheekbones, dark-olive skin, eyes set obliquely in her face, full and luscious red lips, pure symmetricality (except for one unfinished, or possibly damaged, eye), all topped by a unique blue crown that set her queenship apart from every other Egyptian King's Wife, before or after. But Nefertiti was much more than a flawless accompaniment to her god-king or a fertile field for her lord. She would live through an unprecedented storm of events that called upon her to become a steadfast and calm leader who could heal the deep wounds inflicted on her people during the strangest, least traditional time Egypt had ever known. Like so many other women in our story, Nefertiti would receive no credit for this political leadership, even though it was she who started the restoration of a country turned upside down, setting Egypt to rights at its darkest hour.

Nefertiti was born during the reign of strong, centralized kingship, in an ancient Egypt characterized by luxuries beyond reckoning. King Amenhotep III had ruled for almost 40 years, after ascending the throne as a youth. At least two royal sons—Thutmose and Amenhotep—were born to the Great Royal Wife Tiy, in addition to dozens of other princes who would receive no mention in Egyptian documents. Amenhotep III found a calling in temple construction. He commissioned more stone buildings, colossal and life-size statuary, stelae, and monuments than any other king before him, in such high numbers and of such stunning precision of craftsmanship that this embarrassment of riches continues to astound Egyptologists. Amenhotep III found an interest in theology, too, instituting a stronger focus on the solar gods of Egypt, particularly Amun of Thebes and Atum of Heliopolis. This king's Egypt was the land at its very apex—its richest, its most artistic and creative, its most intellectual, its most baroque, its most embellished. He called himself Egypt's Dazzling Sun and, indeed, all of Egypt believed him to be the physical emanation of the light on Earth.

As a boy, the King's Son Amenhotep was second choice, at best. His brother Thutmose had been marked as heir. Without the glare of attention, Prince Amenhotep stood on the sidelines, observing his father's fervent attentions to Egypt's various sun gods. He saw how his father's building agenda focused on solarism and light. The prince was educated during a time of burgeoning religious intellectualism, now so fashionable, in which priests attempted to understand anew the mysteries of the sun's movements, death and rebirth, fertility, life-giving and healing abilities. It's possible that Prince Amenhotep even received a priestly training of some kind. As a King's Son, he would have been an ideal candidate to train into a wealthy and influential high priest's position from which he could act as an extension of the next king's power in temple institutions.

But we have no details of Amenhotep's upbringing as prince; Dynasty 18 Egyptians were circumspect, mentioning little to nothing about the King's Sons in the public records or temple displays if they were not being groomed for the kingship. There were likely between 50 and 100 boys born to Amenhotep III, about whom we know absolutely nothing. Regardless, Prince Amenhotep grew up seeing his father's royal infallibility, his extraordinary achievements, and his religious insights, all during a miraculous reign approaching its 40th year.

Piety and religious fervor were all around him; so too were vast riches, all easily won. King Amenhotep III needed to waste no time on campaigning abroad to gain war booty; he had inherited a ready-made imperial machine that produced income at a steady clip. Nubia and its exploited population were churning out gold and granite; Kush, in modern-day Sudan, was enslaved; the petty kings of the Levant and Syria were paying tribute. Rulers of Canaanite coastal cities were engaged in lucrative trading ventures with Egypt, regularly shipping cedars of Lebanon to the Delta coast. It was a good time to be king. Because his reign was so long, Amenhotep III celebrated no less than three jubilees (the latter two not spaced out at 30-year intervals but held just a few years after the first), and his sons— Amenhotep included—were likely present for all of them.

The king used the jubilees to marry two of his own daughters, bringing them into the royal bed and the royal harem, just as the sun god himself had done with the sky goddess Hathor. The entire court would have watched as the chosen son, the crown prince Thutmose, was brought to the fore, a shining light in his father's eyes. Despite his high birth to the Great Royal Wife Tiy, Prince Amenhotep was just one of many other princes standing in the shadows.

But this was ancient Egypt. It would take just one epidemic, one accident, one infection, to bring another one of the King's Sons to the favored spot, allowing a different boy to become the Golden Horus, the Good God, the Strong Bull of Egypt. As Amenhotep III grew fat and decrepit with his own excesses of food and wine (as his preserved mummy shows), the chosen brother, Thutmose, the crown prince, upon whom his father had pinned all his hopes, died unexpectedly, the cause never recorded, thrusting Egypt into uncertainty and panic about who would fill the position of heir. Whether by the command of the king or by the consensus of the court or order of the divine oracle, Prince Amenhotep was selected as the next crown prince. Perhaps because of his lack of preparation for the job, his father named him as a co-regent alongside him in the last years of his reign.[1] Two kings of the same name, whom Egyptologists call Amenhotep III and IV, sat upon the throne concurrently, clinching the succession and calming the fears of Egypt's stakeholders.

Amenhotep IV was an unexpected king—for his father, for the court, probably even for himself. And because his father had ruled so long, this new sovereign was no boy, but a full-fledged man with mature ideas of his own. If we suppose that he had been born in Year 7 or 8 of his father's reign—speculation based on the young age of Amenhotep III at his succession and his marriage to Tiy in Year 2—then Amenhotep IV was around 30 years of age when he became king, venerable indeed for a new monarch. A younger king would have been more easily influenced by the agendas of those elites and priests around him. But not this son; he would soon bend Egypt to his extraordinary will, almost breaking its back with his demands.

If anything motivated the strange, unprecedented, and radical religious leanings of the new King Amenhotep IV, it was circumstance: the right guy at the right time with the right mindset. Not only was a fully formed and opinionated man now on the throne of Egypt, but he gained this power at a time when Egypt's kingly expenditures had never been more excessive and when Egypt's wealth—in mineral resources from the South, in tribute from the North—had never been greater.

Should we be surprised that a single-minded prince, who grew up with every contrivance wealth could provide, would believe himself beyond reproach of humanity or divinity, able to make shocking new orders that differed radically from what had come before? Like Kim Jong-un of contemporary North Korea, Amenhotep IV was formed by latitude and plenty, surrounded by yes-men and obsequious family members. He had never known anything but a king able to carve his most insane whim into temple stone. His father had even commissioned a unique colossal star chart out of granite, quartzite, and sandstone in his

Theban Temple of Millions of Years. Replete with massive statues of crocodile-hippos and other strange beasts representative of the stellar constellations, accompanied by 730 life-size statues of the female lioness goddess Sakhmet (two for each day of the year: a good fate and a bad), each one with her eyes painted red,[2] it was a magnificent sight. With this much money available to the crown, with no military threats on the horizon, and with everyone believing that kingship was not only unassailable but sacred, Egypt found itself the ideal victim of a willful and mad royal agenda. Like his father, King Amenhotep IV would face no real obstacles to any of the outlandish schemes he concocted; on the contrary, the Egyptian system was perfectly set up to support his wishes in every way possible.

Nefertiti was born into the same wealth and excess, connected to the same royal court. Her parentage goes unrecorded, but she was given the unprecedented honor of a wet nurse and tutor, privileges generally reserved for the King's Children. Yet there is no mention of any royal lineage in her blood. As a girl, Nefertiti no doubt experienced King Amenhotep III's jubilee years, participating in a series of insanely expensive affairs concocted to celebrate Egypt's god-king. During these royal celebrations, the king and his family were paraded through temple avenues, were held aloft in carrying chairs, and engaged in baroque temple rituals in public before the larger populace and in the claustrophobic, smoky, inner sanctuaries where the gods' cult statues dwelled in private.

Every rich Egyptian celebrated right along with the king, drinking and eating to excess, partying as if cost were immaterial. Elites were given palm-size glazed stone scarab beetles, carved with hieroglyphic texts commemorating the abundance that this kingship could afford—for example, the marriage of the king to Syrian princess Gilukhepa, who brought along 317 handmaidens to accompany her to Egypt, or the successful staged-safari hunt of more than a hundred lions by the king, accompanied by the boast that he shot each one himself with his own arrows. This was royal PR, ancient Egyptian style, but recognizable to us as Lifestyles of the Rich and Famous.

In ancient Egypt, rich officials attended various jubilee parades and processions, watched the numerous appearances of the king and his family at the palace window, decked out in their finery, expecting to catch a golden trinket or two thrown down by the god-king and his wife to show their pleasure with their faithful elites. Some of these men even had rituals from the sed festival celebrations carved in all of their intricacies on their own tomb chapel walls as proof of their involvement—kind of like a Gen-Xer crowing about having attended a private Sting concert at an Emirati mansion on a man-made island in the shape of a palm tree off the coast of Dubai. All this conspicuous consumption defined Nefertiti's first decade of life.

Egyptian language, culture, and politics were already thousands of years old by the time King Amenhotep IV became sole king. By this point, people knew what to expect of their divine leader: He would maintain the traditional rituals as the chief priest, interceding with divinities to make sure the Nile crested and receded seasonally, as it should, that the sun rose and set daily, as it should. But this particular king would quickly become an anomaly: a man willing to destroy in order to realize his vision. Amenhotep IV was a radical, allowed to implement the most extreme of religious changes and overturn the most traditional of rites and belief systems, all in a regional state averse to sudden changes, yet willing to do anything their god-king demanded. Amenhotep IV eventually turned himself, his family, his people, even his Great Royal Wife Nefertiti, away from Egypt's many gods.

Nefertiti was selected as Great Royal Wife in Year 4 of his reign. Before that time, there is no reference to any queen at all. Perhaps Amenhotep IV already had a wife closer to his own age, as would be expected of an Egyptian adult male, King's Son or not. The existence of a previous (and unnamed) wife is a more likely scenario than the notion that he was some kind of celibate ascetic philosopher.[3] Whatever the reality of Amenhotep IV's first four years as king, his decision to marry Nefertiti was his new start, resulting in a flurry of bizarre decisions that would come hard and fast, one after the other.

At this point in her life, Nefertiti must have been pliant and easily influenced, just a girl married to an all-powerful god-king. She found herself paired with one of the most resolute, formidable, creative, and indomitable minds in the ancient world, a man who would rip Egypt asunder with his personal fanaticism. He was protected by a supremely well-functioning authoritarian regime. There were no imperial forces or foreign kings poised for invasion. Amenhotep IV was safe to do as he chose, and he would drag his bride, the Great Royal Wife Nefertiti, willingly or not, on his mind-bending journey.

She was a young woman when she began her sexual and domestic relationship with the Egyptian sovereign—as young as 10 or 11 or as old as 15 or 16. Nefertiti had already been in close orbit of the king; her wet nurse had been the wife of the courtier Ay, a man who himself would become known as God's Father, perhaps indicating that he had acted as a tutor of the crown prince Amenhotep as a boy. Ay must have been instrumental in placing Nefertiti in the position of Great Royal Wife. She was a girl with intimate connections to the palace. She may have been groomed for this position from birth.

If her statuary and name (meaning "The Beautiful One Has Come") are to be believed, Nefertiti was stunning to behold. She may have been chosen by the king as his Great Royal Wife for her beauty alone, but the honors given to her as an infant— wet nurse and tutor—make that unlikely. She was born an elite. As a product of the Egyptian court, Nefertiti had been exposed not only to Egyptian luxury but also to ancient Egyptian submission to authoritarian rule. She knew when to keep her mouth shut, how to lower her eyes with grace, when to make eye contact, and when to do what the sun king ordered. Nefertiti knew her place.

Her relationship with King Amenhotep IV seems to have been a success in every way. She was given a visibility and centrality of place that no queen before her had enjoyed, with new reliefs and statuary. And she was a good breeder; Nefertiti granted the king his first daughter, Meritaten, just a year after they married, proving his ability to perform the sacred sexual work he had been put on this Earth to do.

Nefertiti was also her husband's chief priestess and ideological muse. Egyptologists have commented that her name was Hathoric—associated with the Golden Goddess Hathor, who acted as sexual partner to her father, the sun god. Hathor represented the divine feminine essential to any union between the sun and sky, between light and matter.[4] Nefertiti may even have been given this new name by her husband when she entered the harem. She was meant to represent a sacred sexualized aspect for her husband; this is likely why so much of the physical intimacy between the royal couple—kissing and hand-holding, sitting on the king's lap—was later represented in temples and on stelae. Amenhotep IV's marital bed had become a place of divine creation.[5]

Nefertiti's appearance aligned with some new theological strategy of Amenhotep IV, and in Year 5, she joined the king in a glorious sed festival. It was unprecedented to celebrate such a jubilee of royal renewal after only five years as king, but Amenhotep IV threw tradition to the wind with discomforting ease, ordering lavish preparations for an over-the-top royal display of eating, drinking, and dancing, as he had experienced in the reign of his father. He ordered the construction of new temples in eastern Karnak; we can only imagine the consternation of artisans when they heard the tight deadline for completion. Time was so short that they even invented a new building technique, relying on smaller inscribed blocks that Egyptologists call *talatats*, which could be put in place much more quickly.

The new king had big plans. Amenhotep IV was orchestrating a jubilee to reveal his special relationship with a little-known but very material manifestation of the sun god—the Aten, the powerful orb shining in the sky. Indeed, the preserved reliefs depicting this sed festival tell us that the jubilee was not actually meant for *him* personally, but for his god, for the Aten itself who was now made king over all the other gods. Cue the shocked faces of priests and courtiers when they learned that the king was planning a sed festival for a divinity in order to rejigger the hierarchy of the heavens themselves. Amenhotep IV even had his newly elevated divinity's disk adorned with a symbol of kingship—the uraeus, a rearing cobra—at the top of the orb.

During the jubilee festivities, elites must have continuously commented to one another that things were getting very strange. As they watched their king and queen carried in procession along the sacred ways, as they took in the Hathoric dances of semi-nude women to celebrate the shining of the Aten, as they noticed the jarring and startling new images of their king, they must have felt profound change in the air. Even Nefertiti, as young as she was, must have felt a sense of foreboding. She would be right there at the king's side when, in his fifth year, his radicalism truly began to take shape.

Amenhotep IV had already been overseeing a shockingly newfangled temple construction project for years now, and the jubilee was his time to reveal this religious innovation to his people. These new structures were peculiar, constructed in a style supposedly communicated by the god Aten directly to the king, and then from the king to his artisans. With these temples, Amenhotep IV revealed to his people a new, radicalized, physical image of himself as king in his colossal statuary and reliefs. Eschewing the naturalistic full face his father had favored, Amenhotep IV opted for a strangely elongated and pulled visage, marked with slanted, overlong, narrow eyes. Instead of a traditional hieroglyphic body of normalized limbs, Amenhotep IV settled on a lengthening of his person, thinning out his extremities, so that he stood upon stick-narrow ankles and held ritual implements in hands projecting from tiny wrists with alien-like, overly long, and upwardly curved fingers. He didn't thin out his belly or midsection, however; on the contrary, his hips were shown as extraordinarily full, feminine even, each thigh like a fat fowl's drumstick perched on exceedingly narrow calves and ankles, all with the interesting detail of a slightly hyperextended knee. His belly protruded and hung low over his kilt, so much so that his navel was not circular, but flattened into a downward V, re-formed by the weight of the king's prosperity.

Egyptologists have spilled deluges of ink trying to determine the reasons Amenhotep IV ordered himself depicted this way.[6] Had he previously been denied the opportunity to show his body as it really was, only finding the courage or power to depict his true self in Year 5 of his reign? Many theories have been suggested, most of them trying to align his new representation with an actual physiognomy. We read scholarly arguments that the new king was a hermaphrodite, having both male and female anatomy, or that he suffered from a syndrome of some kind (Marfan's and Froelich's syndromes have been suggested, among many others). Later Egyptologists, influenced by the possible identification of Amenhotep IV's nondeformed mummy,[7] have argued instead that the king was using his own body to show himself as both animal and human, male and female, everything that solar light could create.[8] To confuse matters further, he had his Great Royal Wife Nefertiti depicted with the same strange elongation of visage and limbs, her chin so pulled down in some reliefs that it was not only decidedly unattractive but also animalistic.

It seems instead that Amenhotep IV decided to depict himself infused with sunlight, as an otherworldly being made of solar emanations whose body was distorted not by disease but by the golden light of new creation. He was revealed to his people, in his window of appearances, suffused with the rising solar orb behind him, compromising the vision of the people below, deforming and elongating his form. At its most dramatic, it might have seemed to the audience that sunlight was even shooting from the king's and queen's extremities, from the tips of their fingers, from the tops of their crowns. This new portraiture was the king's mechanism of displaying that he and his queen had melded with god and been utterly transformed.[9]

THIS FIRST SED FESTIVAL must have been exhausting for Amenhotep IV's elites, as their king demanded not only blinding rituals to show off his solar merging but also extensive temple offerings under the sun as it traveled through every station in the sky. These rites did not occur in shaded temple courtyards and cool columned offering halls, as before, but instead exposed spectators to the burning and open North African sky. Nefertiti and the king were the only ones standing beneath sunshades as they observed servants and priests scurrying around, piling numerous offering tables to overflowing with bloody haunches of beef, calves' heads, strangled ducks and geese, vegetables, breads and cakes of all kinds, oils, and fruits—all the bounty the sun had produced. The fiery orb would consume it through its solar rays, accompanied, as we can imagine, by flies and the stench of decay. Amenhotep IV created colossal reliefs of himself, his queen, and his children, lifting up offerings of food and drink to their sun god. It was the king's favorite image, reproduced again and again and again, the only difference being the addition of a new Royal Daughter to the scene every couple of years.

While Egypt's elites continued confused, depleted, sore of back, and sunburned, Amenhotep IV was receiving pushback for his reforms, as there are actually cryptic instances of dissent preserved in the Egyptian textual record.[10] What did Nefertiti think of the whole business? It would have been hard for her to criticize this new radical religion of light when it elevated her to a height no King's Wife had ever known, equal in solar fusion even with the king. For his part, Amenhotep IV needed Nefertiti as his female accompaniment in this bizarre new religion; she was even given the unprecedented honor of worship at her own temple at the site of Kom el Nana, then called the Sunshade of the Aten. There she was depicted without the king but with her young daughter, holding her arms up in worship as the life-granting rays of the solar disk consumed the food on the offering table below.[11] Her life as queen must have narrowed to two tasks: first, her husband's religious interests—all the passionate conversations, fervent planning, and solemn rituals revolving around it—and second, procreation with the king to conceive their solar-divine children.

For countless millennia, the people of the Nile had worshipped the spirits of their animals, river, desert, sun, wind, and Earth around them, manifesting into gods and goddesses, eventually coalescing into politically useful divinities like Amun, a solar deity and ruler of the sky; Maat, goddess of truth and justice, who prevented chaos of the universe during its creation; Khonsu, god of the moon, who returned the wounded eye of Horus; Sobek, crocodile god of virulence and the Nile flood; and Isis, reconstituter of her husband Osiris and mistress of magic. High priests and priestesses were appointed to temples around the land to perform intricate and crucial rituals to pull all these gods into the human realm, allowing offerings and appeasement in stone temples, and encouraging the gods to bestow their blessings upon the land with good harvests and easy fortune.[12] Such fervent beliefs translated into sprawling temples throughout Egypt. First constructed of mudbrick, these temples were eventually remade with cool stone walls, pierced by high windows that allowed solar shafts of light to slant in, tempered by the smell of frankincense and myrrh burning in incense lamps, the sounds of chanting, the beating of drums, and the shaking of rattles.

The Egyptian king was believed divine by his people, the gods' Earthly representative; he was also the chief priest of the land, whose presence in cult activity was essential to keep Egypt from descending into chaos. Without the king and his sacred activities, the Egyptians believed their land would be abandoned by their gods, that it would fall into poverty, descend into warring factions, or succumb to foreign invasion, that creation itself could be unmade. In Egypt, the king was the linchpin that connected the ritual machine of divine appeasement with creation itself.

Amenhotep IV was, in the view of his Egyptian courtiers and priests, continuing this trend of sacred exchange between human and god—providing offerings so that Egypt would receive prosperity in return—but there were new disturbing trends on the horizon. The king was favoring one god in particular more than any other—this Aten sun disk. There must have been great anxiety when the king started ignoring the old temples, built upon and added to for millennia by his ancestor kings. Treasury income was already being diverted in large amounts to fund the king's massive building program in Karnak, not to mention what he might have been doing in Egypt's other urban strongholds.

Even authoritarian regimes have their limits, but such a theological experiment could only have been implemented in a place that served its king, no matter how crazy or strange or young or unprepared. An adviser could voice a dissenting opinion, sure, as tales of kingly bravery make clear,[13] but in the end, the king got his way. Royal failures were not mentioned in ancient Egypt. Royal indecision was nonexistent in literary tales. Almost anywhere else on this planet, a king would have been moved aside or shunned or assassinated for turning ideological institutions on their heads and impoverishing the gods themselves. But ancient Egypt remained dictatorial and patriarchal to a fault. (Can you imagine a female leader getting away with any of this?) Egypt was also rich beyond our wildest imagination, and Amenhotep IV must have had some economic wiggle room to maintain some of the old cult while also funding his massive new buildings and his strange sed festival for a sun god.

Revolution is the wrong word to apply to Amenhotep IV's radical changes. This was no grassroots movement; we see no attempt to return religion to the people by its chief priest. No, this was a hegemonic theology, imposed by the king himself upon a people who probably became more unsettled and frightened of it by the day. There was likely too much newness, too much invention, too much oddness for all the elites; people of influence must have started to tell their king, divine or not, what they thought of the whole affair. It seems their comments were not generous or persuasive. In the end, all these opinions were too much for the new king. He decided he needed a clean start; he left his old court cities of Heliopolis, Memphis, and Thebes behind and moved to Middle Egypt as early as Year 5 and as late as Year 8, a time line heavily contested by Egyptologists.[14] No matter how long his runway was, Amenhotep IV tells us in his boundary stelae that no one, absolutely no one, could tell him what to do or how to do it—and that no one could divert him from this ideology granted directly to him by a god.

Bigger change was coming. Soon after his jubilee, the king changed his god-given name from his father's Amenhotep, meaning "Amen Is at Peace," to Akhenaten, meaning "The One Who Is Beneficial to the Aten," a new moniker probably arrived at after hours of divine communion or animated discussion with fellow Aten enthusiasts. The king's new name constituted a bitter response to Amun priests who likely contested his orders at Thebes. Royal name changes like this were unheard of. Slight alterations might be added to the titulary to celebrate some milestone, but such a drastic and elemental change to a king's name was unprecedented in ancient Egypt. Akhenaten didn't leave his queen out, either; her name was emended to the rather unwieldy Neferneferuaten Nefertiti, meaning "The Beauty of the Beautiful Ones of the Aten, The Beauty Has Come."

This change of names was just the start. Akhenaten would show them all; he would rip his new religion out by the roots and plant it elsewhere. This freshly baptized king would leave the urban centers behind, founding a new capital city on virgin soil out in the middle of nowhere, in Middle Egypt. There he created a new sacred city from whole cloth and called it Akhetaten, "The Horizon of the Aten," a name remarkably similar to his own new name, as if king and city were one entity. (The archaeological site is today called Tell el Amarna.) Here, the king would rule with his co-regent, the solar orb itself. His favored elites were brought with him amid, one should assume, a great deal of bribery and/or coercion; Egyptian society was thus flung into disarray. When the social chaos descended, no member of the authoritarian regime mentioned the repercussions in written texts at the time. No papyri preserve the private thoughts of the courtiers, priests, or any other elites during

Akhenaten's momentous move to the new city of Akhetaten, and we should not expect to ever find such accounts.

Out in Middle Egypt, away from the madding crowds, Akhenaten started building new palaces, temples, and bureaucratic structures for his new religious capital. He used the talatats, those light and small stones, to speed the work; a graveyard preserving the skeletons of thousands of children proves that abuse, overwork, and undernourishment of a coerced labor force, probably separated from their protectors, their parents, was the bloody foundation of his new holy city.[15]

Akhenaten shut down, or at least defunded, countless millennia-old temple institutions up and down the Nile, diverting their revenues toward his own maniacal interests, co-opting elites with gifts of wealth to follow him and to embrace his new religion. This king was a radical at the very top of Egypt's social hierarchy, a man who could bend Egypt's agenda, manpower, and extraordinary wealth to his will. Despite the obvious harm he inflicted on Egypt's ideological landscape, this one man was allowed complete latitude to implement his schemes. There were no assassination attempts that we know of, no intense pushback by priestly groups, no organized talk of coups or dissent. All we can see in the historical record is his subjects' obedience during his lifetime (and their revulsion after his death).

Akhenaten built new temples punctuated by a series of gateways that shut out the unclean masses (this wasn't an inclusive cult, after all). Airy courtyards filled with hundreds of altars open to the air and light proliferated, with no closed sanctuary (how could you enclose the sun?). This god had no need of a cult statue. His presence was felt on the skin; it burned the eyes; it warmed the Earth. The Aten's cult effigy would be the human bodies of his Earthly manifestations on Earth: King Akhenaten, his Great Royal Wife Nefertiti, and their daughters. Diplomatic letters (called the Amarna letters in scholarly publications), written in Akkadian, record the complaints of foreign agents at having to stand in the sun during interminable temple rituals.[16] No such complaints were written by Egyptians.

The move to Akhetaten strengthened Nefertiti politically. Akhenaten needed her to implement his audacious plans, and he positioned her next to him everywhere he could. She may have been one of the few people in his court whom he could trust completely, for the simple reason that she was dependent upon him for her own position. One word from him and she would have been demoted, another woman taking her place as Great Royal Wife.

Whether their relationship had that aspect of threat or distrust to it, they were certainly a co-dependent couple. At Akhetaten, Nefertiti was usually depicted at her husband's height, with his same strange bodily features. In some imagery, her crowns make her even taller than her husband. In one stela, now in Berlin, two people with identical body types are shown kissing, both wearing kingly headgear. Because of this stela, some Egyptologists assumed that Akhenaten was a homosexual and that he had crowned his male lover as co-regent. Now we understand that this was a depiction of Akhenaten and his bride Neferneferuaten Nefertiti, wearing the double crown in the manner of the goddesses Mut and Tefnut, protector and con-tainer of the sun.[17] Nefertiti was necessary to his success.

Akhenaten wanted his new city to be perfect—and free from the temptations of the old ways. It was, not surprisingly, quite isolated, far from the halls of power, positioned almost equidis-tant between Thebes and Memphis. He needed a functioning capital, and he needed it fast. At the beginning he must have imported, at great expense, all his luxuries and the people who made them. Glassmakers, weavers, goldsmiths, stone-carvers, engineers, and construction workers would have to start from scratch, dismantling and transporting dozens of high-level workshops, and depriving the elites in the old court centers of their many accustomed luxuries.

Akhenaten built astoundingly large temples in a very short period of time. He had not just one, but at least three palaces constructed for his family and close courtiers. He included government offices, archives, and a diplomatic scribal center: all the things a functioning government would need. He raised a great city from the bare earth, where the king and the Royal Family took center stage—a kind of "pharaohcentrism," as opposed to the old focus on the gods, as was traditional.[18] No longer did the daily or yearly calendar revolve around temple festivals, like the Beautiful Feast of the Valley, when Amun visited the tombs and temples of the ancestors in the land of the dead on the West Bank of Thebes. Now, at the city of Akhetaten, the daily journey of the god took the form of the king and his bride on their chariots of gold and electrum. No Egyptian king had previously been shown riding his chariot into anything but war. Akhenaten and Nefertiti now used the chariot to show their piety for the Aten, as symbol of the sun itself, carrying its chosen representatives in a strange festival procession through the streets of a brand-new sacred city. Akhenaten and his wife were living, human gods, carried past their elites, officials, and laborers, all of them bowing low, scraping their heads before their divine leaders.

Akhenaten obviously enjoyed commissioning depictions of himself and his queen touching each other intimately—even kissing on the lips, unheard of in previous royal imagery (for instance, the sexual consummation as depicted in Hatshepsut's divine birth scenes amounted to the touching of hands). Reliefs are preserved showing the queen sitting coquettishly on her husband's lap, her delicate feet dangling alongside his throne. Some think the sexual congress between Akhenaten and Nefertiti was also considered part of these ritual processions, as they would have been in the old temples between male and female gods.[19]

On the surface, Akhenaten's new religion was one of light and joy and love, and his city was one filled with groundbreaking architecture and fresh ideas: a welcome shake-up of millennia of stodgy status-quo and religious traditionalism. But a closer look at the underbelly of this new city reveals darkness: a lack of care for human life, a religious zeal of a pointed nature focused not on the good of all Egypt, but on its totalitarian leader. Archaeologists have recently uncovered evidence that the demands to build such a great city in so short a time and with, presumably, increasingly limited resources, created corruption and violent duress. Forensic evidence from the interred bodies of the workers used to construct this city show severe repetitive stress injuries, malnutrition, and even repeated traumas. Someone was pushing these people too hard, too fast. They were not fed enough. They were working too young. They were working wounded.[20]

It seems that Akhenaten enticed elites to make the move to Akhetaten through sanctioned bribery. He made them rich (if depictions in their tombs are to be believed). He also gave them free rein to build their homes in his city as they liked. Evidence suggests that he even allowed his elite overseers to build the city according to their own methodology, as long as it happened fast, within budget, and according to Akhenaten's divine plan. Thus, we shouldn't be surprised if many of Akhenaten's loyal officials kept more resources for themselves, skimming off the top to reward their own dissatisfaction at being dragged out to the ends of the Earth at the whim of a madman. The skilled craftsmen didn't seem to have suffered as much as the manual laborers; co-option will always reward those with rare and hard-to-replace abilities. Yes, Akhenaten's religious ideas were groundbreaking and unique, full of light and love. But that solar love was strictly reserved for the Royal Family. Skeletons don't lie. Akhenaten's religious experiment was devastating for the normal working man, woman, and child forced to implement it.

As for his elites, the buy-in is more obvious and still preserved. Numerous scenes from elite tombs at Akhetaten show grateful courtiers receiving solid-gold necklaces tossed nonchalantly from the hands of Akhenaten and Nefertiti from their window of appearances on high. The gold, it seems, pulled military commanders and other opportunistic nobles to the new city, encouraged priests of the old ways to convert to this strange new religion of sunlight, brought bureaucrats who implemented orders, and recruited scribes to execute tax decisions and write diplomatic dispatches.[21]

All the same, rich or not, these educated elites among Akhenaten's co-opted followers must have harbored great anxieties for themselves and their families. All likely worried, in the typical Egyptian manner, about their eternal afterlife. Akhenaten seems to have had no such anxieties; his tomb was considered the epicenter of his divine creation, the alpha and omega of sunlight in the world. He was the god's image on this Earth, and when he would finally be placed in his tomb, he believed light would radiate from his corpse.

AKHENATEN OFTEN SHOWED HIMSELF with his queen. But, like any other king, he, too, had a harem. Few of the wives of that harem were ever named in the documentation, however. Indeed, Akhenaten seems to prefer mentioning only those women in his nuclear family. Only one woman from among his many other wives is named—a certain Kiya, or "Monkey" (maybe a pet-name; maybe her real name). Kiya received the unprecedented title as Akhenaten's "Greatly Beloved Wife," which the Great Royal Wife Nefertiti may have felt was a challenge to her authority as highest-ranking queen. Kiya also had an economic foundation of power in the form of her own estates, because vineyards and agricultural production were made in her name. Whoever she was, she had a short existence at Akhetaten; Kiya's names and images were purposely destroyed, with the name of the king's eldest daughter, Meritaten, often reinscribed over these still legible erasures. Was Nefertiti behind this loss of power for Kiya? British Egyptologist Nicholas Reeves is among those who think so.[22]

Around this time, when she had been chief queen for seven or eight years, Nefertiti would see two of her daughters elevated to the position of Great Royal Wife alongside Akhenaten, presumably taking the title of highest-ranking queen from her. The king's new relationship with his daughters adds an incestuous dimension to those unprecedented images, showing Akhenaten fondly caressing and kissing his little girls. Both of these daughters would bear him children, daughters of their own, it seems—called Meritaten Tasherit, meaning "Little Meritaten," and Ankhesenpaaten Tasherit, meaning "Little Ankhesenpaaten"—both named after their mothers.[23] But what happened to Nefertiti now that she was no longer the Chief Royal Wife in Akhenaten's harem?

Because there is suddenly no more mention of Nefertiti as Great Royal Wife, Egyptologists used to think that she died around Akhenaten's Year 12. There was the added confusion that many of Nefertiti's names were also erased and replaced with her daughters' names, leading some historians to believe that Nefertiti had been assassinated or had fallen out of favor.[24]

But Nefertiti hadn't gone anywhere. She had just reinvented herself into co-king alongside her husband. While ostensibly under his authority, she morphed into something so difficult to link with her previous incarnation that she almost disappeared from our sight.

After Year 12, a new co-king was pictured alongside Akhenaten, named Ankhkheperure Neferneferuaten and now identified by most historians as Nefertiti herself.[25] She had already been given the name Neferneferuaten by her husband, after all. Now, it seems, she abandoned Nefertiti in favor of another cartouche with a second name, the throne name of a king. Akhenaten, it seems, had no one else to trust but his queen to keep his religious experiment going. If Nefertiti really was Neferneferuaten, as so many believe, then Akhenaten needed her completely empowered alongside him as king.

Reeves even suggests that a depiction in one of the tombs at Akhetaten (Meryre II) may depict Nefertiti's ascension to the kingship. Here we see two kings sharing almost the same space on the throne, but with clear delineation of two garments, four hands, four legs, and two bodily contours. From far away, the image looks like just one person; close up, they are a melded pair. It seems that Akhenaten and Nefertiti were now co-kings, somehow communicating their co-rule as one.[26] Another piece of evidence, the so-called co-regency stela, now in the Petrie Museum in London, shows damaged imagery, but double cartouches of Akhenaten plus double cartouches for his co-king. Nefertiti's full name as co-king was absolutely unwieldy: Ankhkheperure mery-Waenre Neferneferuaten Akhetenhys. The stela even shows it had been modified from her queenship to her co-kingship.[27] Nefertiti used to have a single cartouche on this object, as a queen would—but a second one was later squeezed in, befitting Nefertiti's new status as co-king.

Nefertiti's new name was Ankhkheperure, meaning "The Manifestations of Re Are Alive." She was leaving her old self behind, bit by bit. In her new guise as co-king, she had turned away, or been made to turn away, from all ties to her birth family or identity. Since it was Akhenaten who had given her the additional name of Neferneferuaten in Year 5, it must have been he who reinvented her as his co-king—maybe just as cult leader Charles Manson renamed his followers, demanding that they abandon their past lives.

The constant name changing is more than a little confusing for the historians of today. But it also presumably created a conundrum for the ancient Egyptians residing at Akhetaten as well. Their king was forever changing his own epithets every couple of years, dissatisfied, it seems, that his identification really and truly communicated his true piety and beliefs. Indeed, all his alterations smack of a deep uncertainty, of an anxiety that he hadn't gotten it right yet, of the need to constantly mark yet another moment of profound change in his belief system, yet another revelation of his growing relationship to his divinity. Each new name or epithet was encoded with a contextual theological meaning at which we can only guess. Akhenaten styled himself and his female co-king like ancient rock stars who had to keep reinventing themselves to maintain their popularity, like Madonna or Prince, forever trying to redefine their image to fit with what was needed politically and religiously.

Why had Nefertiti even been allowed to become co-regent, an extraordinary step indeed? This was not a situation like Hatshepsut's, who had claimed power as king alongside a boy in his seventh year of reign. It was also not like the crisis of succession that Neferusobek had to solve, as the last member of her dynasty standing. There was no dead king, no young king, no infirm king. This scenario was decidedly different: a woman elevated into the position of sovereign alongside her husband— unidentifiable as queen anymore, but now in the secondary place as the younger co-regent, as if taking the place of the King's Son.

Akhenaten was not utilizing the co-kingship to ensure that his dynasty continued into the future, as every other king before him had done; he was politically securing it to his wife. Indeed, there is no evidence that he had any sons born to Nefertiti from which to choose (although we have to assume there were at least some in his harem, born to lesser wives). However Nefertiti had done it, she had been elevated to a place beyond any of our queens thus far, even Hatshepsut. As the younger monarch, the legacy of this reign would fall to Nefertiti after the king's death.

What compelled such a single-minded ruler as Akhenaten to share power with a woman? He must have felt vulnerable in some way, in need of a partner who could not easily turn on him. He also needed the time and space to form and finesse his Aten religion, it seems. Nefertiti was the younger ruler within the co-kingship in the sense that Akhenaten always took precedence over her. But there is evidence that Nefertiti was the member of the kingly pair who went out into the world to see to the administration of Egypt, ostensibly while Akhenaten closeted himself away in his sacred city, obsessing over his faith. Whatever the realpolitik, they now faced their future together, as king and king.

There was plenty of grief ahead for them both. In Year 13, the deaths began: two daughters, Setepenre and Neferneferuaten the Younger, died, maybe from some epidemic, even plague.[28] Then another daughter, Meketaten, also succumbed, perhaps in childbirth attempting to deliver her father Akhenaten's baby. In Year 14, Akhenaten's mother, the great dowager-queen, Tiy, died. While the Royal Family was wrapped up in the drama of their grief, Egypt suffered a devastating military loss, losing its northernmost territories in Syria.[29] It was at this moment, perhaps filled with doubt and indecision, that Akhenaten went all-in with his new god, becoming even more fanatical and embarking on an anti-polytheistic crusade of violent proportions. Perhaps Akhenaten was attempting to change his fate by atoning to his god for an incomplete ideological construct. It was as if the king believed the Aten had been angered, and thus he searched for a means of repairing his relationship with his divine father. He devised an unyielding, dogmatic, and destructive solution.

From his home base of power at Akhetaten, the king sent his agents out into the world, bearing tools of excision and orders of destruction, to remake all Egyptian temples in the entire land in his image. Akhenaten began a campaign of terror against the

Theban gods Amun and Mut, in particular, ordering workmen with chisels to remove their divine names and images wherever they saw them—even if they had been carved into an obelisk many stories off the ground in hard granite, even if the symbols had been used to spell his own father's name, Amenhotep. Akhenaten even had the word *gods* removed wherever he could: a pointed and frantic attack against polytheism itself.

Akhenaten overlooked nothing. Even small items worn around the neck or placed in a pocket were defaced—and this, more than anything, speaks to a harassed and frightened populace, worried about betrayal from their peers or oversight from their superiors.[30] Temple offerings and funding had already been diverted to Akhetaten and the Aten temples, but surely Akhenaten also sent bureaucrats out to the now-impoverished institutions to make sure that no funds had been overlooked. Temple priests of the old orthodoxy were likely disenfranchised for good, maybe even forced to kill their sacred animals, and almost certainly to send their temple effigies and treasures to the king. The scenario smacks of the destruction brought on by Henry VIII's 16th-century dissolution of the Roman Catholic holdings in Britain and the concomitant social upheaval.

Reeves suggests that the much later, third-century B.C. historian Manetho recorded some of this destruction, mistakenly ascribing blame to the invading Hyksos from centuries previous, rather than to Akhenaten himself. Manetho wrote: "Not only did they set towns and villages on fire, pillaging the temples and mutilating images of the gods without restraint—but they also made a practice of using the sanctuaries as kitchens to roast the

sacred animals which people worshipped, and they would compel the priests and prophets to sacrifice and butcher the beasts,
afterwards casting the men forth naked."[31] If Akhenaten did
indeed order the removal of Egypt's cult statues, we can only
imagine the horror and grief of the priests as they watched
Akhenaten's well-paid military supporters shove their way into
a sacred and silent sanctuary, rip open the shrine, pull out the
solid-gold statue of the god, and throw it in a chest, ready to be
taken to the king, melted down, and reused.

Even in the midst of such horrors and fanaticism, Akhenaten
and his co-king Neferneferuaten were not harmed in turn. If a
political leader had tried such a stunt anywhere else in the world,
he would have been overthrown, killed, ridiculed, imprisoned—
something, anything. If a female leader of Egypt had embarked
upon such free thinking, she would have been suppressed. Only
in a pyramidal and patriarchal regime where the king had an
ideological chokehold on the people, could one man effect such
a fundamental transformation without coup or assassination.

Whether or not it was actually monotheism, Akhenaten
created the world's first religious extremism and the globe's
first iconoclasm. This was a man who did what he wanted,
when he wanted, in the most high-risk, high-reward game
ancient Egypt had ever seen. He was not a revolutionary with
grassroots support, as later fanatics would be, but a radical and
excessive pharaoh with all the wealth that the richest land in
the ancient Mediterranean basin could provide. This man had
the money to quickly implement what so many later shamans
and disheveled prophets in the Levant or Persia could only

imagine. He had an ambitious and unprecedented plan to steer his sacred land of Egypt away from the myriad gods of his fathers and toward his new religion of light. He would change the world from on high, foisting his notions onto an unwilling people. Was he a madman, a genius, a narcissist, a sociopath, or all of the above? We can't know. But Nefertiti would be the one left to clean up his mess.

To make matters that much more apocalyptic, a total eclipse became visible in the Nile Valley toward the end of Akhenaten's reign. On May 14, 1338 B.C., according to modern astronomical calculations, the sun's light was completely blotted from the Earth for an astounding five minutes and 48 seconds, plunging Egypt into darkness and presumably terrorizing the people, priests, and elites with the possibility that the solar light would never shine again. Eclipses only return to a given place every 375 years, making such an occurrence beyond the scope of cultural memory. Without the scientific ability to predict the eclipse, the Egyptians were caught unawares. When the moon's shadow covered the sun for almost six minutes, we can imagine the horror among a populace already weary and frightened of Akhenaten's religious changes. Did the king witness the eclipse and doubt his vision? Was Nefertiti, by his side as co-king, rethinking her faith in her husband? Did anyone try to reevaluate their iconoclasm in light of other forms of divinity? Or did Akhenaten simply see it as further proof that he had to work harder and longer so as not to weaken the sun god even more?

Whatever caused it, it seems the hard edges of Akhenaten's religion may have been softened at the very end of his reign—at

The funerary stela of Queen Merneith, dating to the first dynasty,
circa 2940 B.C. The limestone relief was found at Abydos and
now is stored in the Egyptian Museum in Cairo.
(Kenneth Garrett/National Geographic Creative)

Dating to the reign of Merneith, this burial is representative of those surrounding tombs of Early Dynastic royal tombs. Subsidiary Burial A, from Tomb no. 3503, excavated at Saqqara by Walter B. Emery.
(*Walter B. Emery, courtesy of the Egyptian Exploration Society*)

LEFT: The Narmer Palette, also known as the Great Hierakonpolis Palette, circa 3050 B.C. It is thought to depict the unification of Upper and Lower Egypt. It is now on display at the Egyptian Museum. (*Gianni Dagli Orti/REX/Shutterstock*)
BELOW LEFT: The Palermo Stone, circa 2470 B.C., carved on basalt, contains a list of the kings from the 1st Dynasty through the early 5th Dynasty. It is kept in the Regional Archeological Museum Antonio Salinas in Palermo, Italy. (*DEA Picture Library/Getty*)
BELOW RIGHT: A funerary stela from circa 3800–1710 B.C. shows the stela of King Djet, the Serpent King. (*DEA/G. Dagli Orti/Getty*)

This statue depicts a late 12th Dynasty queen, possibly Neferusobek. It was kept in the Egyptian Museum in Berlin until it was destroyed in an Allied bombing raid in World War II. This is the last remaining image of the piece. *(From Die Plastik der Ägypter by Hedwig Fechheimer, 1920, Bruno Cassirer Verlag, Berlin)*

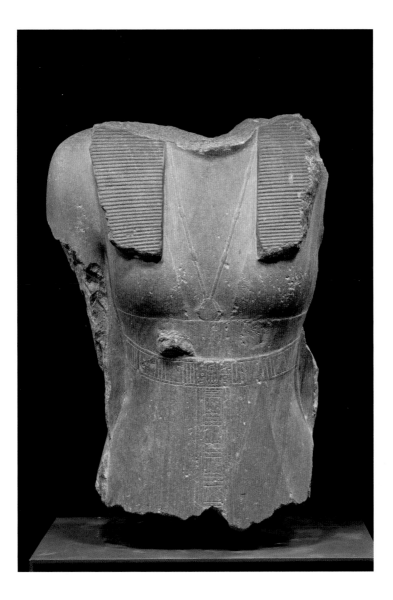

This statue, inscribed for Neferusobek, lacks its head but shows how
the female king layered masculine elements of kingship—including
the Nemes headdress and royal kilt—onto her feminine person.
(© *Musée du Louvre, Dist. RMN-Grand-Palais/Georges Poncet/Art Resource, NY*)

TOP: A relief image from Hatshepsut's Red Chapel at the temple at Karnak near ancient Thebes shows Hatshepsut and Thutmose II as nearly identical figures performing ritual activity. *(Kenneth Garrett/National Geographic Creative)*
ABOVE: An illustration of the limestone Chevier block from the Amun Temple at Karnak shows a relief of Hatshepsut as a feminine monarch wearing ram's horns at the time she took the kingship in the 18th Dynasty. *(Drawing by Deborah Shieh, 2014)*

LEFT: One of at least 10 kneeling granite statues of Hatshepsut shows the queen as a male king wearing a kilt, a false beard, and the white crown of Upper Egypt. The statue rests at the Metropolitan Museum of Art. *(World History Archive/Alamy)* BELOW: An androgynous limestone statue, which sits at the Met, depicts Hatshepsut bare chested as a masculine king, with hints of feminine breasts. *(Artokoloro Quint Lox Limited/Alamy)*

A colossal statue—now on display at the Cairo Museum—
shows Akhenaten, the 18th Dynasty pharaoh who ruled for 17 years.
(*Alfredo Dagli Orti/REX/Shutterstock*)

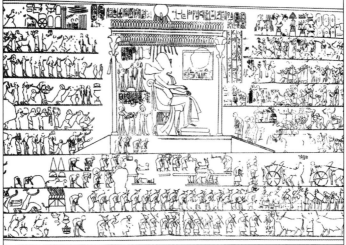

TOP: A small stela, probably used as a home altar, shows Akhenaten and Nefertiti with their eldest daughters being blessed by the Aten—represented by the sun disk and rays. *(Kenneth Garrett)* ABOVE: In an illustration of a relief from the tomb of Meryre II at Tell el Amarna, we see the outlines of two figures sitting so close, side by side, that they seem to be one. Note especially the four legs depicted, clarifying that there are two kings represented here, perhaps Akhenaten and his co-king Nefertiti. *(Drawing by Norman de Garís Davies)*

This bust of Nefertiti, discovered by a team of German archaeologists in 1913, features a slender neck and gracefully proportioned face distinguished by one unfinished eye. The blue cylindrical headpiece graces only images of Nefertiti, to whom it is unique. The bust draws more than 500,000 visitors annually to Berlin's Neues Museum.
(Kenneth Garrett/National Geographic Creative)

A plastered and painted column in the Tomb of Tawosret and Seti II (known as Tomb KV 14 in the Valley of the Kings) shows the female king. Tawosret depicts herself as a female ruler, with both vulture and cobra uraei extending from her diadem, in the manner of Nefertiti before her, as co-king. *(S. Vannini/De Agostini/Getty)*

The sarcophagus lid of King Setnakht II from KV 14 was reinscribed
for him but probably originally made for the female king Tawosret.
(Werner Forman/Universal Images Group/Getty)

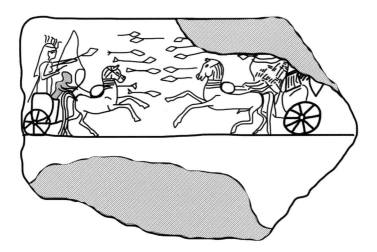

TOP: Two silver bracelets inscribed for King Seti II are etched with scenes of Queen Tawosret making an offering to the king—a vase in her left hand and flower in her right. Seti II holds a cup and leaf. *(Egyptian National Museum, Cairo, Egypt/Bridgeman)*. ABOVE: This 20th Dynasty ostracon in the Egyptian Museum, Cairo (CG 25.125) depicts an Egyptian queen in the midst of battle on a war chariot, firing arrows at the enemy. She protects a small child on her chariot. *(Drawing by Amber Myers Wells, 2018)*

The figure of Prince Seti-Merneptah replaced the figure of the chancellor
Bay in this relief from the shrine of Seti II at Karnak. *(Aidan Dodson)*

In one of the few images that bear her name, Cleopatra is depicted
on the left side of a wall at a temple at Dendera. Her son and heir,
Julius Caesarion, is shown with her.
(George Steinmetz/National Geographic Creative)

A coin shows Cleopatra on one side and Antony on the other, described as Hellenistic rulers. *(UtCon Collection/Alamy)*

least outside of his sacred city.³² Perhaps Akhenaten was in ill health or had fallen into some deep malaise. Maybe that was the reason for the strange co-kingship with Nefertiti in the first place. She was his trusted ally, ostensibly meant to carry out his theological vision. But she was perhaps also someone whom the officials could rely on to make commonsensical decisions, not fanatical and expensive ones. A woman rules differently, after all, even if she's implementing her patriarch's orders.

When Akhenaten did finally die around Year 17, at close to 50 years of age, his daughter-wife Meritaten was probably around 13 years old; the next sister, Ankhesenpaaten, was nine or 10; and his son Tutankhaten—not yet mentioned in any documentation from this time period—was around six.³³ Nefertiti was probably in her mid-twenties to early thirties at the time of the king's death—a transition that is concealed from view. If the Egyptians were going to kill any of their god-kings, Akhenaten would have been the one, given the amount of terror, destabilization, and pain he had unleashed on his people. But there is absolutely no evidence of regicide. If such a thing did happen, it was an inside job, performed by his most trusted allies, in secret and in silence. Whatever the manner of the death, the king was buried in state, albeit in an unfinished tomb in the eastern valley of his sacred city.³⁴

More than anything else, Akhenaten's reign illustrates how Egypt protected its divine kingship at any cost. If a king had to be removed from power, it was done quietly, without claim or fanfare, and with no hint of ownership in any historical records preserved to us of the one behind the scheme. Nefertiti could capitalize on this moment—but to do so, she would have to leave all traces of her wifely connection to the zealot behind. Nefertiti had been co-king; now she could have little connection to the heretic. She had to remake herself completely if she was to become king alone.

♛

HOW WE FOLLOW NEFERTITI beyond Akhenaten's death is strangely colored by which Egyptological school you belong to: French, American, or British.[35] The evidence can be read in so many different ways that a variety of historical stories about Nefertiti have developed. For the most part, I will stick to the narrative established by Nicholas Reeves and the British school because it encompasses all the available evidence— visual and textual.

Much of the confusion stems from the nature of female rule itself. We can't expect the office of kingship to bend and morph to fit the aberrant woman in power. No, the Egyptian woman had to reinvent herself to move into the office at all, often masking her original identity in the process.

The next king to take the throne was called Ankhkheperure Smenkhkare, after whose reign the boy-king Tutankhamun would take the reins of power. Until quite recently, Smenkhkare was believed to have been a male relative of the Dynasty 18 family—a brother of Akhenaten, perhaps. Smenkhkare had wives, too: Meritaten and Ankhesenpaaten, daughters of Akhenaten and Nefertiti. Because of these wives, most Egyptologists have assumed that Smenkhkare was a man, as patriarchy demands and as we expect. But a closer look at the succession crisis at the end of the dynasty and at the throne name of Ankhkheperure—the same one used by Nefertiti as co-king Neferneferuaten—reveals that the mysterious Smenkhkare may have been none other than Nefertiti herself.

Make no mistake, Egyptologists remain locked in fierce disagreement over whether this Smenkhkare was Nefertiti or some male ruler.[36] Some, like Reeves, believe that the real evidence for Smenkhkare as Nefertiti is still waiting to be discovered (but more on that in a moment). The thinking goes like this: If Nefertiti transformed herself so completely from queen to co-regent that she was almost unrecognizable, then maybe she remade herself just as much when she transitioned from co-king to king. All she kept was the throne name Ankhkheperure. The name Nefertiti had long since been discarded with her co-kingship; now as sole king, she abandoned the name Neferneferuaten as well, in favor of Smenkhkare, meaning something like The Ka-Soul of Re Is Restored or The Soul of Re Is Embellished—both potentially useful choices of name for a woman like Nefertiti in a time of profound ideological and political crisis.

If Nefertiti was indeed Ankhkheperure Smenkhkare, then she was in for quite a struggle to heal the wounds that Akhenaten had inflicted on his people. Her sun king husband had instituted unsustainable spending and building. Egypt was bankrupt. Akhenaten had not focused on expanding his sources of wealth to implement his solar vision, as earlier Dynasty 18 kings had done, proving their worth in battle and by generating gold and mineral income. Akhenaten proved nothing; he left behind only ruin and a neglected empire. He had ridden rough-shod over the social balance, brutally oppressing some elites, grossly enriching others. He possessed no humility before the gods; offered no fiscal care; made no attempt to pay for what he purchased. In short, he had left a fiasco in his wake. And it was a woman who started putting things to rights: first as co-king Neferneferuaten and now continuing her ministrations as Smenkhkare.

A rare image of Smenkhkare and his/her Great Royal Wife Meritaten was inscribed in the tomb of Meryre II at Akhenat-en's capital, one of the last images to have been placed in an elite tomb here. A drawing by Norman de Garis Davies shows a figure named Smenkhkare wearing a masculine kilt but also a feminine garment tied under the breast.[37] Is this another instance in which the markers of masculine kingship were lay-ered onto the feminine person, as was done with Hatshepsut and Neferusobek? It seems so.

And yet there is still dissent. One of the main reasons Egyp-tologists have argued against Smenkhkare being Nefertiti is the fact that this king had wives. Indeed, standing beside the king in the tomb scene of Meryre II is an image of Meritaten, retain-ing the label Great Royal Wife. A father marrying his daughter is one thing in an exclusive monarchy—but a mother doing the same? Nothing could be consummated in such a relationship. Nefertiti could have no harem. If a queen was attached to Nefer-titi's kingship, evidently it was because someone needed to occupy the feminine ritual role just as Nefertiti now needed to masculinize herself. Who more trustworthy than a Royal Daughter? As Meritaten had been Great Royal Wife for her father, perhaps she retained that role still, but now alongside her mother.

It was a strange adaptation, perhaps, but functional and not completely unprecedented. Hatshepsut had used her own daughter, Nefrure, in much the same way—although not as a formal wife for herself, but rather as wife to her co-king and as a high priestess for herself. Nefertiti didn't have the luxury of doing everything right; she had to put Egypt's house in order.

One of Nefertiti's first directives, it seems, was to abandon the city of Akhetaten. If it was Nefertiti calling the shots, it makes sense that the deed was done carefully and respectfully: a kind of peace and reconciliation effort to atone for past wrongdoing, to retain the goodwill of the people who had relocated there, to keep from angering the ghost of the king who had created it from the ground up. Archaeologists found the site of Tell el Amarna with the entrances to temples, homes, and palaces carefully bricked up, as if with the intention of returning later for hard-to-pack possessions. Nefertiti, as Smenkhkare, then, may have started to build in earnest at the old capital cities, reinstalling the cult statues of gods like Amun, Mut, and Khonsu at Thebes, or Ptah, Sakhmet, and Nefertum at Memphis. She would have started sending the artisans around to repair the iconoclastic scars her husband had inflicted upon Egypt's sacred spaces. Nefertiti, as Smenkhkare, may have started ordering statuary of the old gods with her portrait, as it was expected to show the gods with the face of the reigning king. Indeed, it is even possible that some of the statues of Amun carved with Tutankhamun's name were actually created during Nefertiti's sole reign, only to be reinscribed with his name or finished for him.[38]

Smenkhkare was now positioned to prepare the next sovereign to rule. She looked to the next generation, to a certain Tutankhaten, a boy of just seven or eight. He was too young to see any of the difficult decision-making through; she therefore tapped her daughter Ankhesenpaaten, who had been a Great Royal Wife to her father—maybe even having borne him a child—to help her young brother Tutankhaten solve problems beyond his abilities and to protect him from avaricious and overbearing advisers. As Smenkhkare ostensibly reconstituted the old Egyptian temple treasuries, rehired the priests, and restocked the agricultural income for divine offerings, she probably prayed for a long life so that she could give the next generation the chance to heal the fissures opened up by her dead husband. Now presumably in her early to mid-thirties, she must have cast a constant and wary eye on the young ones who had grown up in the eye of this Aten hurricane, but who had little understanding of the damage wrought at the storm's edges.

It would take time for the children of Akhenaten to appreciate the need to alleviate Egypt's pain and to form new methods of coping with their father's heretical actions. But Nefertiti's last hope would never become a reality. From all the evidence we have, she died just a few years into her sole reign as Smenkhkare. What can Nefertiti's short reign as sole king say about Egypt's female rulers? She may have attempted to put things right, healing wounds and mending fences. And she probably looked to the next generation, maybe even further out than a man might look—to the future, rather than the immediate, short-term gains of masculine aggression.

The next king we see is Tutankhaten (soon to change his name to the more soothing and restorative Tutankhamun), a boy whose tomb is more famous than he is and whose parentage is argued over more than that of any Egyptian monarch. Some historians discount Nefertiti as Tutankhamun's mother, since he was never pictured with the Royal Family in worship of the Aten. However, Akhenaten had surrounded himself with daughters on purpose, excluding the mention or image of any male offspring, as had all the other Dynasty 18 kings before him. Also problematic is the genetic analysis of Tutankhamun's mummy, which shows him to have been the product of incest. There is no evidence that Nefertiti and Akhenaten were brother and sister, again discounting Nefertiti as the boy's mother.[39] We also have no evidence of any Royal Sister in Akhenaten's harem. But given what we do know about Akhenaten marrying his own daughters, perhaps Nefertiti was Tutankhamun's grandmother. Maybe Nefertiti's daughter Meritaten or Meketaten bore Tutankhaten, making him a product of father-daughter incest and thus fitting the DNA evidence of his body.

If Nefertiti as Smenkhkare ensured Tutankhamun's ascension to the throne, she may have been the only woman in our tale of female kings who was able to pass her rule successfully to her own offspring—not to her son, but to her grandson. It was

Nefertiti to whom the young Tutankhamun would have looked as model and support—not to his father. A grandmother-grandson relationship would also explain the young age of Tutankhamun when he took the throne.[40]

In the end, Nefertiti was not able to undo the damage that her husband had done. She died in the process of restoring Egypt to the old ways. None of these political players would be remembered well by Egypt's historians. Every one of them bore the deep scars of Akhenaten's attempts to remake divinity in his own image. Everyone had suffered. Everyone remembered. All of them—Akhenaten, Nefertiti, Tutankhamun, even the boy-king's advisers Ay and Horemheb—would pay for their participation in the fanatic revelry by being left out of the king lists preserved at later temples.

Indeed, the one and only reason Tutankhamun's reign is so well known today is because his semi-intact tomb was found by Howard Carter in 1922. Without that fabulous discovery, the boy-king would remain as shadowy a figure as Smenkhkare. And the only reason that tomb was hidden so well and for so long was because the Egyptians had erased that king's existence so very well. Akhenaten's hereticism was so reviled, so excised, that even when the Bronze Age Collapse sent Thebes spiraling into crisis and ruin, no Egyptian knew to look to Tutankhamun's tomb for golden treasures, even as they plundered the well-known tombs of other rulers, like Thutmose III and Amenhotep III.

As king, Tutankhamun was married to his own half sister, Ankhesenpaaten, herself to have her name changed to Ankhesenamun, whether she liked it or not, a girl who had already served as Great Royal Wife to her own father, Akhenaten, maybe even bearing him a child. It was this royal pair—Tutankhamun and Ankhesenamun—who stood at attention when they buried mother and grandmother Smenkhkare in the Valley of the Kings. The boy-king presumably performed the sacred opening-of-the-mouth ritual (which was believed to enable the corpse to speak, see, and hear again) on her mummy: a hard responsibility for a young child who must have desperately wished for her to have lived, instead of being thrust onto Egypt's throne before his time.

To the historian familiar with Egypt's patterns of succession, the most compelling thing about Tutankhamun's youthful kingship is the fact that he had no female regent that we can identify as the decision-maker. His own wife, Ankhesenamen, perhaps 14 to 16 years old, was probably skilled enough, having served as Great Royal Wife already (and indeed she may have been placed into this position of authority by Nefertiti herself). But all our evidence shows that Tutankhamun was instead under the tutelage and watch of the elder statesmen Ay and Horemheb, men who had been loyal lieutenants to Akhenaten at his holy city. Perhaps Ay's fatherly relationship to Nefertiti and Akhenaten will help us understand why he ended up ruling for the boy-king.

Ay had acted as God's Father to Akhenaten. He had been a tutor to Nefertiti. He was probably the official in whom Nefertiti had placed her greatest trust when she ascended to ever higher positions of power. He likely helped her negotiate her path from co-kingship to sole kingship. (He may have even helped her rid the world of Akhenaten, but this is pure speculation). He must have supported the boy-king Tutankhamun as well.

Given Ay's support of her family dynasty, maybe Nefertiti never saw it coming that he would not support the authority of her own daughter Ankhesenamun as regent as well, that he would have the hubris to take it for himself instead. But Ay, once a loyal yes-man, would exert his influence over her dynasty and eventually take the throne for himself. Previous dynasties, like the 12th of Neferusobek, had ended with the last standing member of the Royal Family as king, whether male or female. But Dynasty 18 would end in the hands of two nonroyal men in succession. These men took what was not rightfully theirs, upending the women who ruled on behalf of their family lineages.

The last year of Tutankhamun's reign seems to have been filled with a battle of wills between the Royal Family and these upstart lieutenants, waged chiefly by Nefertiti's daughter Ankhesena-mun. Historians have a record of a Hittite letter sent by an Egyptian queen (named Dahamunzu in the Hittite language) to the Hittite king. The letter goes like this: "My husband died. A son I have not. But to you, they say, the sons are many. If you were to give me a son of yours, he would become my husband. Never shall I pick out a servant of mine and make him my husband! . . . I am afraid." This missive was sent to the Hittite king Suppiluliuma, who eventually sent his son Zananza. The Hittite prince died en route, perhaps murdered, maybe even by agents of Ay.[41] If Ankhesenamun was the sovereign in question, as so many Egyptologists have suggested, then she was actively trying to thwart Ay, whom she referred to dismissively as a "servant," from taking the kingship.

Ultimately, Ankhesenamun was kept in her place, becoming instead the Great Royal Wife to Ay when he claimed the throne. This last member of Dynasty 18, Ankhesenamun, the last woman standing, had been ignominiously passed from man to man—from her father, Akhenaten, to her brother, Tutankhamun, and then finally to her brother's regent and adviser, an old warlord, a servant, and a usurper—Ay. Ankhesenamun's grief must have been great, as she herself was skipped over for the kingship—a position she should have occupied, like Neferusobek, made all the worse when she witnessed the tomb prepared for Tutankhamun in the western King's Valley at Thebes (and presumably all of his commissioned funerary goods) taken by King Ay for his own later interment.

As a result, Ankhesenamun's brother, Tutankhamun, was given a hasty burial in the front hallway of Smenkhkare's tomb in the Valley of the Kings (if Nicholas Reeves's theory is correct), using quickly reinscribed objects originally made for his grandmother: a golden mask with a double cobra and vulture uraeus more associated with queenship, as well as a nesting set of coffins with the same markers, refashioned for him. Ankhesenamun would have witnessed the new king Ay perform the opening of the mouth for Tutankhamun at the entrance corridor of her own mother's tomb, in a remade burial chamber widened to fit nesting shrines with Tutankhamun's name newly inscribed. Ankhesenamun, it seems, was powerless to do anything about it.

It is fascinating to contemplate what might have been, had events taken another turn. If Ankhesenamun had been able to grasp the regency herself and rule for her younger brother, if Ay had not been so strong (likely drawing on the support of orthodox priests and haters of the Akhenaten family), we historians would perhaps have been able to identify yet another female king in the records—occurring exactly when we would expect it, at the bitter end of a family lineage. It should have been Ankhesenamun who took on the pharaoh's crown at the unexpected death of Tutankhamun, as was her right as the last member standing of the grand Dynasty 18. This is the place where Egyptian female power would normally have asserted itself—when all hope was lost. But Ankhesenamun was denied: one in a series of events making up a much longer trend as Egyptians of Dynasty 19 and 20 pushed back against female royal power in all its forms.

NEFERTITI'S EXPANDED POLITICAL ROLE is just now being uncovered by archaeologists and historians, and more major discoveries are on the verge of taking place. Egyptologists are engaged in an ongoing and fierce debate about her changing nature, identity, and role. She remains more contested than any other female king of Egypt. The ancient Egyptians haven't helped the situation. When the histories were written and king lists composed generations later, Nefertiti and her heretic husband were removed from most of them, making our job of locating her that much harder. She was not mentioned in any king lists kept in monumental form, in temples, like the one put up by Seti I at Abydos a hundred years later, where perfected story lines of unassailable kingship were inscribed. Only much later administrative histories preserved any possible trace of Nefertiti as a female head of state—but her story is truncated and confused.[42] Indeed, her lifetime will likely remain shrouded until archaeologists can produce a tomb—and maybe even a body. Because of recent archaeological discoveries, that day might actually be closer than we think.

Until recently, the idea that Nefertiti's intact tomb might still be lying in wait in the Valley of the Kings seemed pure archaeological fantasy. Ridiculed and intellectually bloodied in the process of making his case, Nicholas Reeves has put together evidence for a claim that the tomb of the celebrated Tutankhamun—which we know and love so well—was nothing more than the expanded entrance hallway of a much larger and already occupied tomb. Reeves marshals evidence from texts, art history, architectural structure, thermal imaging, and ground-penetrating radar data to argue that behind the rear wall of Tutankhamun's burial chamber lies another tomb: perhaps the tomb of his predecessor, the mysterious Smenkhkare (who could, given the similarity of throne name Ankhkheperure, be Nefertiti herself), at least partially intact. But until someone drills a tiny hole through the back wall of Tutankhamun's burial chamber to see if a treasure trove of fantastic funerary goods or only a rubble-filled corridor lies beyond it, we can only catch a glimpse of Nefertiti as through a fog. Reeves's new revelations have been quashed for now by complicated archaeological politics. But more Egyptologists are starting to see the potential for a find greater even than Tutankhamun's tomb in 1922. Plenty of Egyptologists laugh at the possibility that Nefertiti is behind Tut's burial chamber back wall. I am not one of them.

♛

IN THE END, Nefertiti is all but invisible as a woman of real power, haunting our memories with her beauty, while the remnants of her formidable rule can still be glimpsed in the most famous objects ever discovered by archaeologists anywhere in the world. Tutankhamun's solid-gold coffin and mask with those iconic faces, the delicately carved canopic equipment with tiny golden coffinettes, the inlaid golden throne, all featuring cobra and vulture uraei of a queen.[43] These golden objects, I posit, were not the boy-king's except by happenstance; they were made for Nefertiti as co-king. Hers is the lovely face in the golden mask staring out at us, burned into our mind's eye.[44] But until her tomb as sole king, ostensibly as Smenkhkare, is finally found, Nefertiti will remain known only for her beauty in the Berlin bust, not for her reinstatement of traditional Egyptian religion.

It was Akhenaten, the zealot, who caused his dynasty to fall into a death spin of excess, cruelty, and idolatry from which none of his successors could recover. As her husband's grand experiment unraveled, it would be Nefertiti who, after years of religious fervor and change, became the ultimate reconstructionist, putting to rights all that an overreaching, unchecked, and patriarchal kingship had put awry, and fixing the destructive decisions of her fanatical husband. Indeed, it was a woman who ultimately saved Egypt from its greatest excesses: a Dynasty 18 kingship rich off the spoils of empire, lazy from constant income that was once hard won, but now expected as the due of the god-kings. It was a woman who would set Egypt on its feet again after the people had been forced to doubt their godly leader as never before. More than any other Egyptian queen, it is Nefertiti who represents the epitome of true, successful female power that tapped into the emotions of her people, that embraced multiple perspectives, that reached out in a spirit of reconciliation to those who had been expelled or cast out. Ironically, in so doing, she had to simultaneously morph into a masculinized king who is all but impossible to identify with Nefertiti the queen. Thus, in my mind, it was Nefertiti who tried to preserve her family's lineage, ruling as co-king, even installing the next king. If Tutankhamun had lived longer, if Ay hadn't seized the throne, if Ankhesenamun had claimed a kingship rightfully hers, maybe there would have been more time to save the reputation of Dynasty 18.

CHAPTER 5

TAWOSRET

The Survivor

Many things had changed since the extraordinary highs and lows of Dynasty 18. Indeed, the entire Ramesside Period (Dynasties 19 and 20, starting with King Ramses I and ending with Ramses XI) can be understood as a rebalancing of power after the audacious stunts of kings like Akhenaten. No longer would the Egyptian elites give unbridled power to their king—not even a king like Ramses II, now known as Ramses the Great. From this point on, every Egyptian king would have to work with a stronger and more vocal elite: men and women who now expected recognition for their own work and their own place in society. Egypt's wealthy families, who now felt entitled to hand down their own positions to their eldest sons, would not kowtow to their sovereign (no matter how "great") and would not follow him in overzealous ideological schemes that laid Egypt low. The balance of power had shifted, and not in the king's—or queen's—favor.

It makes sense, then, that political couplings between brother and sister were no longer as commonplace in Dynasties 19 and

20 as they had been previously—particularly in Dynasty 18. Such incestuous unions had maintained power among a select few, royal women among them; the new balance of power tipped toward a broadly construed and decentralized administration of Egypt. These elites would not allow a king to use his close female relatives as arms of his authority and obstacles to their own wide influence.

Distrust of royal women—King's Daughters and King's Sisters—was unwritten but displayed everywhere in Ramesside Egypt. Egyptologists know of no unions between Royal Son and Royal Daughter, thus limiting the kind of concentrated power such relationships could produce at court. When a king of Dynasty 19 or 20 did marry a family member and elevate her to Great Royal Wife, it was usually a daughter—an eminently more controllable entity than a sister—and, even then, only later in a given king's reign. We don't see evidence of any biological issue from such unions, either, as we had in Dynasty 18.

The Royal Family was undoubtedly genetically healthier for avoiding the incest of previous royal generations—and maybe even more attractive. But a lack of brother-sister marriages systematically removed royal women from positions of power, lessening their ability to climb to the highest political office in the land. It also opened the Royal Family up to harm, taking what had been a closed, protectionist system that named only a few, genetically connected people to power, and splaying it wide open into a raging wound with dozens of competitive elements.

Ironically, this new adaptation toward more loosely construed power didn't mean that members of the Royal Family were not interrelated. Indeed, they were all probably connected to one another as first, second, and third cousins. We are simply dealing with a broader, but less incestuous, cluster of elites calling the shots than before. And, in hindsight, we see that incest with strong royal females really had—strangely—been a means of protecting Egyptian kingship itself. That female protection was now crippled.

That wasn't the only thing to have changed from one dynasty to another. Before Dynasty 18, King's Sons were rarely or never mentioned formally as such unless they were marked as heir. Dynasty 18 King's Sons likely served as high officials and priests when they reached adulthood, and were identified on their own monuments (such as tomb chapels or statuary) only by their personal titles and names. This practice must have tamped down the competition at the ever vulnerable time of succession. But with Dynasty 19 we see a momentous change. In the Ramesside Period, King's Sons were publicly identified with abandon, heir or not. They were free to advertise their connection to their father, like a banner to other elites. And there were many such sons in competition with one another, because the harems of Dynasties 19 and 20 seem to have exploded in size and complexity. Everyone wanted a shout-out, and the new decentralized system of power seems to have demanded that these King's Children, the highest of Egypt's elites, be identified to everyone for what they were. Even the King's Daughters were publicly named in temple halls—probably so that their connection to the monarch could be exploited as these girls married into high society, creating households of their own.

No longer do we see a pattern of retaining Royal Daughters in the harem to marry whichever brother became king next. This would have produced more psychologically stable women, we can imagine, because they were now able to form healthy households of their own, instead of remaining shut up in the palace, waiting to marry their brother or father.

But this change also slashed Egyptian women's chances of gaining real political power. It is even possible that royal women were suffering a backlash against the extraordinarily strong female power exercised in Dynasty 18: reactions against women like Ahmes-Nefertari, Hatshepsut, and Nefertiti. Egyptian kings after Hatshepsut—like Thutmose III and Amenhotep II—had already weakened their sisters and daughters, giving limited power to nonroyal women instead, or providing it to their mothers (because what mother would ever act against her own son?).

But Akhenaten undid all of that work when he elevated his great queen Nefertiti, making her a co-ruler. The counterblast against female power started in earnest when Ay refused authority to the King's Daughter, the King's Sister, the King's Wife Ankhesenamun, taking it for himself instead. Dynasty 19 was only a continuation of that trend. The new Ramesside system would not suffer these royal women as rulers. It was a severe but unwritten and unformalized crackdown.

This was the decentralized, competitive context within which Tawosret—a little-known, yet formidable, Egyptian female king—came to power. Used and exploited, she eventually found the strength to pull together the remnants of a failed dynasty in the midst of a civil war between rival factions of Ramses the Great's family. The political disturbance seems decidedly un-Egyptian, particularly since it occurred right after the reign of one of Egypt's longest-lived and most successful monarchs, Ramses II.

The Ramesside political system was not fond of females in power, but Tawosret would nonetheless make it to the very top. Having barely escaped the Amarna period in one piece and suffering through Akhenaten and Nefertiti's joint rule of ideological excess, Egypt was now assiduously and systematically doing everything it could to curtail a woman's authority. Even the great king list of Seti I at the Abydos Temple of Osiris removed the names of recent female kings, including Hatshepsut and Nefertiti (as Smenkhkare, ostensibly), both of whom had nonetheless left Egypt better than they'd found it.

By the time Tawosret's kingly abilities were demanded by circumstance and crisis, she faced a society deeply distrustful of authoritative women and primed to work against female methods of wielding that influence. Tawosret thus had to behave more like a competitive male player than any female king Egypt had yet seen. Her power would be short-lived, but Egypt still needed this woman to rule. It was unavoidable. Even in a time when it seemed prudent not to trust overreaching women and to rely on warlording and competition instead, the systems of divine kingship and a cautious Egyptian society could not do without another woman ruler.

Tawosret follows patterns of many of the women we've discussed. Like Merneith, she acted as regent for a king too young to rule. Like Neferusobek, she held the tattered remnants of a dynasty together, unable to pass any legacy on to a son because the absence of such a boy was the only reason she was in power in the first place. Also like Neferusobek, she ruled alone as king, without any male figure by her side. Like Hatshepsut, she was not the boy-king's mother, on whose behalf she ruled, but one or more steps removed. Also like Hatshepsut, she became God's Wife of Amun, and used her priestly power to vault herself into the kingship. It's almost as if Tawosret were standing on the shoulders of a sisterhood, having learned from each of the female leaders who had come before her.

Tawosret's parentage is unclear. She never claimed to be a King's Daughter or a King's Sister—and if she had such connections to the Royal Family (which almost every operator during the Ramesside period did), she was likely just one of many daughters of Ramses II's 50 or so named sons. We can't expect her to have asserted that she was Ramses the Great's granddaughter, either; there were unwritten rules at this time, it seems, about claiming just any connection to the king, particularly a link two or three steps removed.

Dynasty 19 witnessed a particularly significant and unprecedented adaptation of how the Egyptian Royal Family showed itself to the world. These Ramesside kings depicted their sons and daughters openly, identifying them and picturing them in a visual lineup of royal influence. Ramses II's overt display of his children on his temple walls is practically antithetical to previous patterns of exclusive and closed Egyptian rule.[1] Giving so many royal offspring the opportunity to claim a connection to the king, living or dead, invited extraordinary competition among them—a new destabilizing reality for ancient Egypt. The list of the 50 sons of Ramses II, walking in procession in obeisance to their father, each put in order of birth and named, represented a harbinger of the internal conflict that would burn Egypt from the inside out in the coming generations. Such genealogical publication allowed these sons—all men with their own in-laws, children, and extended familial connections—to create a kind of "parallel administration" of high priests, treasurers, scribes, and military leaders.[2]

Ramses II's long lifetime didn't help matters, either. During his almost-70-year reign, he saw the death of many, if not most, of his sons, most from nothing more serious than illness and old age, but some, perhaps, from more nefarious causes not preserved in our documentation—Royal Brother fighting Royal Brother. Each death of a King's Son snuffed out the hopes of that man's family for more power, each death causing a reshuffling of court hierarchy. In the end, Ramses II's legacy was a mess of his own making: a passel of sons, all named and marked for power, all in competition with one another, all waiting for him to die while they were crown prince. (Watching Dynasty 19 slowly disintegrate from internally created rivalry might even explain the brutal realpolitik of Dynasty 1, which dispatched such potential competitors to the throne as sacrificed tomb attendants.)

During the Ramesside Period, as the King's Sons reached adulthood, there are suggestions of fraternal feuds. Details are sketchy, but we can recognize that Egypt was inviting problems it didn't need. This was a time of unchecked male aggression, with no mothers, wives, or sisters holding them back from the fight. Sometimes it is better for everyone to have a strong woman telling you what to do.

The Ramesside queen was now passive within the halls of power, not taking on positions of economic might or priestly ritual responsibilities. She served her lord as a caregiver, help-mate, and sexual exciter, and she was represented as such. The harem was her arena of competition, even though the harem could no longer launch her into positions of real political power. Nefertari, the Great Royal Wife of Ramses II, must have ruled over the other queens and children of that harem in Dynasty 19—but there are no texts chronicling her actions or strategy. Harem management had now become quite a big job; Ramses II depicted his 50 sons and 50 daughters in mul-tiple temples (and these were just the ones worthy of publica-tion to Egyptian elites). The production of 100 children did not just happen; it demanded planning, effort, time, and hun-dreds of women at one's disposal. This was the Ramesside king's new reproductive strategy: Invite elites and officials to send their daughters to his harem, elevate a Great Royal Wife from among those girls, populate the harems around Egypt with hundreds more beauties from Egypt's villages and towns, start the production of children by visiting the harem often, organize the children into hierarchical order, dole out offices and income as the male children come of age, use the females as a social mechanism of connecting the interrelated families together in alliances and redistributions of wealth, and do not elevate any Royal Daughters to priestly positions of significance that they might use to expand their own power. This latter strategy is an interesting one; if the kingship was in any way vulnerable, it would have been wise for the king to use his daughters or sisters to protect his dynasty. But this attitude was no longer socially acceptable; these royal women were now melted into elite Egyptian society, no longer kept apart.[3]

Tawosret likely began her life during the latter years of Ramses II's 67-year reign. (This was a king so long lived that he may have come to the throne as an adolescent, requiring a regent to call the shots, for a few years at least. His mother, Tuya, may be a rare instance of early Dynasty 19 female power.) No other females were invited into positions of authority in Ramses' administration. Ramses II's wife, Nefertari, would be celebrated for her beauty as an adornment of her king, a producer of children, a fertile field for her lord—not as a high priestess or anything approaching an equal. Her depictions alongside her husband are usually much smaller. No longer do we see king and queen as partners of equal stature; now the queen is diminutive in comparison, relegated to a tiny statue alongside the king's lower leg, not even reaching his knee. Exceptions are made for Nefertari's temple at Abu Simbel and in other places. But, overall, it's clear that something had shifted against expressions of female power, even in statuary and reliefs.

TAWOSRET MAY HAVE BEEN too young to understand the details of Ramesside family hierarchies, but she would have learned fast. She likely saw the frustration and anxiety in the adults around her as Ramses II continued to live on and on while all his elder sons died. She was probably linked in some way to everyone she knew—as cousin, aunt, niece, sister, daughter. Everyone in the Ramesside elite circles was related, and those connections were likely carefully documented within the family (albeit in no form easily deciphered by historians).[4] Within every new administration, each family would have looked to its own connection to the king, whether direct or circuitous, each with its own patriarch, its own King's Son. They would have known what number their patriarch was in the line of succession, how his income compared with his brothers', and how his political connections to those brothers functioned. The extended Ramesside family would have been one of ever forming and splintering alliances of King's Sons: some short-lived, others seemingly unbreakable. King's Daughters, on the other hand, were no longer of much consequence politically.

As King Ramses II approached his 80th year of life (around 1200 B.C.), 12 crown princes were named and died in succession. Each death caused a mini-upheaval of anxiety as all the hierarchies and successions had to be rejiggered. Finally, the title of crown prince landed on the 13th son—a certain Merneptah—who got the position in Year 55 of his father's reign. Merneptah, probably already quite mature himself, had to wait another 12 years for his father to die. Like Edward VII after his long-lived mother, Queen Victoria. Or Prince Charles, waiting decades while Elizabeth II reigns on and on. It's amazing the crown prince had any life himself left to give his country and his family as king. When he ascended the throne, he must have been 40 or 50 years old, with a wife and grown sons of his own, each with their own household and mini-bastions of power. He probably had dozens of children, grandchildren, and even great-grandchildren, all of whom now expected a slice of the pie. Although the appearances of a strong and centralized kingship were kept up in Dynasty 19, although decorum was maintained by these distinguished elites, the slices were getting awfully thin with so many players, and the fighting for each morsel became ever more fierce.

Extraordinarily, throughout most of Egyptian history, the men who had seized the kingship originated in the South. But now the balance of power looked northward. In Dynasty 19, the monarchy was remade by men of the North: by Ramses I and his son Seti I, men who came from the eastern Delta, who had Levantine connections, who were named after Canaanite storm gods equated with Seth. From the North, too, new problems were arising. A mass migration of epic proportions was brewing. Originating in climate change that brought on repeated droughts, crop failures, and famine, tens of thousands of people were starting to relocate, coming first from Europe and moving into the Middle East in wave after wave of invasions by ship and on foot.[5] These newcomers were called Peoples of the Sea, and they would change the politics and landscape of Egypt forever.

King Merneptah, already old, was called upon to repel a mighty coalition of Sea Peoples who invaded the Egyptian Delta. Some of them now self-identified as Libyan, having already settled there for some generations. Others were newcomers, identified by strange tribal names like Peleset or Sherden or Meshwesh, which the Egyptians would translate into their archaic hieroglyphic system of writing. Whatever these invaders were called and wherever they came from, their advance was brutal and relentless, as a persistent onslaught of humanity entered Egypt. Scores of them were killed, but more still found a way to settle in Egypt's Delta. Many brought their women, children, and livestock in a desperate attempt to find a sustainable life; their military invasion was only a secondary result of an unwieldy population crisis. Starting with the reign of Merneptah, the Egyptian army suffered a series of assaults by these Sea Peoples.[6] Egypt's day in the sun as unassailable ruler of the Mediterranean, African, and Near Eastern worlds was over. From here on out in its history, Egypt would always be bracing for the next attack from outside its borders.

As a child, Tawosret likely heard the adults in her family talking in hushed and worried tones about the invasions. Just the name of the Sea Peoples would have struck fear in the mind of a child. But Tawosret also heard her family speak of a great triumph won by their king Merneptah against the People of the Sea. Probably in a coordinated attempt to keep Egypt's northern border safe from further aggression, Merneptah then engaged in a campaign to Egypt's northeast, sending his troops into the Levant, the land of Canaan, after which he recorded the various cities and polities vanquished on a stone victory stela that he would set up at his Temple of Millions of Years in Thebes.[7] The stela mentions strongholds like Gezer and Ashkelon, seized by Egypt. Even a tribal people of Israel (written *Ysryr*) are mentioned as having submitted to Egypt's control; the stone inscription documents that many live captives were brought back to Egypt, probably as slaves and servants in Egypt's fine houses, estates, and urban spaces (including their new growing capital city of Pi-Ramses in the northeastern Delta, the Pithom of the Bible). It was a triumph, and Tawosret would have seen the evidence of it all around her; maybe her family even took some of these Canaanite slaves into her home. Egypt was still strong and wealthy; there were reminders of that daily.

As a girl, Tawosret probably heard how King Merneptah had respected the peace treaty originally set up by Ramses II by shipping masses of grain to the kings of Hatti in Anatolia as famine had settled upon their lands. The Hittites were an old rival, but the threat of the Sea Peoples seems to have prompted even bitter enemies to forge protective alliances. And Egypt still had plenty of grain to send to their suffering new allies— certainly more than other polities in the ancient Near East. Egypt was one of the lucky ones; the years to come would see the fall of great ruling houses and governments all around the Mediterranean.

The Egyptians' other source of continued stability was in the South, enabled by their unflagging exploitation of Nubia and Kush. If Egypt kept these lands under its control, it would have plenty of mineral wealth with which to trade influence. As a

young girl, Tawosret may have heard that Merneptah had successfully put down a revolt in Nubia in his sixth year—an absolute necessity to keep the gold mines productive and wealth
flowing into Egypt. The revolt was suppressed; that was good
news. But it seems the Nubians sensed a new weakness in their
Egyptian neighbors.

Tawosret's Egypt was now unavoidably globalized, replete
with foreign peoples and decision-makers. Levantine, Canaanite, Syrian, Libyan, Nubian, Kushite, and even Sea Peoples'
influences were growing in Egyptian spheres of power. Many of
the people with whom Tawosret interacted at court would have
come from elsewhere. Egypt has always had connections with
the Levant—but there were arguably more back and forth movements of people at this point than at any other.

If we are to pick any one time for the biblical stories preserved
in the Exodus, this would be it.[8] If Jewish cultural memory has
preserved any kernels of historical truth within its fantastical
tales of survival, parted seas, and Egyptian military destruction,
it could be found in Merneptah's Egypt, when tens of thousands
of Levantine people were brought in as captives, many ultimately
sent into slavery in Egypt's urban spaces, where more established
and Egyptianized Levantines already acted as scribes and officials
for the Egyptian crown. Perhaps some of these foreign peoples
really did build the capital of Pi-Ramses, the biblical Pithom,
creating a cultural memory that they were forced to make mud-
bricks without any chaff, as recorded in the Book of Exodus.

To Tawosret's young eyes, everything probably seemed to be
working just fine. Rebellions had been put down; invasions had

been repelled; allies were fed; oaths were upheld; temples were built; monumental statuary was raised. She would only learn later, when it was too late for anyone to do anything about it, that it had all been a facade: the seeds of Egypt's destruction had already been sown. Merneptah's own Temple of Millions of Years was largely quarried from Amenhotep III's Temple of Millions of Years, pieced together from reused blocks and recarved colossi. Not only that, the social destabilization brought on by Ramses II's overly long rule, of brother feuding with brother, was still plaguing Egypt. When Merneptah eventually died at 60 or 70 years of age, most of his own sons had predeceased him. This dangerous cycle would continue.

Merneptah had named a crown prince on his public monuments: a son named Seti-Merneptah, whom Egyptologists call Seti II. Already a mature man with his own wife and grown children, Seti II seems to have been named king immediately upon his father's death. And this is when Tawosret enters our story—because even though Seti II already had a wife, she must have been old at this point, ostensibly beyond childbearing years. The Egyptian king was expected to create new offspring, to stock his harem with children and future heirs. The fact that he was an old man mattered not a bit. But he needed to take a young Great Royal Wife—none other than Tawosret, who suddenly found herself in the unenviable position of serving as one of two great queens: one aged, the other juvenile.

It was probably a difficult situation for everyone as two Great Royal Wives, two leaders of the king's harem, two arbiters of his children and many wives, tried to cooperate with each other.

The elder queen (probably a woman named Takhat) would have had the authority and experience to manipulate the younger Tawosret. But the younger girl had the power of her beauty and youth. Maybe the women even headed up different harem palaces to avoid conflict—one in the North at the court of Pi-Ramses and the other in the South at Thebes. We don't know the details, but it was clearly a poor beginning, and Merneptah's extended family was put in the position of having to choose between them. Ancient Egypt was rife for a brutal showdown, split down the middle into competing halves.

As is typical, the Egyptian documentation—so intent on broadcasting a perfect and unassailable divine kingship—kept the realpolitik of the story almost completely closeted. Egyptologists are forced to ferret out the real narrative by examining the written remnants of the conflict; namely, which cartouche names had been scratched out and which names had been put in their places as well as documenting when and where these erasures happened—a tedious way to reconstruct history.

Not everyone in Egypt accepted the claim of Seti II to the throne. His reign was contested. Egyptologists have found evidence that another individual, a man named Amunmesses, claimed to be king, in Thebes at least and maybe elsewhere, too, during the first year of Seti II. This southern king, Amunmesses, had southern military connections—particularly the political rule of Nubia and control of its gold. It seems he was descended from Ramses II, like everyone else in the court. But some Egyptologists[9] even believe that Amunmesses was the son of the already ancient King Seti II himself, a son who lost all his chances at power when a new Great Royal Wife was named and honored over his own mother. This is the kind of destabilization produced when Egyptian kings lived too long, leaving a large number of established and empowered adult children who didn't take kindly to being passed over.

The exact source of the family rift and royal rivalry remains vexingly unclear. It could have been when Tawosret was named Great Royal Wife in addition to another woman, or when Tawosret was given the unprecedented honor of a tomb in the Valley of the Kings as a mere queen.[10] Or perhaps Amunmesses saw the writing on the wall when word spread that Tawosret was with child, knowing that he and his kin would be cut out of the succession.

As an official administering Egypt's southern province of Nubia, Amunmesses had enough access to military, riches, and manpower, not to mention political connections, to take the kingship in Egypt's southern Nile Valley. His handiwork is all over Thebes, where he left a significant amount of monumental statuary, stelae, and temples for one whose reign was so short and contested.

All the evidence suggests that Egypt had entered a civil war, and maybe even one between father and son—between Seti II, son of Merneptah and named heir to the throne, and Amunmesses, the powerful King's Son of Kush, the viceroy of the South. North versus South. According to scattered and broken evidence, Amunmesses first declared his rival kingship within the king's first year from his stronghold in Nubia. Fighting continued until Amunmesses took Thebes and the surrounding territories a year and a half later. The Egyptian people—used to continuity and centrality of rule and having faith in their government institutions—found that conviction shattered. Egypt was shaken to the core as two rival kings ruled Egypt simultaneously, one from the Delta and another from the Nile Valley, just a generation after their greatest king's lifetime.[11]

The younger Great Royal Wife Tawosret knew the next Egyptian king would ideally come from her womb. She was in the right place at the right time. Her husband, Seti II, was mature but not decrepit. Tawosret likely did everything in her power to produce Egypt's next crown prince, beautifying and seducing, strategizing and conniving.

But what do we know with any certainty? Amunmesses had control of all the gold mines and was busy constructing grand statuary and adding on to Egypt's stately temples in Thebes—a sure sign that there was income to secure raw materials and to pay craftsmen. Egyptologists always use material production to measure power: If statues were being built in good numbers, other things were going well, too. Amunmesses was even able to commence construction of his Temple of Millions of Years and his tomb in the Valley of the Kings; simultaneously, he ordered a halt to construction of his competitors' tombs—those of Seti II and his queen Tawosret—in the same royal valley.[12]

None of it would matter. After a few years of playing king in Thebes, Amunmesses was defeated by Seti II and his greater military resources. Whether there was a final showdown between the two rivals, whether words were spoken, in public or private, whether there was a final public execution of Amunmesses, we will never know. We only learn that Egypt had all too easily split into warring factions, and that authority had suddenly shifted back to Seti II and Egypt's North. Not long after his victory, Seti II would begin his campaign of erasure and reinscription, essentially putting his name onto all the cartouches and on all the statues, stelae, and reliefs that Amunmesses had carved in Thebes during his short reign—often so poorly executed that Egyptologists can still see traces of the old name underneath. Even Amunmesses' tomb was ordered ritually emasculated and destroyed: hieroglyphs shaved and cut, names removed. One wonders if Amunmesses was even given a real and proper burial; betraying the king was generally not the way to earn a spot in the afterlife.

Seti II now had control of a united Egypt, but he still didn't feel that his power was consolidated. Indeed, given how many Thebans must have rallied around Amunmesses and his rebellion, Seti II may have found it prudent to keep a closer eye on the southern regions. And this is when a new and ferocious player appeared on the scene: The Great Overseer of the Seal of the Entire Land, a man named Bay. The "seal" that he oversaw was a control mechanism, a kind of visual lock and key, to protect temple and palace treasuries where all the gold, silver, and other easily fungible goods were kept. To oversee all the seals implied rule over all the treasuries in the land—containing Egypt's vast reserves of precious metal, turquoise and carnelian, lapis lazuli and bronze, frankincense and myrrh.

Bay was a chancellor, a money man, a kind of Egyptian chief financial officer who doled out wealth and thus influence. It seems he was sent to Thebes to consolidate the king's power. He likely relished the opportunity to boost his own personal ambitions. When Bay ordered the removal of a carving of Seti II's crown prince on Karnak Temple, he had it redone with his own image.[13] To remove a crown prince and replace it with a nonroyal official was unprecedented. The conservative Thebans must have been shocked.

To put a chancellor—a treasurer—in such a holy place reserved for kings and their chosen successors was strange indeed. It smacked not only of this man's narcissistic intent but also of how money now controlled everyone in Egypt during this period. Suddenly, a financial trader was in charge of Thebes. That this official, Bay, may have been of foreign origin—Syrian or Levantine, relocated perhaps to the Northeast Delta of Egypt—makes the narrative that much more extraordinary. Seti II was, it seems, relying on a foreign finance mercenary to see his plans fulfilled in Thebes and elsewhere—maybe because there was no one he could trust among his extended Ramesside family, many of whom had already flouted his authority. Maybe Seti II had used a foreign mercenary army to defeat Amunmesses in the first place; perhaps this was Bay's reward for raising those forces. No matter how he came to power, the shrine that Bay had redone with his own image was located at the very front of Karnak Temple, on the most public procession way possible. Bay was making sure that every Theban witnessed his power and influence over the crown.

However long Bay had been in Egypt, and however Egyptianized he actually was, later texts would focus on his foreign origins and disparagingly call him a Syrian.[14] Nonetheless, Seti II seems to have owed him something, and something big, because Bay was given free rein to implement his control over the South after the reconsolidation of power, and to show his place in society in ways unheard of before. Not only did Bay display his images along the Theban processional thoroughfares in the company of the king himself, but he also had the audacity to represent himself the very same size and stature as the king—something no man had done before in Egyptian history.

It hadn't taken Egypt long to go from the days of groveling to Akhenaten to insurrections against the crown and rivaling the king's authority in image, word, and deed. And there were to be more unprecedented actions by the upstart chancellor: Even though he was nonroyal, Bay ordered a tomb for himself in the sacred Valley of the Kings with a straight axis in the manner of a monarch's, right next to that of the king and queen. For the orthodox Thebans, the presumption of this foreign man from the North must have been insufferable.

Given that she was Great Royal Wife and that all hopes of an uncontested dynastic continuation hinged on her, we have to imagine that Tawosret still spent as much time with her husband Seti II as possible, trying for that royal heir. But we never see any record of their relationship or that she bore him any sons. Time was running out. A civil war is exhausting, but a civil war against one's own son would have been soul-destroying. Whatever the actual circumstances, Seti II would not live much longer. Evidence in his tomb in the Valley of the Kings suggests that an order had been given at some point to speed up the work, but it wouldn't matter. There was no more time to complete the massive project; the king was dead—and in only his sixth year. As it has been with so many men throughout human history, most of Seti II's existence on the throne had been spent fighting for control of Egypt, rather than ruling it.

♛

EGYPT WAS PLUNGED INTO UNCERTAINTY. The next king—Siptah—was not only a mere child but also disabled with a clubfoot, probably stemming from cerebral palsy. His parentage is, astoundingly, unrecorded. The father could have been Seti II or even Amunmesses; the mother was decidedly not Tawosret. Was the kid even a King's Son? Against all odds, Tawosret ended up acting as the boy's regent. Around the same time, she was named God's Wife of Amun at Thebes, ostensibly moving her from the harem palaces of Pi-Ramses in the North down to her own bastion of power at Thebes in the South. Tawosret would share the same priestly position once held by Hatshepsut herself—and, like her, she would utilize it to gain further authority as time went on.

Tawosret's new position must have seemed strange and even imperious to the elites and priests of Thebes, since the office of God's Wife of Amun hadn't been used as an arm of royal political power for quite some time. Indeed, the post seems to have been baldly manufactured to justify Tawosret's role as acting regent to a boy who was not her own son and may not have even been a prince (just as Hatshepsut had used the religious position to rule for her nephew). Assuming Siptah was expected to spend most of his time as king at Pi-Ramses in the North, how was this arrangement to work? Was Tawosret an absent God's Wife of Amun, a high priestess in name only, helping Siptah rule from the Delta? Or was she a regent in name only, staying down South while Siptah was in Pi-Ramses with Bay, the Syrian constantly hovering and monitoring the throne room? Either way, Tawosret certainly didn't leave many monuments of herself at Thebes as regent. And, in the end, all the evidence suggests that it was Bay who exercised real control of the country.

Even if Tawosret was accepted as regent to Siptah by the Egyptians—since she did hold the title "The Great Noble-woman of Every Land," which many historians believe is representative of queen regency during Dynasty 19—it seems that Bay was nonetheless calling all the shots. Just as he had done with the short-lived elderly Seti II's kingship, Bay made sure to visually and publicly mark Siptah's kingship with his own presence. In every published temple image of the young king, the chancellor haunts his steps, appearing right behind him in numerous scenes—in carvings at Aswan and Gebel el Silsila. At the latter location, Bay even includes the unique and extraordinary inscription that he was the one "who established the king on the seat of his father whom he loved"—an unprecedented claim of king-maker. The chancellor's audacity knew no bounds. No commoner had ever taken such public and visible liberty in regard to the Egyptian kingship before.

Who was this Siptah that Bay could take such advantage of the young king?[15] Some Egyptologists have suggested that Bay was Siptah's uncle, a blood relation through his mother.[16] We will probably never know who Siptah was—Seti's son? Amunmesses' son? Bay's nephew?—and it doesn't really matter. The material point is this: This boy, Siptah, seemed to have been a tailor-made vehicle for Bay to achieve informal, yet grandiose power, making himself not only indispensable to a weak king but also the true authority over all of Egypt. Bay knew it. It was a canny move to choose a child-king: a boy for whom decisions had to be made by a female regent, who in turn could be easily manipulated by the chancellor himself. The dowager-queen Tawosret had no claim to authority from her own lineage; she was no King's Daughter, no King's Sister, no King's Mother. She was just a dead king's wife. Her position as high priestess was likely conjured by Bay, too. Bay ably positioned Siptah and Tawosret to give the appearance of keeping to traditional ways of ancient Egyptian rule, while simultaneously allowing the exercise of that power by someone wholly unconnected to the Royal Family—and perhaps not even Egyptian, to boot.

The whole game—the defeat of Amunmesses, the choice of Siptah as the new king, the choice of Tawosret as regent—seems to have been engineered by Bay. Now the ambitious chancellor had a new young monarch—a 10-year-old at accession, more or less, according to the preserved mummy—whom he could completely dominate. As for Tawosret, she had not been brought up for such a position of power within the Royal Family; the society in which she was raised frowned upon giving women such authority. She had no role models of this kind of politicking.

Moreover, she was likely still a young woman at this point, probably in her early twenties, perhaps overwhelmed by the frightening upheavals that set members of her family against one another. We can imagine Bay exploiting her inexperience and fears with impunity, using her as his political tool.

Tawosret already knew she had failed as Great Royal Wife to produce a son; Seti II was dead. Assuming that Bay had picked the next king himself, as he claims in the texts, then he would have chosen one who needed his protection, who needed his "eye on him," as he would say (in a text he had carved at Deir el Bahari at the Temple of Mentuhotep II).[17] Let's also assume that Bay had chosen Tawosret to be regent with the same strategic knowledge about her character and potential for being controlled. He was essential to her position; she had no justification, truly, to act as queen-regent. Bay was the one who engineered the whole thing, cornering both Siptah and Tawosret into absolute dependence upon him—not only for their authority, but for their very lives: a skillful manufacture of indispensability.[18]

Tawosret found herself in a sticky situation. She was no longer chief queen. She was named decision-maker over an immature monarch who was not her own child, so her claim to the regency was remote at best. The child in question was probably not even the son of the previous king, her dead husband. And the boy Siptah was weak. Everyone would have seen his disabilities with their own eyes as he limped around the throne room. Tawosret was the regent for a king nobody expected, to whom she was in no way related, protected by a man feared and hated from north to south (as brutal erasures of Bay's name would later show). Subsequent king lists wouldn't even include King Siptah, although Seti II himself was listed—certainly unexpected if Siptah had the backing of the Egyptian people as Seti's heir. Siptah was nothing more than a pawn of Bay's, and Tawosret was quickly on her way to becoming the same thing. Siptah was Bay's pet project, not hers.

Although Tawosret had little grasp of the political realities, Egyptian culture still demanded that Bay pay the proper respect to the country's queen-regent. So every time Bay ordered himself depicted in large scale in a public Egyptian temple, he put Tawosret's image alongside him—at Abu Simbel, at Amada, even in the Valley of the Kings. Some have seen these paired, mirror images of Bay and Tawosret as representative of a political partnership, presuming complicity on the part of Tawosret and even assuming a sexual relationship between the two.[19] These paired images should instead be seen as our first clear example of a royal female manipulated as a pawn for power by an outsider. Tawosret was a front, a human shield, a ruse. She was Bay's means to acquire all the power, while she only held the traditional appearance of that power as her dead husband's chief queen. It wasn't the first time in human history that a woman with a formal title of power found herself under the control of a man with no claim to it. But, sometimes, women can gain mastery of the system and fight back.

Apparently, Tawosret still had a few cards up her sleeve. As Bay grew more and more empowered, she bided her time, waiting years before she struck back, according to evidence in her tomb in the Valley of the Kings, which shows only increasing expansion and decoration of her architectural space as queen.[20] Our first significant news comes from Deir el Medina, from which we have a record dated to Year 5 of Siptah that "The scribe of the Tomb Paser said: Pharaoh, life, prosperity and health, has killed the great enemy, Bay."[21] No reasons or details were given. The text in question was found at a workmen's village, not in the palace or a great temple—and it was just a simple ink-drawn memo on a limestone chip, a note preserved by the men who were building tombs belonging to all the interested parties: Siptah, Tawosret, and Bay.

We can be sure that the Deir el Medina artisans stopped work on Bay's tomb immediately, once the Syrian chancellor had been put down. Maybe the tomb craftsmen even had a little party to celebrate the man's death. All the glory for the act was given to King Siptah, the "pharaoh" mentioned in their text, who at this stage was a boy approaching a mere 15 years of age. But it was almost certainly Tawosret who had ordered the extermination of this interloper, this foreigner, from the Egyptian halls of power. She had finally had enough of his control, found new supporters to rally around her, and somehow engineered a way to be free of him.

Egyptian posterity would not remember Bay well. The Great Harris Papyrus, written in the reign of Ramses IV, a few generations after this messy history, includes the following intriguing passage: "Then another time came consisting of empty years when Irsu [The One Who Made Himself], a Syrian, was among them as a chief, having put the whole land into subjugation before him; each joined with his companion in plundering their goods, and they treated the gods as they did men, and no offerings were made in the temples."[22]

If your rule constituted "empty years," you were not a popular leader. As soon as Bay was gone, the orders went out to have him erased from temples throughout Egypt. Indeed, the triple bark shrine at Karnak, built by Seti II, still bears the scars of his removal (although careful scrutiny reveals his name and the ghost of his image). Bay was chiseled away from statuary and temples all over Egypt's South—at Deir el Bahari, at Amada, at Karnak. His tomb in the Valley of the Kings was defaced.

Tawosret was now free to train and educate her young charge, King Siptah, as she saw fit. He had almost reached his majority anyway. But less than two years later, Siptah was dead, too—not yet into his sixth year of kingship, maybe not even 16 years of age. There are no explanations given in the formal textual record, but there are clues as to how Tawosret felt about the boy, if not about the nature of his death. Orders had already been given to remove all the references to the young king not only from Tawosret's tomb, where they were replaced with those of her dead husband, Seti II, but also from Siptah's own tomb as well. Siptah's coffins, sarcophagi, and canopic chest were found by archaeologists smashed and washed into a crevice in the Valley of the Kings.[23] That insult might very well have been the result of later tomb robbery—but the erasure of the young king's name from his own tomb smacks of something else: a desire to deny the boy his place as king. Or, Tawosret was now publicly claiming her status as a female king, justifying her ability to take the throne as the previous Great Royal Wife of the dead king Seti II on monuments throughout Egypt. She now needed to create a new royal lineage for herself, and quickly: one that completely removed King Siptah and went straight from Seti II to herself as female sovereign.

Tawosret might represent that one unique instance of an Egyptian queen who decided not only to seize power by force but also to refuse to share that power with any male partner. Even though Siptah is credited with killing Bay, Tawosret was no doubt a part of the scheme, if not the perpetrator. And even though there is no direct evidence that she had Siptah killed, circumstantial evidence abounds. As soon as Siptah was gone from the scene, Tawosret was able to set herself up as a female king—with a series of new names ostensibly granted in temple rituals throughout Egypt. Her kingly monikers connect her to Heliopolis to the North (Horus name: "Strong Bull Beloved of Maat, Beautiful as King Like Atum") and Thebes in the South (throne name: "Daughter of Re, Beloved of Amun"). She even changed her given name at her ascension, becoming Tawosret-Beloved-of-Mut, a shout-out to Amun's bloodthirsty and violent consort resident at Thebes. Indeed, by connecting her person to the lioness goddess Mut, Tawosret may have been effectively communicating her modus operandi to her elites; Mut was capable of brutal acts, to be sure, but only on behalf of what was right and true, only in the interest of her husband-father, the sun god.

When she took the kingship, Tawosret tells us obliquely that she was only acting in the interest of the true family lineage. She enlarged her Valley of Kings tomb, cutting it deeper into the mountainside and adding the Book of the Amduat and the Book of Gates: both texts previously used only for monarchs, not meant for queens and not formerly inscribed in her sepulcher. She had her own images in her tomb modified, ordering the king's blue crown carved onto her head, her figures transformed into monarchical images of power. She even ordered a Temple of Millions of Years for herself at the edge of the inundation in western Thebes, distributing many foundation depositions to sanctify the space, putting up a mudbrick pylon to add monumentality and majesty to the temple where she would be worshipped as a god.

Tawosret also commissioned new statues of herself as king, one of which survives: a piece showing her as a woman with breasts, tight waist, full hips, and narrow shoulders, but dressed in the masculine long pleated kilt, shirt, and apron favored by kings like Ramses II. With this gesture, she was visually claiming descent from the great god-king of her dynasty. Indeed, her statue resembles similar examples of the great Ramses—a point that she couldn't have made often enough to justify a new and vulnerable female kingship. Her new royal names are preserved on the surface of that one remaining statue, found by archaeologists near Heliopolis in the vicinity of modern-day Cairo.[24]

Like Hatshepsut before her, Tawosret recorded the years of her reign using those of the previous king, signaling to her people that the child-king's rule was immaterial: His reign had happened under her watch and no one else's. His Year 6 was her Year 6. Unlike Hatshepsut, however, she ruled (or decided to rule, if she did have the boy assassinated) without a male counterpart on the throne next to her. But in such an unprotected and unjustified position within such a competitive political sphere, it seems she couldn't last long. Despite her youth, she reigned as king only two to four years after the death of the young Siptah.[25] This underscores an important pattern: There is no evidence of any Egyptian woman ruling alone for longer than a few years. Only those accompanied by a male—Merneith, Hatshepsut, Nefertiti, Cleopatra—held on to power for a decade or more. Those who attempted to go it alone all met their ends after four years tops, including Neferusobek. Whether they were assassinated, unsupported, thwarted, or debilitated as a result of their femininity and/or inability to quickly sire a multitude of heirs, the rule of these solitary pathbreaking women was always bleak and short.

Why are human societies so happy to be quickly rid of female rule? Jezebel's daughter Athaliah, for instance, ruled Judah in the eighth century B.C. for just a few years in protection of her son, an immature king. She was killed alongside the boy by Yahweh priest Jehu who claimed the throne after her. And there is the case of Shajar al-Darr of Egypt of the 13th century. Once a slave who married a sultan, she was raised up as monarch by her elites in Cairo after her husband's murder; she ruled only a short time when need and crisis demanded it, cruelly and duplicitously shunted aside as soon as it was expedient. Shajar al-Darr would have met her end stripped naked and beaten, her corpse thrown from Cairo's citadel to rot, if her people had not lovingly buried her.

Many of history's women could rise to power only within extraordinary crisis and, when the immediate predicament had abated, were unceremoniously pushed aside. Indeed, the catastrophe itself was usually blamed on the woman's rule, a Catch-22 if there ever was one. And yet, the fact that Tawosret was able to take the throne alone at all is a testament to ancient Egypt's deference to royal lineage, if not also the status quo. This was a country in the habit of giving power to the one who was already exercising it, but also a country that bestowed authority on a woman only when politics was at its lowest point and when discretion and prudence were required above all else. They took on female rule only when conditions were bleak. Without Bay and Siptah around anymore, Tawosret was the only one there to do the job. Indeed, we should assume that she and her supporters had already set up her kingship before she dispatched Bay and even Siptah (if she was the one who ordered the hit). And it seems that most priests and courtiers went along with Tawosret as king, if only to avoid outright civil war between the remaining factions of Ramses the Great's family—but also in deference to her, realizing that she would rule differently from all the avaricious and bloodthirsty warriors who had come before her, her presumed assassinations notwithstanding.

Still, Tawosret possessed one massive liability that Neferusobek and Hatshepsut did not share. She was not a King's Daughter or a King's Sister, but a Royal Widow: a sliver of a justification for being the last woman of Dynasty 19 left standing.

Tawosret was scrappy and brave, able to take great risks and to capitalize on her efforts. But, despite all that, her kingship was short. Little of substance was accomplished during her reign. Little was built. Her imagery was never masculinized like Hatshepsut's, because she had no male counterpart who was growing older and stronger to match, no long kingship to equal. She showed herself, like Neferusobek before her, as a woman with the elements of kingship layered upon her feminine person. She never tried to become the masculinized king of her people. Not only did she not have enough time; it's likely she didn't have enough political support to show herself this way. We should remember that Hatshepsut's manly images were an overt allusion to exactly that kind of masculine power, not indications of weakness or insecurity of a woman trying to become what she was not, or desperate yearnings to cross-dress. Hatshepsut could show herself as a male king because she was truly indomitable.

Tawosret was no Hatshepsut, and everybody knew it. Plus, her people likely believed that it was she who had removed the boy-king from power. If we suspect it thousands of years hence, the ancient Egyptians must have suspected it as well. Tawosret did not hold the high ground. From the beginning, her power was exercised from a defensive stance. But this queen accomplished what no Egyptian woman before her could: She took the kingship out of her own ambition. Make no mistake: Tawosret still became king, a woman who ruled the world. But her ability to dominate Egypt was more limited than that of any other Egyptian woman leader before or after.

Tawosret would have no legacy, no children. If she was still of childbearing age when she took the kingship (very likely) and hoped to bear a son, then that plan hadn't worked. Any sexual-romantic partner of King Tawosret would have been looked upon with great suspicion anyway, and there is no record of such a man. The next king would not be her son. Instead, we see a continuation of the power of that mighty and overly large extended family of Ramses the Great. Tawosret's death is not explained to us, but we can suspect that she was removed from power violently because her rule was seen as illegitimate. A stela from Elephantine tells us, in oblique terms, how Tawosret was taken down: "the land had been in confusion . . . [the great god] stretched out his arm and selected his majesty in life, prosperity, health from among the millions . . . Fear of him seized the hearts of combatants before him; they fled like sparrows with a falcon after them."[26] Thus, we are to understand that a warlord arose from among the strongmen left in Ramses the Great's extended family, took down Tawosret and her supporters, and had himself installed in her place. This warlord's name was Setnakht, meaning "Seth Is Mighty," founder of Dynasty 20. For once, the Egyptians were not (that) shy about telling us that a king vanquished another ruler by force (but they still don't explicitly reveal in writing from whom Setnakht took the throne).

In a later text—the same Great Harris Papyrus that mentioned Irsu the Syrian (Bay)—we are told that after those empty years, this new King Setnakht "cleansed" the throne of Egypt.[27] Tawosret herself was likely counted among those rebels whom Setnakht killed. It was she who was cleansed from the great throne. Who was this Setnakht? He may have been a royal insider, a courtier of Tawosret, even, someone who walked the palace environs. He may have been one of many men shocked by Tawosret's decisions and antics. Indeed, we might even assume that it was Tawosret's ambitious overreach, her killing of a boy-king, possibly, that caused many men at her court—men from the family of Ramses II—to take matters into their own hands and strike back against her. Indeed, it seems Setnakht wasn't able to finally destroy Tawosret until the second year of his own reign. Did Setnakht have himself crowned, then contest Tawosret in another civil war? If so, she lasted for a little while, but eventually lost the throne and the support of her people.

Tawosret's ambition went much too far in its perceived narcissism and self-interest to maintain any positive memory in Egyptian history. And she was taken down for it. This highlights an uncomfortable truth: Even in ancient Egypt, women could not show political intent. Ultimately, Tawosret disrespected the office of the regency, acting not as the protector but as the aggressor. Tawosret is the only woman in our story who broke the unspoken pact that allowed repeated bursts of female power in ancient Egypt: that she should act only on behalf of a Royal Family member, that she deny any personal interest in such power, that she build consensus and act for the good of all. And she was punished for it.

When Setnakht, a new king of a new dynasty, took over, his own throne names broadcast his achievements and justification for power. He was The One Powerful of Arm Who Drives Out His Rebels and The One Who Smites the Nine Bows Who Oppose Kingship. Unlike Tawosret, he would see no censure for his ambitions or outright claims to have committed violence because he did it against a rebel (Tawosret) in support of divine kingship. The double standard is clear: Violence is excusable for men. In fact, it makes them seem more powerful. But a woman's militarism is considered so aberrant that it's unsettling. When Setnakht died after just a few years of rule, he was buried in Tawosret's old royal tomb, by order of his son Ramses III. The tomb was quickly altered for his use, the Deir el Medina workmen simply covering over the female king Tawosret's images with plaster, which they carved to fit the masculine Setnakht, a rush job to bury a warrior in someone else's royal tomb. It is because so much of this plaster has now fallen away that Egyptologists can reconstruct much of the confusing story.

But there is something strange in the alteration of Tawosret's tomb that speaks to her value to her people. The queen's names here and elsewhere were never intentionally destroyed. Indeed, there was no purposeful hacking away at any of Tawosret's monuments, few that they were. Her preserved statue bears no scars of erasure. And later, in the reign of Ramses VI, Tawosret was still mentioned in contemporary texts with her name in a cartouche. She was not called the enemy or any other disparaging names in these later texts. She may even have been depicted in a later Dynasty 20 ostracon, which shows a drawing of a queen with a boy riding a chariot, shooting at an enemy in a chariot opposite her.[28] Tawosret also makes an appearance in the later fourth-century king list of Manetho as Thuoris, a legendary man of Thebes. It seems her aggressive deeds were just too manly, leaving behind a cultural memory that erased her femininity entirely.

A sliver of Tawosret lasted into Egypt's collective consciousness, escaping total censure and removal. Maybe, just maybe,

Siptah had died a natural death, leaving Tawosret holding the bag and all the suspicion for causing the boy-king's demise. We Egyptologists still suspect her, after all; maybe the ancient Egyptians did, too.

♛

IN THE END, whether she killed Siptah or not is immaterial. Tawosret served as a representative of a weakened dynasty, crippled by infighting. She is a product of disastrous and apocalyptic times, teetering on the brink of collapse, not of her own overreach. No surprise that her husband before her, Seti II, had also been weak and ineffectual. No surprise that her young charge, Siptah, was feeble as well. And yet it is Tawosret who is blamed for the dynasty's collapse, not the male rulers before her. Tawosret lived through a civil war, took power back from the mercenary Bay, and went on to hold the highest position in the land, albeit for a short time. She was the victim of bad times, decentralization, war, and tumult—and she was, it seems, remembered only for those very things. The Egyptians might even have blamed her for the very crisis that characterized her reign, conveniently forgetting that it is only when there were political problems that women were allowed into the game at all.

Tawosret should be remembered for having created her own luck. She eliminated threats, but instead of building a foundation of future power, she was tainted by the suspicion of her violent acts. She was the last best hope for Dynasty 19: a prudent female ruler who seized the limited opportunities available to her. But, rather unfortunately, she is remembered for her lack of success and her gender—and not much else. History shows her as reactionary, not strategic. We remember her as a pawn of a larger struggle she didn't or couldn't control.

But what's truly astounding is that a woman could play in this high-stakes mess of a political game at all—particularly at a time when decentralization and internal family feuding barred royal women from recognized positions of power. If anything, Tawosret was a real and viable political player. In the midst of this complicated political arena, she is perhaps the most masculine of our female kings in her strategy and execution: getting down to their level, getting her hands dirty, transcending the normal female ways of ruling.

And so it is no surprise that after Tawosret, we won't see another female king enter the Egyptian scene until the Ptolemaic Dynasty, more than a thousand years later—and, given the Macedonian descent and political system, in an entirely different form. But that doesn't mean Egyptian women had no power in the intervening millennium. It just means they weren't able to hold it formally as king. Instead, women resorted to subterfuge, knives in the dark, conspiracy, even regicide.

Such women would rise up in Dynasty 20, when there was a brutal and murderous attempt to wrest the kingship from Ramses III, the son of Setnakht himself. The participants were revealed and their plans thwarted—but not without the assassination of the king himself. King Ramses III of Dynasty 20 was killed in a conspiracy hatched within his own Theban harem.[29] Indeed, recent examinations of his mummy have revealed a slash in his throat—certainly deep enough to have dispatched him. And archaeologists have uncovered reams of papyrus documenting a series of trials accusing Egyptian harem women, court officials, and Royal Sons of collusion, sorcery, and violence against the king. The charges are never explicitly clarified, as we should expect in ancient Egyptian texts where such sensitive matters were not openly discussed. Word of the grisly deed had likely already spread to all who needed to know; no reason to put such shameful acts against the king into writing, giving it more power than it already had.

Piecing together the documentation and filling in the unwritten gaps, it seems a queen named Tiy had worked assiduously and secretly to hatch a plot to assassinate Ramses III and get her son onto the throne. There were many people accused of involvement, which makes sense. None of the conspirators had any real positions of power, as Tawosret had as Great Royal Wife. Eliminating the king—in this case during a ritual at the temple or during a harem visit at the same temple palace—was likely the easiest part of the plot; the more difficult action would have been to engineer the chosen son past his brothers on to the Egyptian throne. We can probably assume that many sons of Ramses III were also targeted by the conspirators—threatened with violence or collusion. All this implies that the royal succession had only become even more politically complicated than in Tawosret's time.

The people involved in the plot were accused of using witchcraft—dark magic, if you like—to enchant those they needed to influence, to confuse them. They made figures out of wax to control their victims. The trial included interrogations to extract the full story from all those involved, to make sure they named names. That questioning was almost certainly accompanied by torture. The end result for all those accused was death—either suicide by one's own hand or execution as the Egyptians chose to dispatch it: being impaled on a sharpened spike slid through the upper abdomen and balanced between the ribs. It was a slow, cruel, and public death—the Egyptian version of crucifixion. The court documents even tell us that some of the judges were accused of corruption and payoffs—maybe even given sexual favors by women of the harem to deliver a better verdict to their friends and family. Trying to influence the judges didn't work. There were three hearings, all long and involved, and 38 people were sentenced to death.

Ironically, it was also during the reign of Ramses III that scenes from a royal harem were depicted for the first time in the Egyptian record.[30] The representations appear on the second floor of the gateway in front of the king's Temple of Millions of Years, a gateway shaped like a defensive tower. In the depictions, Ramses III seems quite pleased with his situation, a bland smile on his face as he fondles and caresses his beauties. Scene after scene shows naked women in the company of the king: playing a board game called *senet*, playing instruments, or offering food or other luxuries. All have fabulously baroque hairstyles. Each young lady is shown as prepubescent and fresh. The king is always depicted seated on his throne, never standing, and always completely clothed in full regalia. In some scenes, he might chuck one of the ladies under the chin. In others, he fondles their nether regions (these images have been vandalized by later Christians, no doubt offended by the subject matter). The depictions are staid; no orgies or sexual intercourse are shown. But everywhere there are the subtle markers of what the harem provided to the king: women shaking vaginally shaped rattles or holding vaginally shaped flowers.

The sexual congress was ordained by the gods. Their king was the Bull of Egypt, able and meant to populate the royal nurseries with hundreds of his offspring. This was a place of beauty and divinely inspired procreation. But these idealized scenes leave out the dangers that a coterie of partially enfranchised women with conflicting agendas could inflict upon a king who, lured by sex, could be dispatched before he even knew what had happened to him.

This is the kind of female power many men still fear today—those deep, dark actions that women are often forced into to make their own luck, to change their fate. Such underhanded measures are even today seen as quintessentially feminine, yet particularly un-Egyptian. Taking a step back, however, we understand that the subterfuge was reflective of a fragmented and overly large extended family of inside players. All had competing agendas; all possessed some small measure of power in an increasingly deregulated system; and all were vying for the same prize: the kingship itself. Tawosret's truncated kingship had just been a cautionary precursor of the bloody twists and turns that female power was to take at the end of Egypt's 20th dynasty.

But what became of those capable and respected female kings of Egypt? Would such imperious women ever ascend the throne of Egypt again? Would the country ever need them to? As Egypt entered the age of empires, women were systematically barred from the kingship; there was simply no point of entry for them. With a nonexistent or weakened native Egyptian dynasty, there was no strong monarchy in need of feminine protection. Instead, the country found itself buffeted about in a global game of domination. The Assyrians invaded in 676 B.C., sacking Thebes in 663 B.C. The pylons of Karnak still bear the scars of burning flagpoles against stone. The Egyptians then had to scramble to repel two Babylonian invasions of Egyptian lands—one in 601 B.C. and another in 569 B.C. Disaster would strike again when the Babylonian Empire fell to the resurgent Persians, who themselves defeated the Egyptian army in 525 B.C.

Throughout such constant assault, the age of female rule was seemingly over. Egypt was now just a prize being passed from one imperial, male-dominated hand to another. Dynasties couldn't maintain themselves for longer than a few generations—and without that unyielding authoritarian core, the royal female was, ironically, just as emasculated. But the Egyptians never forgot that women were meant to rule over their lands—in peace and security, with protective bloodlust and righteous revenge—and that goddesses were expected to play a part in ruling the divine order.

When all seemed lost, Egyptian priests began focusing on the divine feminine in new temple constructions. They bent their theological energies to depicting and serving the heavenly mother, relying on the protective embrace and violent defense that only the goddess could provide to her king. In many ways, this time period of imperial pummeling became Egypt's renaissance of female power, at least in the world of the gods.

During this period, cultural and religious attention was lavished on the goddess. The Mammissi—a temple that celebrated the feminine aspects of kingly creation, protection, and training—was invented around this time. Notions of female creation were analyzed, pored over, glossed, and reimagined by priests. New temples were built that granted substantial and profound new responsibility to the divine feminine. This was the age of Mut, the lioness goddess of Karnak; of Opet, a grandly pregnant hippo goddess who could contain and protect new life, given new temples at Karnak; and of Hathor, a gentle cow goddess who represented sexualized beauty incarnate and daughterly subservience at new temple structures at Dendera.

Egypt prepared itself—body and soul—for female power to rise again within its palace walls. Alexander the Great would take Egypt next, and after his death, the Ptolemaic Dynasty of Macedonian Greeks would rule Egypt for 300 years. The royal women would rise again—this time not just to protect their family interests but to reward their own personal ambitions. When we finally see another powerful woman on the throne of Egypt, she will surpass everything we have seen thus far.

CHAPTER 6

CLEOPATRA

Drama Queen

Cleopatra nearly had it all. She fought against the longest odds in our story thus far, and she almost triumphed.

Her accomplishments are many. She seized Egypt on the cusp of its absorption into the Roman Empire, and she manipulated statesmen of that empire to fight off Roman domination. She used all her wiles and diplomatic skills to keep Egypt whole and unoccupied for two decades.

Cleopatra is the only woman in these pages to have expanded her dynasty using her own procreative abilities, placing herself at the center of the wheel of power as the producer of future kings. She is the only one to attempt—and accomplish (in the short term, anyway)—succession via her own children, as a man would. She combined brilliant leadership with a productive womb, impregnated by powerful men to whom she was never subservient as wife. She used those men to maintain and strengthen her superior position as queen of all Egypt. And if either of those men—Julius Caesar or Mark Antony—had been better able to protect themselves and implement their own political and military strategies, Cleopatra would be remembered differently today.

The first Roman warlord chosen by Cleopatra—Caesar—was assassinated by his own kinsmen for taking too much power; the second, Antony, overreached in his disastrous attempts to take vast lands in Central Asia, as had his hero before him, Alexander the Great. If these warriors had lived longer and thrived, Cleopatra would have expanded her power, not relinquished it. (Though, of course, if they hadn't connected themselves with this drama queen, they might not have had such starkly drawn targets on their backs, either.)

Cleopatra was the first female ruler of Egypt in centuries. Native rule had been returned to the land of the Nile after more than 500 years of imperial domination by the Assyrians, the Babylonians, the Persians—even the Macedonians. Indeed, the scourge of ongoing outside control was so reviled in Egypt that when Alexander the Great appeared in 332 B.C., although a foreigner himself, the Nile dwellers greeted him with open arms because at least he styled himself as an Egyptian god-king and savior from Persian oppression. But if Alexander's conquests had lasted, Egypt would have been counted as just another province in the Macedonian Empire.

But this was not to be. At the young emperor's untimely death, Alexander's lands were split into multiple parts and doled out to his deputies. Macedonia and Greece went to Cassander; Anatolia went to Lysimachus; Persia and Central Asia went to Seleucus; Egypt went to Ptolemy and his successors.

The Ptolemaic family was in no way native Egyptian, but native rule had nonetheless been returned to Egypt for the simple reason that the family lived and worked in Alexandria on the western Mediterranean coast. These Macedonians used Egypt as their base of power, rather than exploiting it from afar. They learned from their mentor Alexander that they had to set themselves up as Egyptian god-kings if they were to seduce the Egyptians into accepting them, embracing all the baroque regalia, hard-to-balance crowns, and archaic rituals. And so we should not be surprised, with a living Horus once again occupying the Egyptian throne, that powerful royal females also returned to the scene for the first time in a thousand years.

Cleopatra VII, as she is called by historians, was a woman of unique and prolific talents. She would act as head of state politically, of course. But she held ideological power, too; images of her were set up in temples of mother goddesses throughout Egypt and even in Rome. She raised and controlled her own armies and navies, even traveling with her men and making decisions about strategy and positioning, granting this woman the unexpected bonus of military experience. And when the Nile flood was functioning, her country was capable of producing more easily grown grain than anywhere else in the Mediterranean. When Egypt's mines were working at full tilt, gold was easily acquired and plentiful, an economic power that made all of Rome sit up and listen.

And then there was her sexual power. This woman didn't hide from her sensual nature or procreative abilities. She is arguably the first of our Egyptian queens to have openly used her feminine charms to ensnare and control. (Of course, she

was also the first who had to resort to using her sexual allure—
but, we should remember, the first for whom there is a written
record of sexual dalliances at all.) Cleopatra's emotionality
earned her a reputation, to be sure. But it also won her the
protection and offspring of powerful Roman men who helped
her survive in a more complicated and globalized world than
Egypt had ever known.

Cleopatra built upon what all the other Egyptian queens
had already achieved: Merneith's ability to establish her son
in royal power; Neferusobek's survival as the last ruler standing in her dynasty; Hatshepsut's climb to the pinnacle of
political power using the males around her as stepping-stones;
Nefertiti's transformation of herself as she aged, not to mention her salvaging the nation from the political mess left by
the men around her; and Tawosret's scrappy potential to act
as an aggressive, even masculine, political operator. Cleopatra
stood on all these women's shoulders and almost transcended
them all.

She was also perhaps the first Egyptian queen to openly show
her own ambition: to her Ptolemaic court, to her Egyptian
people, to the Romans, to the world. There is little dissembling
in her own Egyptian narratives, little apology for her power:
She made few coy statements that she was only doing as the
gods asked, few defensive claims that she didn't want the
authority for herself. Cleopatra was no martyr. Her bald ambition translated directly into survival. Having grown up in the
vicious snake pit of her Ptolemaic Family, she had learned to
fight a never ending series of tiny and ruthless battles, always

looking out for number one, even if she had to murder brothers and sisters along the way.

Thus far, each of the queens has told us her story through buildings and tombs, statues and reliefs, mummies and stelae—but without letters or speeches, memoirs, or any humanized firsthand accounts, only the idealized narrative or what archaeological stone can tell. In Cleopatra's case, we finally possess personal narratives, texts that record her thoughts as she made certain decisions, that explain why her lovers and opponents acted the ways they did, that provide eyewitness recollections.

But not one of these personal texts was authored by the queen herself or by those with a pro-Egyptian mind-set. Indeed, Cleopatra's reign presents historians with a different challenge, in that we are overwhelmed with a mass of personal details, almost all of which come from Roman politicians or rhetoricians opposed to her agenda and outside of her cultural milieu. The texts written by Plutarch and Cassius Dio,[1] for instance, are colored by the deep wounds inflicted in costly Roman civil wars—not to mention the profound belief in Roman exceptionalism, Rome's heartfelt xenophobia and distrust of the East, and its elemental opposition to kingship in any form (even as the Roman Republic itself was inexorably moving toward just such a consolidation of power under one man).

These ancient historians included detailed accounts of Cleopatra's flagrant and ostentatious displays of wealth, her squandering of her country's precious resources on her own selfish whims, her tendency to engage in revelry for weeks at a time, her ability to seduce men so that they lost all reason and rationality, her power to poison good Roman men's souls with her degenerative ways, her ambition for rule at all costs, her melodramatic bouts of hormonal fury or manipulation, her insatiable sexual hunger, her disregard for her children when committing suicide to avoid being displayed as a trophy of war. All of it was written by Romans, so all of it must be regarded with suspicion.

If we are to arrive at Cleopatra's story, fairly analyzed, the modern historian would do well to throw out any and all Roman sources that discuss her personality, limiting themselves to the basic facts. In this way, her story will present us with a challenge no different from Hatshepsut's or Tawosret's, characterized by a dearth of sources that reveal the real humanity of the women involved. This doesn't mean we can't look at her decision-making process, her strategy, her scheming; we just won't do it through the eyes of her political enemies.

As any Egyptian monarch would, Cleopatra played it close to the vest, always representing herself as fully in control, idealized, godlike, perfect. No Egyptian texts revealed, or would ever discuss, personality, worldly motives, or shortcomings. Any formally shared personal opinions would have been out of character with an authoritarian regime like Egypt's, over which Cleopatra ruled. But even if we remove the Roman propaganda from this discussion, there is more than enough to go on. We can resuscitate her as a woman of power who served her Egyptian people, who used her resources as well as could be expected, and who came extraordinarily close to winning the high-stakes political game she was playing.

Indeed, like Cleopatra, modern female politicians know that a focus on personality is detrimental to their campaigns, lest they be seen as hormonal beasts, unable to think clearly and govern decisively. But if a male politician displays his feelings—like tears shed at the appropriate place and time—it can be a boon to political strategy, just as a male politician's extramarital interests and activities might be lauded as manly and representative of his real-world power, while a woman's extramarital affairs would be understood as destabilizing and deviant. Cleopatra knew all the double standards, too.

♛

IF EGYPT HAD CHANGED dramatically between Nefertiti in Dynasty 18 and Tawosret in Dynasty 19, we can only imagine the onslaught of alterations experienced by the time the Ptolemaic family took control. We now find ourselves in a globalized Egypt that had suffered through a series of imperial onslaughts, already chewed up and spit out by at least four foreign systems of exploitation. But with the Ptolemaic Dynasty (305–30 B.C.), homebound rule was reestablished in Egypt,[2] once again providing a connection between the king and the god Horus, the queen and the goddess Isis. The Ptolemaic Family resuscitated the system in which the wives, daughters, sisters, and mothers could rally around their god-king as a fierce goddess-queen herself.

Despite their Greek origins, the Ptolemies embraced Egypt's archaic system of divine kingship with open arms. They were descended from the power of Alexander the Great, a man anointed by the oracle of Amun at the far-flung temple in Siwa Oasis. The Ptolemies brought back divine kingship with a vengeance. And a strong queen always rose up when there was a god-king to protect, and maybe also to dominate.

Indeed, this is likely the greatest tragedy in our tale of women who ruled the Egyptian world: Females were allowed to govern consistently and regularly only in systems of deep social inequality, characterized by the most brutal forms of authoritarian power. Women were largely shut out of decentralized governments, like the Greek democratic systems or the Roman oligarchy. In these more broad-based conceptions of power, when one man fell, another would take his place, leaving little need for a woman to fill a gap to protect a family dynasty or ensure a royal succession. Kingship was different; this power was limited to a few, within a family dynasty made up of men and women. In this context, women could serve a real purpose. Alexander the Great descended from just such a line of strong Macedonian kings, demanding that his mother Olympias act as a ruthless political operative herself. This was the kind of regime Alexander had planted in the Egyptian soil when he conquered it—one of exclusivity and totalitarianism and loyalty.

The Ptolemies styled themselves as Egyptian kings of old, often abandoning their native Greek outfits and dressing the part. They inhabited the archaic god-king character with relish, wearing all the extravagant crowns and collars, and even engaging in repeated incestuous brother-sister marriages. The Ptolemaic Dynasty was an extraordinary mix of an Egyptian prudent fondness for the status quo and the hypercompetitive Greek world of political decentralization. There were back-biting and competing entourages, assassinations, even regi-cides—but despite all that, the Ptolemaic was still the longest-lived dynasty in all of ancient Egypt, lasting around 300 years in total.

The Ptolemies lived in a world that was cruelly competitive—but that savagery pointed inward, to the Macedonian court circles. Egypt's geographic location and easy grain still allowed for a long-lived family lineage protected from outside invasion, if not from their own knives in the dark. The Ptolemaic insti-tution of kingship would thus rely on the royal female in the same way as the Egyptians of old did, using queens and prin-cesses to protect, nurture, buoy, and even control the divine monarchy. The agendas of all the royal participants were intertwined. Even when constantly trying to terminate each other, these Ptolemaic Egyptian kings engaged in that most ancient Egyptian form of protectionism: a close-knit and deeply incestuous Royal Family, as in Dynasty 18, when Royal Sons and Daughters kept power exclusive and exceptional, cutting other elites out.

The Ptolemaic court was located in Alexandria, that great harbor city founded by Alexander, who had briefly seized the entire known ancient world, only to die of sickness in Babylon, young and full of promise. He never got to see his newly founded Egyptian port grow into a metropolis of intellectualism, trade, and ritual activity. Alexandria's halls of power and culture were the epicenter of influence in the eastern Mediterranean. The city was rich. It was diverse. It was commercial. It had such a functioning industry that the city housed a substantial middle class—a first for Egypt, whose agrarian economy had thus far only supported a mass of underemployed and overexploited peasants. This new working class had power of its own, and Alexandria suffered from frequent revolts against royal power when it was overtaxed and underfunded.

But this was a yes-we-can city; it was full of learning and opinions and wealth and people from every corner of the globe, all trying to find a scheme or make a deal. There was a massive lighthouse, the tallest building of its time, listed by ancient authors as one of the Seven Wonders of the World (the second tallest being the Great Pyramid at Giza, also one of the Wonders). This was a new city, shiny and bright, and its youth settled upon it like an unsteady chip on its shoulder. Like a defensive teenager, Alexandria felt the need to build bigger and more ostentatiously than Byblos or Babylon, quickly acquiring the trappings expected in venerable urban centers. No surprise that the city ended up being home to the most massive and complete library in the entire Mediterranean. It was as if the Ptolemies knew their city lacked veneer and experience in comparison to the old stalwarts of the ancient world. It was full of money but lacking respect: the Dubai of its time. And so, like Abu Dhabi, it lured scientists and intellectuals with quick cash to bulk up its worth in acquired scrolls and volumes from neglected foreign collections.

Alexandria had the latest in modern inventions, too. It was set up on a grid, quarters set aside for certain ethnic populations, including Greek, Jewish, and Egyptian, and areas delineated for particular trades, like metalworking, tanning, and jewelry making. When the Nile cut through the city, its dirty river water had already traveled thousands of miles from Lake Victoria and the Ethiopian highlands. But an engineered lake to the south made sure that the city received a clean water supply, as well as fresh air.

Alexandria was a port city; it was situated to look outside of Egypt, not into it. Arguably the first non-navel-gazing center of power ever built in Egypt,[3] it was situated closer to Rome, Athens, Ephesus, and Ashkelon than to Abydos and Thebes. It was a schizophrenic place—located in Egypt but perched on its very edge, participating in archaic rites of divine kingship but led by people of Macedonian descent within a hypercompetitive and fragmented court. The Ptolemies built traditional temples around the land of Egypt, but injected new Mediterranean theologies into its harbor city. So it should come as no surprise that, as time went on, the pharaoh, though ensconced in Alexandria, looked to Rome more and more as a protector, moneylender, and arms dealer, only glancing south occasionally to extract much-needed African gold and grain to send to the Mediterranean as installments and kickbacks.

Alexandria soon found itself in a precarious position; it was a potential asset to an avaricious Rome that was currently absorbing the entire Mediterranean into its empire. Egypt was the breadbasket of the Mediterranean, but it was no easy conquest, even for Rome at the height of its imperial expansion. Even when Alexandria and its kings were in debt to Latin moneylenders more than the value of their own city, even when they had mortgaged the entire island of Cyprus away, there was little the Romans could really do to make the Egyptians pay them back in full. They couldn't annex the land of Egypt very easily, as they had Gaul and Britain. Egypt was old and established, not some disorganized collection of chieftains and barbarians, easily cowed with fancy legal arguments, overwrought systems of taxation, and efficient armed forces. It possessed its own sophistication as the oldest regional state in the world, the ultimate originator of complex governmental systems. Not only that, every Roman senator knew that whoever won Egypt as provincial governor would have the necessary might to take over the entire known world. Annexing Egypt would only set up one of their own senatorial warlords with far too much power. With so much internal competition in Rome, it remained easier just to allow the native rule of the riverine country to continue on a while longer under the Ptolemies. For Rome, Egypt was the proverbial can kicked down the road.

The city of Rome was much less ostentatious than Alexandria—marshy and plagued by malarial outbreaks, its famous monuments only now being constructed with grand marble columns and decorative friezes. But Rome's citizens considered themselves morally superior to Egypt, from what we can see in their diatribes about Eastern excess and political decadence. It certainly doesn't seem as if the Egyptians thought themselves inferior to Rome in any way. When Cleopatra accompanied her father, Ptolemy XII, to Rome in 58 B.C. when she was just 11 or 12 years old, she must have been sorely unimpressed with the Latin city, with its dirty, damp streets and lack of majestic structures.

Cleopatra learned about her family's convoluted power dynamic with Rome at a young age. Indeed, her greatest weakness had nothing to do with her character. As Egypt's last Ptolemaic ruler, she had inherited an economically debilitated Egypt. Ptolemy XII was in astronomical debt to wealthy Roman elites, reportedly with numbers so high that Rome could legally step in and take control of Egypt at any time. The debt didn't necessarily stem from wasteful spending but from a series of extreme droughts that Egypt was experiencing. The Nile had been consistently low during the reign of Cleopatra's father and into her own reign. Egypt, once known as a place where plump kernels of wheat and barley were easily and quickly grown, was now reduced to bare survival. Sometimes the Nile waters rose too little to allow much land to be farmed; sometimes they didn't rise at all. There was no agricultural surplus in the days of Ptolemy XII and Cleopatra. To make matters worse, the Ptolemaic solution was generally to levy more taxes on its people, particularly those in its urban centers, placing more stress on an already difficult situation.[4] It is no surprise that Egypt would lose its native control to a voracious empire at this most vulnerable point when its great river, its raison d'être, had failed it. Whether Cleopatra was a long-term thinker or not, she realized that her only chance at survival was to be found outside of her Royal Family—even outside of Egypt itself.

Thus, she tried to get away from the Ptolemies early and often. Cleopatra grew up in a context of extreme distrust and danger, constantly on the lookout for potential enemies and poisoned food or drink. Her father's queen—Cleopatra V—disappeared from the textual record around the time of Cleopatra's birth, only to reappear as Ptolemy XII's children were trying to take the throne from him. None of the Pharaoh's Sons or Daughters would die a natural death; Cleopatra is said to have killed herself. All the others would be eliminated in battle or through assassination by their own family members, most before reaching adulthood. To grow up amid such fear and anxiety would have formed a certain kind of person: a survivor, to be sure, but for those who pulled through into adulthood, a creative strategist—someone who could put her emotions aside when necessary and deal with the dire situation at hand.

Ptolemaic life was one of persistent PTSD. There were duplicitous alliances, blades slipped between the ribs, and extensive poison lore, reaching the level of domestic chemical warfare.[5] Every Royal Family member had his or her own entourage, an essential part of the competitive scheme; each Ptolemaic son or daughter had a group of hangers-on, some of them Greek intellectuals acting as tutors or strategists, others generals, others moneymen or administrators. Every Ptolemaic child, it seems, relied on a group of adults from the population of Alexandria to watch over them in childhood; to oversee their education in rhetoric, politics, and foreign languages; and to forward their own suit as their patron prince or princess grew old enough to enter the political fray. Even before a given Ptolemaic princess was mature enough to fight her own battles, a member of the entourage could do it for her. Alexandria was full of informal warmongering, waged by advisers who worked in the shadows, whispering about potential dangers, strategizing about how to push their candidate to the top of the royal heap, removing enemies, slandering an opponent, building alliances against a competitor.

Such an existence must have been soul-destroying. Brother killed sister. Wife worked against husband. Father executed daughter. And, all the while, these family members were inbred in a self-protective system of royal incest to keep outside competition from coming into the family.[6] To be a Ptolemy was a difficult and dangerous thing.

Given their long-lived dynasty, it is surprising that these Greek-speaking pharaohs did not implement the most important part of the ancient Egyptian system of successful kingship, the element that guaranteed its long-term success: the harem. Such a collection of women would have invited too many potential problems and potential players for the Ptolemies, perhaps. Instead of securing many heirs from multiple women simultaneously, these kings officially married only one woman at a time, even if it was their own half or full-blood sister, resorting instead to informal methods of procreation on the side (with the understanding that the products of unsanctioned unions would always bear the politically devastating mark of a bastard). There is no biological way that a 300-year-old dynasty could have survived from one generation to another riddled with incest. Mistresses to the king would indeed bear sons to their Ptolemaic lords—not legal heirs, to be sure, but sometimes the best choice of next king, bastard or not. Cleopatra VII herself was probably the result of a mistress-pharaoh relationship, rather than from the sanctioned union of Ptolemy XII with his cousin and niece Cleopatra V.[7] (This means that Cleopatra VII may have been one-quarter to one-half Egyptian—which might explain why she was said to speak Egyptian when all of her Ptolemaic predecessors had not bothered to learn the language of the land over which they ruled.)[8]

Regardless of the ethnic or legal origins of these Ptolemaic monarchs, the family officially kept to what some Egyptologists have called "serial monogamy,"[9] marrying one sister or brother or cousin or niece or uncle at a time. When these alliances went south, there were many methods to correct the situation and start fresh with a new partner. They could divorce, as the Romans did. Or, in typical Ptolemaic fashion, they could just kill the spouse. Some 2,000 years later, Henry VIII of the Elizabethan English court would also find himself boxed into a monogamous system—but his creative means of ending his relationships had nothing on the Ptolemies. Murder at the hands of a royal partner was a startlingly common way to die for Macedonian rulers of Egypt.

Even if the Ptolemies never subscribed to Egyptian intensified forms of child production, they divinized their royal selves formally and early in their dynasty, understanding that religious power was an excellent foil to their dirty realpolitik. Ptolemy II created a temple cult for the pharaohs of his family; this cult included the women of their family in a prominent way, providing the Ptolemaic queens with as much ideological influence as their menfolk. Ptolemy II and his sister-wife Arsinoe II were named living *theoi adelphoi*, "sibling divinities," pictured on coinage together or conducting highly visible temple festivals side by side.[10]

In many ways, all the infighting between royal Ptolemaic Family members made the women in their family that much more robust politically. The queens brokered alliances, settled disputes, or destroyed opponents. The political game was one of partnerships and social backing. Indeed, none of the Ptolemaic royalty was an individual unto him- or herself. Each one of them had lands, income, supporters, tutors, administrators, and connections, all of which they were constantly trying to manipulate, co-opt, or seize outright from the other, like the tangled and overlapping family lineages of modern-day Saudi Arabia. Thus, each tiny disagreement between members of the Royal Family set off waves of dissent and fragmentation at court, resulting in changes of ownership in property, the reassignment of certain priestly titles, or the transfer of a particular administrator. With so much at stake, it was therefore wise to use royal marriage to build factions at court and avoid any such loss of people and income. A brother might be married to his sister to shore up his position, because that sister might have had more power in terms of land and supporters. Indeed, Ptolemy VI had to treat his sister Cleopatra II like an equal.[11]

And when Ptolemy VIII eventually defeated his brother and became king, he married that same sister Cleopatra II, erstwhile queen to Ptolemy VI. Cleopatra II thus transferred her allegiance and partnership from one brother to another. But both of these men needed her support as queen and her extended alliances.

There was considerable power embedded in each Ptolemaic royal female, and sometimes they used that power against each other. This was no sisterhood. For example, Cleopatra III challenged her own mother, Cleopatra II, deposing her as queen and marrying her mother's brother Ptolemy VIII, to solidify her nascent power. Cleopatra III then named herself Isis incarnate, creating a temple cult in which she was the goddess's living embodiment.

The story doesn't end with the other family members accepting their weakened status. To the contrary, the deposed mother, Cleopatra II, led an armed rebellion against the uncle-niece pair, successfully driving them both out of Egypt. Ptolemy VIII retaliated against the elder queen by murdering his own son by the woman, as the boy was now an obvious threat to his throne. He dismembered his son's body, cutting off the boy's head, hands, and feet, and sent the grisly package to Cleopatra II in Alexandria at court on her birthday.

Eventually, the uncle-niece pair raised their own army to drive Cleopatra II from Egypt and the throne, until she publicly reconciled with both her brother Ptolemy VIII and her daughter Cleopatra III. Strangely, the story ends with all of them ruling from Alexandria together in a brutalized threesome of distrust and pain. If nothing else, the Ptolemies led complicated and perilous lives, in which family loyalty meant everything and nothing. This was the cultural context in which Cleopatra VII grew up, and the kind of life she herself could expect.

♛

IN 80 B.C., PTOLEMY XII was crowned king, even though he was the illegitimate son of Ptolemy IX. (Every other possible candidate was dead—many murdered.) He inherited a massive financial tab at his ascension, and when he offered the island of Cyprus to Rome to settle that debt, he was forced into exile by angry Alexandrian courtiers in 58 B.C. He fled to his creditors in Rome.

Ptolemy XII had three daughters and two sons, many of whom would try to benefit from his absence from Egypt. His eldest daughter, Cleopatra VI, moved in first to take his throne, but she was murdered for her overreach, perhaps by agents of her younger sister, Berenike IV. With her sister and father gone, Berenike opportunistically seized the throne for herself. Normally, such a coup would be supported by marriage to another family member, but her brothers were only three or four years old at the time. Berenike attempted to rule alone for a while, but there was significant pressure from Alexandrian advisers that she marry and share her throne with a man. She wed a cousin—a prince named Seleucid from the empire of the same name in Syria, a powerful match for two powerful Macedonian families. Then, within a week of their marriage, she had him strangled. She next married a man named Archelaos, who hailed from a powerful kingdom in Anatolia; she never allowed him to actually act as co-regent, keeping him meekly in his place. Fierce as she was, Cleopatra's sister Berenike didn't rule long. When Ptolemy XII returned to Alexandria with the help of Rome in 55 B.C. (savvy creditors need their debtors to have a guaranteed source of income, after all), he had his daughter eliminated, reclaiming his place on the throne.

Alliances were everything in Ptolemaic Egypt, and it was always prudent to consolidate the help of supporters. Therefore, when Ptolemy XII reclaimed his kingship, he felt it expedient to share the power—to diversify his portfolio, if you will, naming as his co-ruler the 14-year-old Cleopatra VII. There's no evidence that she shared her father's bed, but she was probably sitting next to her father when her sister was beheaded for acting against him.

Around this time, Cleopatra first met Mark Antony, a handsome 25-year-old Roman officer, sent to Alexandria to secure Roman interests in Egypt militarily and diplomatically. Antony would later claim that he fell in love with her at this time; Cleopatra never specified that she reciprocated Antony's affections, but they may have started a friendship then. Cleopatra was certainly young when they first met, but already learned in the ways of the ruthless world she occupied. She had absorbed multiple strategies of self-protection and alliance building, understanding the need to curry Rome's favor while accepting the necessary cruelties of life on the throne. She likely grasped the justification for Berenike's execution. In many ways, Cleopatra's Egypt had returned full circle to the days of Queen Merneith of Dynasty I with its violent dispatch of close family members who might claim the throne. When you have power, you have much to protect.

Cleopatra must have known that Egypt was the prize at the center of an increasingly perilous Roman game of domination. She watched the warlords circle around her country hungrily, none daring to seize it outright. Cleopatra thus realized that she could look to Rome for military and monetary support, turning competing Roman interests in Egypt to Ptolemaic advantage. But to whom should she turn? Rome was now a moving target, embroiled in its own power politics, civil wars, and rapidly changing government structures. How was Cleopatra to interact with an empire that constantly changed its own rules of command, much as current leaders tried to rejigger policies and relationships as Obama's United States became Trump's United States? How could Cleopatra work with a Rome that was quickly and painfully moving in fits and starts from a republic with its decentralized, often combative, senatorial rule, into a centralized, authoritarian regime, soon to have an emperor at its head? No one knew that the war to take over Egypt would end up creating Rome's first hereditary monarchy, but everyone in power understood that the dynamic between Rome and Egypt was somehow essential to them all.

Cleopatra observed her father, Ptolemy XII, address this political reality firsthand, attempting to choose the best of the competing Roman senators as his strategic partner. Egypt would soon find itself at the center of Rome's greatest transformation as Cleopatra's decisions pushed Rome over the edge into the very authoritarianism it claimed to despise. But, at this point, Rome was still a (barely) functioning republic, working diplomatically with Egypt's kings as allied monarchs. Under the weight of massive debts, Ptolemy XII was compelled to keep his will in Rome.

In that will, he named joint heirs—his daughter Cleopatra VII and his young son Ptolemy XIII—to be under the guardianship of the Roman people when they took over Egypt as king and queen. Thus, when the elder Ptolemy died, Rome had the legal excuse it needed to intervene directly in Egyptian politics, as caretakers of the new, and young, monarchs. It was no different than what Rome had done to Queen Boudica of Britain, using legal fine print to claim that, without sons, the female monarch had no heirs and Rome could formally annex the British territory into their growing empire under the watch of provincial governors.[12] Legal subterfuge was a favored tactic of the Romans. But Egypt would be a more formidable opponent: more than able to engage in complicated legal arguments, to be sure, but also able to create more complex global alliances—with Libya, Phoenicia, or fellow Latins—that would be difficult for Rome to break.

Ptolemy XII seems to have known that his death was not far off because shortly beforehand, he formally named his two eldest children *Theoi Neoi Philadelphos*—"New Gods" and "Loving Siblings"—throwing the 18-year-old Cleopatra into a political (and ideally amorous) relationship with her own brother. The pairing would almost be the end of her. When their father died the following year, Cleopatra was the more experienced of the two siblings, but Ptolemy XIII's entourage moved against her quickly, wanting the kingship secured without her interference or alliance. They wanted Cleopatra dead.

Meanwhile, Rome's civil war had heated up. Pompey and Julius Caesar were using the entire Mediterranean as their personal battlefield. We see an oft-repeated and dire choice: Which of two Roman warlords should the young king Ptolemy XIII back? He (or, better stated, his advisers) chose Pompey, an old ally of his father's, providing the Roman warrior with ships, troops, and supplies. Cleopatra was still officially a co-ruler with Ptolemy XIII, and while all the evidence suggests that she went along with the choice to back Pompey, too, she was nevertheless looking for another alliance. Indeed, there are whispers that Cleopatra tried out some of her best political machinations at an early age (perhaps even having a sexual affair with Pompey's son, Gnaeus Pompey, when he visited Egypt in 49 B.C.)[13] If this is true, it would fit with Cleopatra's pattern of emotional-political diplomacy; it would have also been a clever method of breaking the alliance between Pompey and her brother, and moving Pompey's support, and affections, toward her alone.

The political plotting between Cleopatra VII and Ptolemy XIII was heating up in Alexandria. Cleopatra made the next move: Records show that she had herself named sole ruler on many monuments just a few months after their accession as co-rulers. Ptolemy struck back, and with more ammunition, getting Pompey to legally abandon Cleopatra as co-ruler and thus violating the terms of their father's will. It may have been an easy task, given Rome's general distrust of female leadership. Ptolemy XIII was named sole ruler, with Pompey's military backing. Cleopatra fled into exile, leaving Alexandria and moving south to Thebes, the heartland of Egypt's early kings, and then on to Syria, where she relied on allies who had, thankfully for her, been betrayed by Pompey more than once. There she managed to raise an army in opposition to her brother—no small feat for a woman in her early twenties, banished from her land. With a formidable force behind her, she marched through the Sinai back to Egypt, setting up camp in the eastern Egyptian Delta, cooking up schemes to take back her throne in Alexandria.

But events would soon take place beyond the control of either Egyptian monarch, changing not just the rules of the game, but the players involved. Pompey and Julius Caesar met in battle in Greece. The clash resulted in a devastating loss for Pompey, who, upon fleeing the battlefield, decided that his best refuge would be Egypt (interesting how so many Romans found exile in Egypt, while so many Ptolemaic kings found their refuge in Rome).

This was obviously a problem for Ptolemy XIII, who did not want to get on the wrong side of Rome. The young pharaoh's entourage quickly realized that they had backed the wrong Roman horse. They had a few choices before them when Pompey's ships arrived in their harbor. They could reject Pompey outright, not allowing him to use Alexandria as a base to rebuild his power. Or they could kill the fallen general, demonstrating to the winning Roman warlord whose side they were really on.

Ptolemy chose the more dramatic option, sending a gruesome gift of Pompey's severed head to Julius Caesar, who, according to Roman historian Cassius Dio, wept when he saw his father-in-law's visage.[14] The Romans, it seems, were involved in their own treacherous competitions between family members. Maybe this is why the Romans and Ptolemies understood each other so well: They were aligned on the level of strategy and political need.

There had been a third choice, of course, which, to their detriment, Ptolemy XIII and his advisers seem not to have considered. They could have delivered Pompey to Julius Caesar alive. Let's call it a culture clash, a misunderstanding of the methodology of Roman political conflict that pitted family member against family member, but still demanded an honorable and legal fight to the end. This would be the undoing of many a Mediterranean king who saw the safe and quick dispatch of a rival, even illegal and underhanded, as the best way out. Julius Caesar, for his part, had to openly and officially reject the duplicitous murder of his father-in-law, even if he benefited from the action.

The murder of Pompey had clarified many things. When Julius Caesar arrived in Alexandria, he was immediately more sympathetic to Cleopatra and distrustful of Ptolemy and his advisers. Encamped in the Delta, Cleopatra's spies reported what happened when Caesar entered the palace. She would have known that her brother and his supporters had miscalculated with their crass and juvenile gift of Pompey's severed head, and, filing that information away, she decided it was time to make her move. She had herself smuggled into Alexandria (maybe in a bedsack, according to Plutarch's account, not rolled in a carpet as in the Hollywood version), in order to meet with Julius Caesar in person. It was perfect. Caesar was in Egypt. He was upset with her brother. She was positioned in the eastern Delta with an army. It was time to strike.

There was reason for Ptolemy and his advisers to panic. When they found out that Cleopatra had beaten them to an up-close and personal diplomatic meeting, they must have known it was already over. Cleopatra's negotiations, whatever form they may have taken, were successful. Caesar produced her father's will (he had brought the document with him; Romans love hard legal evidence) and demanded that Cleopatra VII and Ptolemy XIII act as co-rulers. To lessen Ptolemaic power, and possibly to fragment the family, Caesar sent the two younger siblings Arsinoe IV and Ptolemy XIV—at this point around 13 and 11 years old, respectively—to the island of Cyprus to act as co-rulers there of a new and separate kingdom. This may have been the beginning of the bad blood between Cleopatra and her younger brother and sister, or at least the reason for the later rivalry. Or perhaps a brutal Ptolemaic upbringing had already poisoned all of them against one another. No matter what, none of the children of Ptolemy XII had any qualms about killing their siblings.

Ptolemy XIII did not even wait for Caesar to leave Egypt before he attacked Cleopatra. While Caesar and Cleopatra were ensconced in the palace, Ptolemy started what historians now call the Alexandrian War in 48 B.C., blocking the Roman general in at the harbor and cutting off his supplies. Caesar, in turn, burned down (all or partially) the famous Library of Alexandria when he used flaming arrows in retaliation. This would prove to be yet another a massive miscalculation on the part of Ptolemy XIII's advisers; all they ended up achieving was to throw Caesar and Cleopatra into each other's defense (and arms) for about four months. She was 21 years old; he 52. Caesar's many allies in the East aligned with Cleopatra's interests, and when word got through, they sent armies from Anatolia, Syria, and the Levant to serve them both, attacking the army of Ptolemy XIII and Arsinoe IV, who had now joined her brother in fighting Cleopatra. The boy-king was killed, the princess captured and displayed in Caesar's Roman triumph in 46 B.C. in chains, after which Arsinoe was sent into exile to the Temple of Artemis at Ephesus in Anatolia.

When Caesar revealed himself to the people of Alexandria as triumphant, the locals rejoiced. Cleopatra had not only backed the right warlord, but she was probably already pregnant with his child. What queen needed a husband when she could produce a baby with Rome's most powerful statesman? Cleopatra is the first woman ruler discussed in these pages who used her procreative abilities to her political benefit, as a man would have. Discussions of Cleopatra's beauty are meaningless; we will never know what she really looked like. Pretty or not, she was alluring, charming, and diplomatically astute enough to seduce Rome's most powerful men. So when Caesar placed her younger brother,

Ptolemy XIV, on the throne alongside her, claiming it would fulfill the will of her father, she likely didn't complain, understanding the political need (from Rome's perspective, at least) for her to make a formal alliance with the boy—all the while knowing that procreation with her brother was not only unnecessary but biologically impossible with a baby already on the way. In any case, she and Caesar were already living together in the palace at Alexandria during the early days of her co-kingship with her brother.

Cleopatra knew, and undoubtedly made sure that Caesar understood, that she was carrying his child, potentially a son. Thus far in his life, Caesar had produced only one living daughter. Cleopatra's unborn child therefore had a 50 percent shot at being the blood heir of Julius Caesar. The only issue was legality. Caesar had a Roman wife; he could not marry Cleopatra, who, in turn, could not marry him, because she was already formally attached to her brother. The illegitimacy of Cleopatra's son by Julius Caesar would, arguably, be her greatest undoing, but there was no way to have avoided it. Marriage would only have weakened her own authority over Egypt, as it would have Caesar's in Rome.

Caesar never explained his feelings about Cleopatra's pregnancy in any documents preserved today, but he did linger in Egypt far longer than he needed to, enjoying elaborate Nile cruises that went far south into Sudan. He satisfied his interest in geography as they traveled closer and closer to the source of the Nile, all the while watching Cleopatra grow large with her first child, his baby. Caesar eventually found the political sense to leave Egypt and return to Rome before the birth, but he left four Roman legions in his place (each legion made up of thousands of men). The army protected Cleopatra and his unborn child in his absence—but it was also a clear signal to Egypt that Rome was now in charge of its future and would watch closely over its investment.

In 47 B.C., Cleopatra bore a son whom she named Ptolemy Caesar Theos Philopater Philometor—"Ptolemy Caesar, The God Who Loves His Father and Mother"—leaving no doubt about the baby's parentage and her aspirations for his legacy. She even had coins issued, in Cyprus at least, that showed her nursing her baby in the manner of Isis feeding Horus. Greek-speaking Egyptians called him Caesarion, "little Caesar." Everyone knew who the father was; what nobody knew were the implications of the progeny.

With Caesar gone from Egypt, Cleopatra and her brother Ptolemy XIV kept up the pretense of co-rule, even traveling together to Rome in 46 B.C. The boy-king must have known that his older sister was protected by the great politician and didn't seem to have attempted any power plays—at least not yet. Given the long and enduring Ptolemaic record of assassinations, we can be assured that Cleopatra kept the infant as close to her as possible at all times. The baby went to Rome with his mother, and his existence must have colored every encounter she had there.

Caesar never recorded his feelings for Cleopatra or her son, but he did have a golden statue of Cleopatra installed in the Forum in his newly constructed Temple of Venus the Mother, essentially proclaiming his Egyptian lover as maternal goddess to his Roman people. His foreign political entanglements were becoming highly visible to everyone in Rome.

Julius Caesar needed Egypt's wealth to continue his consolidation of power; Egypt's indebtedness to Rome could be manipulated to his political benefit, and he knew it. His placement of a statue of Cleopatra was a statement on many levels. Even if he never formally claimed Caesarion as his son, putting Cleopatra's image in a temple of Venus broadcast his personal connection with the African agricultural powerhouse to rival senatorial warlords. Everything had shifted. Caesar was able to rule Egypt behind the throne and collect the rewards of that governance. The public display of his connection to Cleopatra, political or otherwise, along with his extended dictatorial powers, were too much for his Roman political competitors. Julius Caesar was killed by his fellow senators in Rome in 44 B.C. while Cleopatra was in town on another visit, accompanied by their three-year-old son. Cleopatra had likely gone to Rome in an attempt to get Caesar to recognize the boy as his son and heir; she would leave Italy with nothing. Even if the urban people of Rome rallied around her as a mother-goddess (for which there is no direct evidence),[15] the elites of Rome made sure that the Egyptian queen was left with no Roman support or legal standing.

With hindsight, we can see that Cleopatra's strategy of aligning herself with the most successful and decorated Roman warrior was doomed to fail, regardless of which statesmen she chose; every time she linked herself with a Roman man, he would be marked with a bright target on his back as a high-level threat in need of elimination. Cleopatra wasn't the curse of these men; Egypt's wealth was. We can only wonder if Cleopatra, or her Roman suitors, ever became aware of this essential fact.

CLEOPATRA NO LONGER had a Roman protector. The men who killed Caesar were after Egypt—and her. She had to consolidate her power.

Killing her brother and co-ruler Ptolemy XIV was the first step. She used poison; it was quickly done. But instead of becoming sole ruler of Egypt, Cleopatra knew that it would be easier to keep power with a male presence by her side. Thus, she elevated her young son Caesarion to co-ruler. Given that he was known by all as Julius Caesar's offspring, this created an interesting and new political relationship with Rome. Like Hatshepsut, Cleopatra knew she could never rule alone—or at least she understood enough to keep up the pretense that she never ruled alone. Now she had to decide again which side of the complicated and ever shifting Roman civil war to take. She had chosen the right side before when her brother had not, only to see her man eliminated. She now decided to back those who were against Caesar's assassination: Mark Antony and Octavian, the latter Caesar's legal heir and nephew—a canny choice because these men would defeat Brutus and his co-conspirators at the Battle of Philippi in 42 B.C. It was also a complicated choice, as her son, now Ptolemy XV, was also Caesar's son.

Mark Antony, who had been Julius Caesar's right-hand man, was now the most powerful of the Roman warlords and thus a perfect political match for Cleopatra. It seems he knew they were well-suited to each other, too. He made the first move, writing her to leave Alexandria and come to him in Greece. He needed a way to remunerate his troops and pay off allies in the East; she needed a Roman protector. But she had doubts about Mark Antony's long-term future. She played hard to get, ignoring his requests until he finally sent a personal messenger to Egypt. That in itself illustrates their power dynamic. She may have needed a Roman ally, but Cleopatra must have known that he required her money more. Knowing exactly what Antony was looking for in a potential political partner—quick cash—Cleopatra made sure that her arrival in Tarsus was a display of wealth and excess. She arrived in a lavish, over-the-top river barge procession, dressed up as a goddess, according to eyewitness accounts. Word of this ostentatious display spread back to Rome, where people discussed the immorality of Cleopatra's overspending.[16] But if she did indeed put on such a conspicuous spectacle, she knew what she was doing. She had to make herself indispensable to Mark Antony—indeed, to any Roman warlord. She was essentially broadcasting her wealth to give her chosen partner no option but to work with her politically.

We might judge such opulence as wasteful, but such displays were carefully orchestrated to snare a Roman warlord with the promise of easy money. Lest we be seduced into thinking that Romans were all disgusted by such shows of wealth because they only prized simple, hardy farm living, as many ancient historians claimed, we should remember that later imperial Rome and its emperors would soon enjoy their own ultra-luxurious lifestyles of villas and sexual proclivities and profligacy. As for Cleopatra, her strategy worked in the short term. Longer term, it would be her—and Egypt's—undoing.

Antony was 41 and Cleopatra 28: a good match in terms of world experience and force of personality. Like Caesar, Antony was married—perfect for her needs. An unattached man would only bring her serious problems.

The Roman world was quickly spiraling out of control, and all those on the outer fringes were pulled into the vortex with it. Antony needed monetary support in his bid to take the eastern Mediterranean and destroy his Roman rivals. According to Plutarch, Antony and Cleopatra spent their time in Tarsus trying to outdo each other with lavish celebrations. Cleopatra won the battle of excess. The Roman accounts tell us that Mark Antony and his soldiers were even allowed to take the golden plates and furnishings from Cleopatra's banquets with them. Cleopatra was essentially buying her next romantic conquest. Once she had secured the Roman warrior and put him in her pocket, it was time to make her next big move: She asked Mark Antony to kill her sister Arsinoe, dwelling nearby in exile in Ephesus. There must have been a reason for her to strike so aggressively; perhaps she had news that Arsinoe was forging another Roman alliance to take her Egyptian throne. Arsinoe's elimination served Mark Antony as well, because no Roman could work against him by supporting Cleopatra's younger sister as contender for Egyptian rule. Once the woman was dead—killed in her early thirties on the steps of the Temple of Artemis, where she had taken refuge—Cleopatra ruled uncontested, alongside her son Caesarion, with no living Ptolemaic threats to her throne.

In 41 B.C., Mark Antony visited Alexandria and stayed at the palace with Cleopatra. He brought no legions, probably understanding that such overt military claims to Egypt would only get him killed back in Rome, as it had Caesar. As for Cleopatra, she was simply doing what her father before her had done—creating a close and personal relationship with Rome and thus protecting her rule. During this meeting, an alliance was formed. She gave Antony ships and grain; in turn, he restored Ptolemaic lands that had been lost, something he could legally do as a member of a triumvirate with Octavian and Lepidus. In her mind, the alliance with Rome must have seemed like the best solution, something that had worked for her father and had protected Egypt for centuries.

The added twist, the thing that upped the ante, was that Cleopatra was a woman of childbearing years, inserting a sexually procreative element into these political relationships. Cleopatra had already borne a child with Julius Caesar. He was now seven years old, a vulnerable and young heir. She would need more children to solidify her position in the long term. She had no harem to turn to; her womb was her only salvation. She would instead need to choose her partners carefully.

Mark Antony's visit in Egypt lasted through the winter of 41–40 B.C. The Roman records of his time in the Delta are filled with descriptions of feasting and excess: details that must have excited the elites in Rome, who were obsessed with overt displays of money and power. Word would soon spread back to Rome that Cleopatra not only forged a new political alliance with Antony but also was pregnant. They had heard this story before. Rumors spread like lightning; she had snared another good Roman man. It should come as no surprise that other powerful Romans, particularly Octavian, would see the potential danger in allowing a hybrid Roman-Egyptian dynasty of kings to rise in the East. Antony's close connection with Egypt would enrich him in the short term, helping him fund his forces. But in the long term it would also make him a target among his Roman peers, just as it had Julius Caesar.

Both Antony and Cleopatra must have known this. When he left Alexandria in 40 B.C., with a fleet of 200 ships provided by the queen, the Roman civil war was flaring up again. Obviously, Antony got what he wanted out of the partnership. Cleopatra also got what she wanted. She would soon bear him twins.

Antony nonetheless saw the political imprudence of his Egyptian connection and put Cleopatra out of his mind for more than three years, resolutely staying away from North Africa. Back at home, he had a giant mess to clean up. He had to deal with the effects of a disastrous war started by his own wife, Fulvia, against his ally Octavian. Fulvia had died after the battle; Antony was now a widower, able to take a new wife. To solidify a rapprochement between the two warlords with split power between East and West, the Senate demanded that Antony marry Octavian's sister, Octavia. This was all part of a typical

Roman tactic of serial monogamy—marriages that linked powerful elite families together and thereby limited competition for power and resources. To negotiate power alliances within a landscape of shifting loyalties, Roman men and women married, divorced, and remarried with ease, creating alliances and offspring with other families. It was not unusual for a Roman patrician to have had three or four partners by the end of his or her life, producing children with each of them. It was also not untoward for the Senate to order a marriage between feuding families, even if a divorce was required in the process, hoping to unite agendas and stem future violence. Unsurprisingly, many such coerced political marriages were ineffectual and bitter. Antony's marriage to Octavia would be one of these.

We have no idea what Cleopatra's reaction was when she heard of Antony's union with Octavia, or whether it mattered to her at all. This was a woman who understood political alliance through marriage; she would have expected such a partnership between Roman rivals. The progenitor of her first child had been married to another; now the second one was as well. Antony had been married when he sired her twins, in any case. Cleopatra didn't fuss about the illegitimacy of her children, all of whom were formally bastards in the Roman and Ptolemaic legal spheres. It didn't seem to matter in her Egyptian world, now defensively shoring up power against so many outside aggressors. Caesarion was acting as divine co-king unimpeded, bastard or not, and was now approaching the age of 10. With her sexual conquest of Antony, she now had two more children to add to her little stable of heirs—the twins, whom she named

Alexander and Cleopatra. Cleopatra VII had a very effective womb and a strong constitution; birthing twins in the ancient world was fraught with danger. But it seems that Cleopatra was somehow strategic in her pregnancies, preventing or eliminating those from men who would not benefit her position politically, and only keeping those babies who would help her act as ruler of Egypt with no husband. At this point, Cleopatra's lack of a formal husband was perhaps the best part of her strategy for a woman in power.

But Mark Antony would soon have need of Cleopatra again. In 37 B.C., he desperately required money and resources to wage war on Syria. He sent for Cleopatra to come to him in Antioch, in Anatolia. She arrived with all three of her children. He acknowledged the twins as his own, adding "sun" and "moon" to their names (Alexander Helios and Cleopatra Selena), ostensibly influenced by a total solar eclipse he had witnessed while abroad.[17]

In return for her support of his military endeavors, Antony was very generous. Cleopatra was one of many allied monarchs set up by Antony in the eastern Mediterranean, all meant to be friendly to Rome, but she benefited more than any of the others. With legal backing from Rome as a triumvir, Antony essentially restored Egypt's Ptolemaic Empire to what it had been 200 years before, granting back parts of the Phoenician and Levantine coast, extensive lands in inland Syria, large swaths of Arabia, parts of Crete, and Libya.[18]

It was a significant move for Antony from the perspective of the Romans. In many ways, the lands weren't his to give, but governed by provincial rulers from Rome. Legally, he was triumvir and fully able to make such a determination, but it was a deeply destabilizing decision and transparent to any Roman as patently self-serving. Antony couldn't have these lands transferred to his own personal rule without starting a war. And he couldn't control their present rulers the way he could Cleopatra. By giving these Eastern lands to her, he created a money- and power-laundering system that benefited himself, funneling the increased wealth through her new empire to his personal and growing military needs.

Antony's ruse doesn't seem to have worked. Word flew back to Rome of the land donations he had given Cleopatra. The Roman people would also learn that Antony had acknowledged the twins as his own—problematic, to say the least, in this Latin land of conservative family values. The Eastern dynasty of Cleopatra and Antony had been officially declared. The target on Antony's back came into clearer focus for Octavian.

While Antony was on a military campaign, Cleopatra returned to Egypt, heavily pregnant, to deliver yet another of Mark Antony's sons. This one she named Ptolemy Philadelphos, after one of her greatest ancestors, Ptolemy II Philadelphos, a clear shout-out to that time hundreds of years before when Egypt had the entire eastern Mediterranean in its mighty grasp. For Cleopatra, things couldn't have looked better. She had her Ptolemaic Empire restored; she could count on the protection of one of Rome's strongest warlords; she nurtured three children connected directly to the power of Rome; her co-king was the son of the martyred and sainted Julius Caesar himself, now about 12 or 13 years old and gaining in maturity and experience by the day. Her heirs were growing up, becoming wise to the ways of the world, ready to help her administer her great holdings, and, somehow, perhaps at her own design, not in competition with one another body and soul, as she had been with her own siblings. And Antony's ambitions to take over the world in the manner of Alexander the Great had only just begun.

The Roman Senate demanded that Antony invade and take Parthia in Northwest Asia to expand the glory of the Roman Empire. Antony assented. Octavian must have known that Antony was walking into a death trap. Previous campaigns against Parthia had ended in chaos and destruction. This one would be no different. Over the next few years, Antony repeatedly and unsuccessfully beat his head against this brick wall, attempting to secure Roman dominance over the area, depleting his vast resources, losing legions of men, and weakening himself politically in the process. Even though Cleopatra didn't accompany the expedition, the Romans blamed the failure on her directly, claiming that Antony was so overcome with his desire to return to her that he lost all reason and strategic thinking, that she had addled his mind with Egyptian magic and even intoxicants, that she had simply emasculated him. As Jezebel had done to King Ahab when she encouraged him to worship other gods besides Yahweh, as Delilah had ruined the strength of Samson, a woman can be a mind-bending seductress of her man. Such perceptions continue in our minds: First Lady

Mary Todd Lincoln was blamed for Abraham Lincoln's battle failures in the U.S. Civil War, Edward VIII was thought to have abdicated only after manipulation by his divorcée love Wallis Simpson, and Bill Clinton allegedly only strayed because of coldhearted Hillary.

When Antony did finally return from the front, Cleopatra met him on the Levantine coast with supplies for him and his men. She herself probably knew the Parthian cause to be futile at this point, but she had bet everything she possessed on this Roman warlord. Mark Antony was her last, best ally in her fight to keep Egypt free from imperial occupation. Whatever the nature of their personal relationship, she had funded his latest military bid; they had three children together and were poised to create an Eastern dynasty to rival Rome. She had no choice but to support Antony's ambitions in any way she could, no matter how foolhardy.

As for Antony, his military disaster was so complete and so ignominious that a return to Rome was apparently out of the question. He slunk off to Alexandria, instead, to lick his wounds. He would never see Rome again. It's at this point of the history that we read accounts from Roman authors about Cleopatra's manipulation to keep Antony by her side in Egypt, despite repeated and anxious calls from his Roman wife for him to return home to her. Cleopatra is said to have used tears, weight loss, and hysterics to turn his attentions to her instead.[19] Whether any of this is true or more Roman slander doesn't really matter. Antony stayed in Alexandria. Antony and Cleopatra looked to their future together as a political partnership.

Antony's next move was a brief campaign into Armenia, where he captured a recalcitrant king and his family and brought them to Egypt for a triumph in Alexandria. If he couldn't return to Rome, it seems he still needed a way to showcase at least some of his victories.

There were two political problems with this stunt of Antony's. First, the triumph was a particularly Roman thing and to celebrate it abroad, in Egypt—to actually present the captives of a land dominated by Rome to a foreign queen as she sat upon her golden throne—was beyond problematic to the Roman senators, proud of their Republic and distrustful of any kingly state. It smacked of disloyalty to his Latin homeland, if not outright treason. Second, everyone in Rome knew this triumph for the farce that it was. The details of Antony's defeat in Parthia had already spread far and wide; the display of one provincial Royal Family from an adjacent region in golden chains and Antony's appearance in the ceremonies as the god Dionysus himself just gave more political fodder to his rival Octavian, who could present Antony's corruption by this seductress of the East and his transformation into a degenerate king with aspirations to take over the Mediterranean. Octavian referred to Antony's Alexandrian displays dismissively as "a sort of triumph."[20] Octavian was certainly winning the propaganda war in Rome.

Cleopatra may have realized at this point that her partner was a liability, that the Parthian campaigns had transformed Antony into the weaker of the two Roman rivals. Always able to pivot, however, in 34 B.C. she created a grand ceremony to broadcast Egypt's control of extensive lands in the eastern Mediterranean, publicly granting each of her children a parcel of her vast empire to rule. She created an enormous spectacle, doing what she did best: claiming the appearance of power as the means of getting it.

Cleopatra and Antony sat in the stately marble gymnasium of Alexandria, both upon golden thrones, according to the Roman accounts, Cleopatra's four children seated on smaller thrones in front of them. The ceremony was over-the-top in its ostentatious display, again imitating her most successful ancestor Ptolemy II, who had held similar luxurious events. Cleopatra was grandly and publicly named queen of Egypt, Cyprus, Libya, and Syria. The 13-year-old Caesarion was named king of Egypt alongside Cleopatra, as Ptolemy XV. Six-year-old Alexander Helios was named king of Armenia, Media, and Parthia, although the last territories were obviously far from theirs. Six-year-old Cleopatra Selena was called ruler of Crete and Cyrene in modern-day Libya. Even the two-year-old Ptolemy Philadelphos was named king of Syria and Anatolia: an open threat to Rome's power because Cleopatra's ceremony nominally stripped the territory from Roman provincial control. The couple even memorialized this event with new coinage that displayed both Antony and Cleopatra as Hellenistic king and queen. We can be sure that these coins found their way back to Rome and its cocktail parties and formal political arenas for discussion, as did the account of Antony sitting on a throne like an archaic despot. Antony himself wrote to Rome asking that these Eastern territories be formally redistributed to Cleopatra and her children, shocking his fellow elites with his presumption and overreach—and his poor judgment in Roman affairs of state.

Now that the pair had decided to openly declare their dynastic ambitions in the eastern Mediterranean, this was all Rome could talk about. The Senate furiously discussed the legalities of Antony's action to grant power to Cleopatra and her children over these lands. Though absent, Antony still had a large number of political supporters in Rome, and they fought for their man in the Senate debates. Accusations and counter-accusations flew between men loyal to each side. One of the main arguments made on Antony's side was that Caesarion was the true blood heir of Julius Caesar, whether a bastard or not: an open affront to Octavian and his legal claim. Everything was spiraling toward a final confrontation between Antony and Octavian.

Cleopatra now haunted every discussion of Roman politics. She had borne the only known son of Julius Caesar. Her other children by Antony were being used as props for her territorial aspirations. Antony lived with her in Alexandria, not having been back in Rome for years, ignoring his Roman wife and relying on supporters in the Senate to make his case for him. It was with inevitable war looming and within a bitterly divided Rome that Cleopatra's reputation took the worst beating. Indeed, she was used by Octavian and his supporters as a "fake news" cipher to deflect their lowest attacks on Antony to her and away from their Roman compatriot, who was still a well-loved and popular war hero, despite his embarrassing losses in

Parthia. She was the best political gift Antony could ever have given Octavian. It was Cleopatra, Octavian argued, who had used her seduction and witchcraft to corrupt one of Rome's best leaders, to make him abandon his sense to such an extent that he was defeated in Parthia. It was all because of a foreign and degenerate woman that Rome was broken and suffering: her foreign ways, her excesses, her selfishness, her demands for attention; her arrogance and cruelty, her female inconstancy and hysteria—all of it were bringing Rome to its knees. She had to be stopped. In other words, most of what we know about Cleopatra was manufactured or exaggerated for political reasons, to create a case against Antony without actually speaking against him directly.[21]

If Cleopatra was now realizing that Antony was a liability to her, then Antony was probably now aware that his partnership with the queen was deeply problematic for him in Rome. His reputation among his compatriots was in tatters. This upstart female queen was a problem; the Romans viewed any kind of female rule with suspicion. Indeed, women didn't really find a place in political power in Rome until rule coalesced under an emperor—and, even then, they only acted to influence that man as an emperor's wife, daughter, sister, or mother, never as a ruler in her own right. At this point in Rome's republic, female rule was antithetical to conservative Roman values and laws. Cleopatra represented everything that good Roman elites feared.

Why is it easier to blame a woman than to confront the flaws of our men in power? Woody Allen comes to mind, a genius of a filmmaker whose problematic sexual interests have been ignored or blamed on "hysterical" women, like Mia Farrow. Or Martin Luther King Jr., whose sexual dalliances we discount. Or Mohandas Gandhi, who admitted to beating his wife in his own autobiography, an admission that caused many to come to his defense, nonetheless, with the claim that his wife created the circumstances that led to the abuse. We don't like to take down our masculine heroes; scapegoating a woman is always easier. Cleopatra would have known this, as we do.

When Antony sent an official letter of divorce to Octavia (which the Romans, of course, claimed Cleopatra instigated), it seems to have been the last straw. Octavian raided the Temple of the Vestal Virgins to seize Antony's will, even taking it by force from the reluctant priestesses. When the will was read aloud by Octavian, and Antony's last wishes were revealed, Rome was shocked. Antony had claimed Caesarion as heir of Julius Caesar, declaring that the distribution of Eastern lands to Cleopatra's children was legal, and that he wished to be buried in Alexandria with Cleopatra, not in Rome. Historians have discussed ad nauseam whether the will presented by Octavian was authentic or falsified. We will never know. What we do know is that Octavian used the document to suggest that not only did Antony desire to be king of the Mediterranean world, alongside his dissolute Egyptian queen, but that he would then move the Roman capital to Alexandria. Antony was not present in Rome to defend himself; his lingering existence in Egypt damned him.

The Senate was properly impressed by Octavian's Vestal Virgin stunt, and war was declared specifically on Cleopatra and Egypt, *not* on their erstwhile senator, Mark Antony. It was a stroke of political genius to vilify the woman, Cleopatra, all the while allowing Octavian to commit to military aggression against his compatriot with impunity. No longer in partnership with Octavian and its now-defunct triumvirate, no longer a consul or a senator, Antony was now truly dependent upon Cleopatra for everything: his military spending and support, his living quarters, her connections to the Eastern lands. Egypt's Eastern allies initially supported the cause against Rome, many donating ships, men, and supplies, probably hoping against hope to get rid of Roman domination of their lands once and for all. As the entire world geared up for an epic confrontation, many of Cleopatra's allies must have noticed that Alexandria's navy—though larger than the Romans' in the number of ships—was hastily assembled, reliant on untrained draftees, slow-moving, and a poor match for the well-trained naval strike force of Octavian.

There is a great deal of he said/she said about the run-up to the Battle of Actium, with some ancient authors observing that Antony had wanted to attack Octavian's ships in port in Italy, but that Cleopatra dissuaded him, preferring instead to fight farther east. There is also the story that Antony and his supporters preferred to engage in a land battle with their superior infantry troops, but that Cleopatra did not want to give Octavian a clear path to her beloved Egypt, demanding a naval battle at Actium instead.[22] Whatever the reality and whatever Cleopatra's say in the matter, the end result was obvious to everyone before the battle had even taken place. It was so clear that Antony and Cleopatra would lose that a number of key supporters defected to Octavian in the days before the battle.

When the navies finally clashed, the pair was soundly defeated. The eyewitness account that Cleopatra escaped and cut through Octavian's line, with most of her faster ships, sailing as fast as she could back to Egypt in the middle of a losing battle, was used effectively by Roman propagandists to accuse her of subterfuge, faithlessness, and abandonment. Antony, it was said, followed her out of the harbor, overcome by the defeat, unable to concoct any strategy whatsoever. The key takeaway is that Antony was more invested in the military solution than was Cleopatra, who was more interested in escaping from the battle with much of her fleet intact. A woman's move, to be sure, but who could blame her sensible choice?

Both Antony and Cleopatra attempted to rebound. Antony headed to Libya to collect infantry to defend Egypt from a land attack. Cleopatra entered the harbors of Alexandria, sails and flags raised as if in victory, ready to raise more funds for a counterattack.

But both Antony and Cleopatra were met with immediate and dire obstacles. Word had already spread to the Roman commander in Libya that Antony was hoping to commandeer his forces; the general refused to receive Antony, instead formally switching his allegiance to Octavian. The same happened with every Roman legion and ally they had once counted on in the eastern Mediterranean. From Albania to Judea, everyone defected to what they saw as the winning side. Bystander Roman accounts say that Antony had to be forcibly restrained from committing suicide when news of the betrayals poured in. He was brought to Alexandria where he apparently sat in depressed and drunken silence.

Cleopatra and Antony were now alone in their Egyptian harbor city with no powerful friends and no allies, just their citizenry. And as soon as they got word of the latest events, the population of Alexandria would have looked to their own self-preservation, too, just as the rest of the eastern Mediterranean did. How the children of Cleopatra received this news is anyone's guess, but the reaction can't have been positive. They were Ptolemies, and they must have known the repercussions. These young people had all been lauded as monarchs in their own rights, strategically placed by their own mother as pieces on the game board. Now, it was a waiting game for each child to receive his or her fate. It would be a long, cruel year of waiting—hoping to devise an exit strategy and, eventually, finding none.

In the absence of a clear-thinking Antony, it was Cleopatra, it is said, who attempted negotiation with Octavian. She wanted him to make her son Caesarion king of Egypt after her own proffered exile, hoping that the Romans would continue to leave Egypt formally unoccupied if it resumed its old ways as an obedient and cooperative ally of Rome. There are accounts that she tried to plan an escape for herself to Ethiopia or India—but, if true, Cleopatra eventually had to abandon these plans and deal directly with Octavian. Antony was of no help to the queen whatsoever, according to the Roman stories, holed up in his drunken malaise. Cleopatra was left to pick up the pieces of their disastrous military defeat.

Roman accounts tell us that Cleopatra repeatedly wrote to Octavian, camped on the island of Rhodes, asking him to spare her children. He didn't write back. Antony wrote to Octavian, too, but his messengers were all killed: a diplomatic insult of the highest order. Eventually, Octavian sent word to Cleopatra that she should execute Antony if she wanted to spare herself and her family. If this is true—and how can we really know in such a one-sided history?—she wouldn't or couldn't follow through on the request, even, it seems, if it would have saved her children and her land. Indeed, what was once her greatest asset—her son Caesarion—was now a massive liability. She would have done better to have had inbred children with her Macedonian brother, handing Egypt off safely to their pure Ptolemaic rule. How could Cleopatra have expected Octavian to support a pharaoh who could later claim to be rightful blood heir to Julius Caesar, who could threaten power in the heart of Rome itself?

Cleopatra was utterly boxed in by the decisions she had made over the previous decades. Her children's descent from Roman men would ultimately spell her ruin. The Roman accounts suggest that Cleopatra either didn't understand or didn't care what would eventually happen to her own children as she repeatedly tried to establish them in power positions in her absence. But remember, these are Roman accounts of Cleopatra's desperate strategies. The alternative story, and one we should assume first, is that she was keenly aware of the politics involved. Maybe she did indeed offer Antony to his rival Octavian. Maybe she even

suggested another of her children to rule Egypt besides Caesarion. If such was the case, Octavian never presented those
negotiation attempts of Cleopatra's for public consumption, nor
should we expect him to have done so. The Roman propaganda
war was already won. Octavian could essentially make up any
story he liked. We are told that when she learned Octavian
would display her as a captive in his triumph in Rome, Cleopatra
began planning her suicide.[23]

There were more military operations before the end. In 30
B.C., Octavian sent a land army from the Levant, through the
Sinai, to Alexandria. Even though Antony won this battle, his
troops understood what he himself could not. First, his navy
defected to Octavian; then his cavalry of trained elites, probably
his best men, did the same. It was all over. Antony stabbed
himself in the stomach, according to Roman reports, hoping for
a hero's death. Instead, he won only a slow and lingering demise;
he was brought to Alexandria to die. According to the romantic
and melodramatic stories, he was raised into the upper window
of Cleopatra's last refuge: her own tomb in Alexandria, in which
she cowered with a few of her servants and all of her vast,
hoarded treasury. She was selfish to the last, the Romans tell us,
the doors bolted from the inside with some trick mechanism
that could not, we are told, be unlocked. Egyptian witchcraft at
its finest, apparently.

There are reports that, around this time, Cleopatra had
already begun investigating the best poisons, trying them out
on servants to determine the most painless means of suicide:
more useful ammunition for Octavian to build a case of a cruel

and self-interested woman, keen only on sheltering herself from all the pain she herself had wrought. We also hear that Cleopatra threatened Octavian with the destruction of her entire treasury, which she said she would burn to the ground, thus depriving him of her vast riches when he took her palace: another useful trope to paint her as nihilistic and selfish, even into death. Whether any of these stories have kernels of truth, we will never know, but their Roman origins make all of them highly suspect.[24] The truth is this: Cleopatra now found herself trapped in Alexandria, trying to strategize a way out of a deep, dark hole from which she could not extricate herself or her children.

♛

WHEN OCTAVIAN FINALLY ARRIVED in Alexandria, he was presented with a complicated political situation, at least from the Roman perspective. Taking Egypt outright would imbalance Roman power among its elites, putting too much economic authority into the hands of one man: himself. If Octavian entertained ideas of keeping Cleopatra alive as ruler of Egypt, as a means of laundering her money into his coffers without Roman suspicion, as Antony had done, the existence of her children made that impossible. Cleopatra had borne Julius Caesar his only living son; she had borne Mark Antony three more children. She was enmeshed with Roman politics genealogically as no previous ally monarch had been; Octavian could not safely keep her as queen of Egypt, nor could he keep Caesarion as king without threat to his own position in Rome. And yet there was no other candidate among her children to take the kingship. All were potential direct threats to his own leadership as offspring of a beloved Roman general.

Octavian had no choice but to take Egypt outright and rule it directly as a Roman province. Given that he had already quashed all real and credible threats from other Roman warlords, seizing the land of the Nile was finally possible. It was the conquest of Egypt that granted Octavian that singular power of centralized imperial rule as Princeps, first among many, Caesar's heir, and the first leader of a growing empire. In many ways, it was Cleopatra herself who unwittingly created the first in a very long line of Roman emperors.

Caesarion, now a young adult, had already fled south with his own entourage of supporters. He was a king in exile, this Ptolemy XV. Cleopatra's three younger children with Antony were held by Octavian as hostages, awaiting transport to Rome. It was at this point that Cleopatra manufactured a means, although she was supposedly closely watched, of killing herself—maybe by snake bite, maybe by a dose of poison she had managed to get into her hands, maybe by some other means unknown to history. If she had planned on killing her children, too, she didn't have the heart for it. If the Romans dispatched her themselves and blamed it on suicide, we have no account of it. In any case, the Roman narrative is full of her shameful scheming and interest in painless death and decadent glamour, even at her end, at 39.[25] We hear that she indulged in a special bath, put on her finest garments, and that her last meal was extravagant, maybe even including a basket of figs with the means of her suicide—an asp—hidden inside, so that when Octavian's men found her dead inside her mausoleum, she was decked out in her full royal regalia, crowns and all, beautiful and beyond their care. Or so Octavian would have us believe.

The means of her death has been rehashed ad nauseam. Most historians simply try to figure out how a self-involved, cowardly, deceitful woman would have contrived her own end. But the mechanism of death is meaningless; the Roman Empire killed her, outright or obliquely. Cleopatra's end was not unusual for the Romans and their voracious imperial machine. She was just another in a long line of rulers mowed down by a rapacious expansion. She tried her best to overcome that military might, even weaving her own interests and offspring in with theirs, creating a rival dynasty of sons and daughters bred from Rome's best men. She almost pulled it off; she nearly became the only woman in our story to create her own dynasty. But she was vanquished like all the other female pharaohs, not to mention all the other women leaders who dared to take on Rome.

After her death, a general named Cornelius Gallup was put in charge of the army and administration of Egypt. No longer did pharaohs decide Egypt's fate; this was now a bureaucrat's task. Egyptian funds now went directly to Roman veterans and Roman causes. With Egypt's absorption into the Roman Empire, Egyptian native rule had ended, not to return until 2,000 years later, in 1950 of the Common Era, with the end of British occupation.

Cleopatra's son Caesarion was scurrying south when he received a note to return posthaste, that Octavian would make him king to rule Egypt after his mother. Whether his entourage knew this to be a ruse or not is immaterial. They all apparently turned around, returning to Alexandria and Octavian, who knew there could only be one heir to Caesar: himself. Accounts tell us that the boy was killed on the road back.[26] Again, even this story may be false and self-serving, given how artfully it represents Caesarion's naiveté.

Octavian made sure to root out every potential Ptolemaic monarch waiting in the wings, even killing a 16-year-old cousin of Cleopatra (a boy historians have named Pedubast of Alexandria), so that there could be no attempts to take back the Egyptian kingship. Octavian annihilated the Ptolemaic line, taking Egypt for himself, transforming himself into the only living heir of Caesar. It's at this point that the name of his uncle Julius Caesar would become synonymous with centralized imperial power in Rome; Octavian would take on a newly invented title of Caesar Augustus, or Caesar the Great, heir of the great senator and warlord killed in Rome on the Ides of March in 44 B.C., later memorialized with the month (August) in which Octavian had won a final series of great battles over Mark Antony and Cleopatra. Julius Caesar became a god incarnate, deified by Octavian when a comet, later called the Julian Star, appeared during the funeral games held in his honor. Octavian was thus able to name himself *Divi Filius*: "Son of God." It was a brilliant public relations scheme.

Rome had Egypt to thank not only for its new authoritarian regime, but also for the means of its presentation as divinely given. Averse to kingship, the Romans simply reinvented any despotic titles, using the name Caesar to address their ruler instead. Rome's new imperial rule was a dynastic monarchy dressed up in legal niceties of heir designation and Julian cults— but, make no mistake: It was still a kingship.

Alexander Helios and Cleopatra Selena, the sun and moon, children of Antony, were marched in the Roman triumph of Octavian of 29 B.C., their disgrace visible to every citizen of the great city of Rome. They were allowed to live with Octavia, Mark Antony's ex-wife and widow. As the good Roman matri- arch, the Melanie Hamilton to Scarlett O'Hara's Cleopatra, she brought them up as her own children. Alexander Helios doesn't appear in any of the texts soon thereafter; nor does his younger brother, Ptolemy Philadelphos. Maybe Octavian had something to do with that, maybe not. Only Cleopatra Selena lived on, eventually marrying King Juba I of Numidia in North Africa, bearing a son, audaciously named Ptolemy, who would later be executed by Emperor Caligula[27]—because Cleopatra's grandson, and Mark Antony's as well, of course, was still considered a threat to Roman imperial power. The Ptolemaic-Roman family that had almost built a dynasty in opposition to Rome had finally been pulled out by the roots with this last extermination.

♛

DESPITE ALL THE SUCCESSFUL sexual strategy, the battles won, the children brought up, the alliances made, Cleopatra failed nonetheless. Her downfall was brought about by two major factors: first and foremost, the Nile and its lack of water. Long-term climatic changes had already spelled her doom before she even took the throne and started strategizing. Without access to easily grown grain (in Egypt, money more or less grew on trees), she would always be walking uphill as Egypt's real base of power was its agricultural surplus. Second, Cleopatra was trying to negotiate her place in terms of a powerful, growing, and ever evolving Roman Empire, making her dependent on successful relationships with Roman creditors and warlords in a globalized Mediterranean that could change on a dime, depending on Rome's own confusing, internal politics. Egypt wasn't the only game in town in the ancient world. It had to play second fiddle to a number of more powerful states and empires, always trying to buy them off with cash and favors. If Cleopatra had not had to depend on the cooperation of a variety of ambitious and fallible men, maybe this whole story would have turned out differently. As it was, native rule of Ptolemaic Egypt was a tightrope walk between the competing agendas of feuding super-empires.

But in the end, it was the military hubris of her chosen Roman partner in war and in child-making that proved Egypt's tragic downfall. The need to fight Marc Antony's battles weakened Cleopatra beyond repair, destroying her ability to protect Egypt from Roman domination. Her true and abiding love for the man may have driven the final nail into Egypt's coffin, causing Cleopatra to give too much, to overlook glaring and fatal flaws in her paramour. But how can we judge the authenticity of Cleopatra's human affection for Antony so many thousands of years in the future, sullied by pages of Roman propaganda, not to mention

Shakespearean stage treatments and Hollywood renditions? Without Antony's vulnerability (or without Octavian's brilliance), maybe Cleopatra could have built a powerful Eastern competitor to the Roman Empire and passed the whole show on to her eldest son, Caesarion. But Egypt would soon be brought to its knees, folded into yet another empire. Cleopatra would be the last woman to rule her Egyptian world.

Unlike the other women in our story, however, Cleopatra has a rich afterlife. Her opposition to Rome set her up as a hero and martyr for peoples of the East. Queen Zenobia of Palmyra modeled herself on the Egyptian queen, claiming genealogical descent from Cleopatra, as she fought against Rome during the third century.[28] Cleopatra's identification with the goddess Isis may have had the longest afterlife of all; indeed, her identification with the divinity likely helped to export the Isis cult throughout the Roman Empire and thus to the rest of the world. After her death, the mystery cult of the Egyptian goddess took off like wildfire:[29] no accident, as Cleopatra was seen as a protector of her children; of her lover (like Osiris); and of her son (like Horus), who, against all odds, somehow defeated a mighty empire in eternity, if not in her lifetime. Indeed, Jesus of Galilee lived around the same time as Cleopatra and also fought the great Roman Empire in his own way—and he also lost, only to be martyred and later worshipped in his own popular mystery cult. Human beliefs aside, the comparisons of history and context between Cleopatra and Jesus Christ are striking.

If we ignore the Roman misinformation and propaganda campaign against her, Cleopatra's legacy is rich in meaning. She created a means for people to connect to female power in the form of the goddess, as Hatshepsut had done before her in the goddess Mut's temple with her Festivals of Drunkenness, in Nefertiti's reversion to the old ways of worship. Hatshepsut's name we cannot pronounce. But Cleopatra's name comes to our lips easily as a greedy slut, a capricious and inconstant emotional female force, a degenerate queen—but also, for many on the losing side against Rome, as fierce protector, insurrectionist, rebel, brilliant strategist, and attempted savior of her people—a dichotomy of perception that women still contend with today. Roman poets eulogized her. Shakespeare wrote plays about her. Elizabeth Taylor found in her the role of a lifetime. Cleopatra's ending is tragic only because she came so close to achieving so much. She was such a threat to Rome that her suicide may very well have been a regicide. How are we ever to know, when every good trait of Cleopatra was so utterly extinguished?

EPILOGUE

Why Women Should Rule the World

The Egyptians never wrote any laws or diatribes against female leadership, and their institution of kingship was flexible enough for a woman (on occasion) to fill the role. They allowed women to serve when necessity dictated. Women were able to take positions of real political power in ancient Egypt from the very beginning of its state formation.

There was still the expected backlash against these women, to be sure. Each time a female pharaoh was pushed back down again, another somehow found a way to ascend once more, only to be suppressed again. This process was repeated at the highest political level six or seven times during 3,000 years of Egypt's complex history. The stakes rose higher for these female sovereigns with every push, demanding that each woman use a different strategy and claim more power through time. Merneith, the first woman to rule as head of state, couldn't claim the title of king—but, by the end, Cleopatra found herself the most audacious of them all. Her fall was also the most brutal of them all—a smackdown not just of powerful Egyptian women, but of native rule itself.

Arguably, the most real and lasting gift that Egypt's female rulers gave to the world was the empowered divine feminine. The Isis cult spread throughout the ancient Mediterranean, honoring the actions of a vibrant goddess. Notions of female power also found their way into Christianity's Mother Mary figure, a woman capable of bearing God incarnate on Earth, through no procreative ability of her own, just as Nut bore the sun god, by means of her selfless devotion to her deity and her people, and her strength to see it through against all odds.

It's important to recognize that divine kingship—of Osiris or Horus, or of Jesus as king of the Jews—automatically demands divine queenship to protect it. One needs the other, like two sides of a coin, and so the protective, sexualized, and strong female was maintained within Christianity, just as it was in ancient Egyptian theologies. Her power was not taken away but fostered, because it was wielded in protection of the family, of the dynasty, of Christ. On the other hand, if disconnected from masculine power, that same female power can be rejected with vehement hostility—as Hatshepsut's authority led to her erasure by her nephew, as Tawosret's independent ambition to rule on her own terms demanded her violent removal, as Cleopatra's power over Roman warlords required the manufacture of a skillful (if self-absorbed) suicide.

On the other hand, if female power is used in support of the (rightful) masculine leader, we laud it as righteous and good. Mary fearlessly protected her son Jesus: when Herod wanted to kill him, when the holy family was forced into exile in Egypt, even when Jesus was sought by Jewish and Roman authorities before his execution. Or, in the modern world, when the dutiful daughter of the assassinated general steps up for general elections to save her family dynasty, she is thus loved by her people. Women are judged—good or bad—by that vital question: Did she act selfishly?

Alone or in the service of others, the ancient Egyptians knew to embrace and utilize all female talents, including emotionality, a mercurial nature, and an ability to softly nurture or ferociously kill when circumstance demanded it. The feminine nature is seen by many of us today as a liability—for example, a woman's propensity to weep at charged work meetings, rather than get angry and slam a fist on the table. Her likelihood to change her mind is seen not as building consensus, but as dangerous indecisiveness. But to the ancient Egyptians, this aspect was the key to a woman's utility: the quality that allowed her to connect to the other side of an issue; to take her time to make the best decision; to give her the ability to nurture, to nag, to fight, to hold a grudge against, and to love.

The Egyptian female could be witch or goddess, ferocious protector or vulnerable woman, temptress or mother. The Egyptians saw the advantages of this multiplicity—duplicity, even—rather than its detriments. The ability of other places and peoples to figure this out depends on a reckoning that female power is best wielded in our darkest moments, usually when all hope is lost. Egypt was an old and venerable land that forced this power on a people whether they wanted it or not; the agreement of the ruled people was never sought. They had to submit to their female mistresses. Authoritarianism is thus one answer.

But maybe Egypt also traversed more end times than other places, moving through the shadow of death and finding resilience on the other side. Maybe we think we are invincible, that we don't need our mothers, sisters, and daughters telling us what to do. The long-lived Egyptians had been through it all: ups and downs, triumphs and abject failures. They knew a woman's power could be the last hope of a people.

The women in these pages—Merneith, Neferusobek, Hatshepsut, Nefertiti, Tawosret, and Cleopatra—together form a mighty epic that ends in tragedy: not because they failed (in fact, some were extraordinarily successful, saving their land and their dynasty), but because they are remembered as failures or have been forgotten, expunged from reliefs and statues. And it took nothing less than a dictatorial regime to compel people to accept female power at its most fierce.

These mighty Egyptian monarchs have many lessons for us if we want to move toward full and total equality for both genders in our halls of power; they can provide great insight into our current and fierce aversions to female rule, particularly within modern democratic systems. Perhaps we assume these powerful women are serving only their own family members in nepotistic self-interest, making any female ambition for power somehow distasteful or deceitful. Or maybe we don't believe women belong in the arena of mud-slinging and personal takedowns, so common in our modern decentralized political mess. Just as we exclude women from modern military combat, we feel they are too gentle for the political arena, too. No doubt, we expect women to serve their children and grandchildren and distrust those who say they want to pursue larger ambitions.

In competitive and decentralized societies like our own, even brilliant and educated women are sometimes blocked from the start by our own misperceptions of their intentions. The ongoing wage gap; the epidemics of sexual harassment and assault; the lack of female representation in government; the dearth of women in business leadership positions; the belief that women can't compete in science, technology, or math because of their female cognitive structures—all are evidence of an immature humankind that hasn't yet learned to appreciate what's good for it.

I often end public lectures with a meme that a friend of mine posted on Facebook. It's a series of emojis. The top part is titled "A Man's Day" and shows a bunch of blandly pleased faces, none too happy, none too sad. The bottom part, called "A Woman's Day," features face after face drastically different from one another: one ecstatically happy, the next brutally angry, the next weeping and distraught, and on and on from one feeling to another.

This, right here, in visual form, is the reason we keep women from power. We think of them as emotionally incapable of ruling over us—their highs too high, their lows too low, their feelings too acute. And yet the ancient Egyptians never accused women of being too emotional to rule. They knew the truth: It is the men who all too easily allow their thin-skinned sensibilities and lust for power and domination over their enemies to lead them to maim and murder and rape.

Not only have studies proven that men are expected to be less emotional; they actually *are* less in touch with their emotions.[1] Men don't suffer as many mood swings as women in a given day—but, then again, which gender commits the most violence and murder in human society? Which gender yields the most suicide bombers? Which gender is the most common serial killer? Which is more active in fomenting and continuing war? The answer is obvious and demands that we turn our perception of female emotionality on its head. Emotional roller-coastering is what allows females to *feel* such acts before committing them—to revel in deep anger and express it to friends and family, instead of pushing it down until it explodes in an act of domestic or community violence; to express profound personal insecurities to others, rather than repressing the emotions, only to see them surface in bullying and picking fights.

Many studies show that women might even have a biological predisposition to indecision, to more nuanced thinking—to knowing that one can and should ask for a variety of opinions on a problem.[2] That very prudence can save lives. Male decisiveness is exactly what pushes the button launching the nuclear missiles; female doubt pulls the hand away and reconsiders, thinking it over just one more time. The female of our species may have a greater need to be liked, rather than respected and feared: an amenability that can be easily abused by lovers, husbands, and children alike. But it is this bridge-building that creates truth and reconciliation, instead of scorched earth.

Women are not driven by honor as much as by empathy and pragmatic protection of the family. Merneith's fierce protection of her son's kingship overrode her softer emotions toward her compatriots. Neferusobek was likely allowed to close out her family dynasty because she ruled without domineering aggression. Hatshepsut enriched all her elites, wanting them to enjoy a queen-regent's rule. Nefertiti called a halt to her husband's fanatical agenda and built consensus with priests long excluded from Egypt's religious life. Tawosret may have lost to Setnakht because she lacked a certain ruthlessness that he possessed. And Cleopatra used every ounce of her female abilities to read faces and create romantic interest to connect her land's continued survival with powerful men of Rome, linking national security with family togetherness.

Both stereotypes and the studies alike indicate that women don't interrupt as much; they listen more. They immediately recognize facial expressions that many men miss entirely. These traits are sometimes discussed in negative terms (for example, that they need to be more aggressive and speak up more, lest all their ideas be taken by their colleagues; that they need to masculinize to advance in this patriarchal world).[3] But the ancient Egyptians knew that mercurial, protective, and cautious female thought patterns could also be seen in positive terms—especially when they stop people from drawing harsh lines in the sand, pulling the gun out of its holster, or tearing up the peace treaty in violent anger. We need to stop misperceiving feminine emotionality as weak and deceitful when it is the most construc-tive way forward in days of crisis.

Ancient Egyptian monarchs proved that women do rule dif-ferently. They didn't demand hundreds of lovers to sexually service them, like Harvey Weinstein or a king in his harem. They ruled on behalf of family members, not just for themselves. For the most part, they avoided war, rather than jumping into the melee. And they were called upon precisely when their people were at their most vulnerable.

Of course, there are exceptions: Some women exhibit more masculine behavior on the social gradient, and vice versa. And, yes, evolutionary biology has been harshly criticized as another easy way of keeping a woman down, of telling a girl that her brain simply isn't capable of following a STEM career path.[4] Or that because she is more likely to hold a grudge, she is not suited to the business world. Or that because she is penetrable, she cannot serve in combat forces. In fact, what seems unstable and scary is actually a woman's strength: her main means of connect-ing with the myriad emotions of the world. What is going to save us from the apocalypses of global warming, mass migration, constant warfare, corporate populism, and nuclear aggression more than female hesitancy and nonaggression? We should try it; it might help.

The ancient Egyptians brilliantly used female power to avoid potential aggression from men, to avoid war, to get through a crisis, to keep a culture going for more than 3,000 years. They may have treated their female rulers poorly after the fact. But the Egyptians knew that women avoid risk, steer clear of shock and awe. Women were regularly chosen as pharaoh for this very reason. They don't typically wage war, rape, or throttle; they rule pragmatically; they don't hog all the credit. Society won't let them. They avoid owning their ambition; society would excoriate them for displaying it. In Egypt, such women were the salvation of a people again and again. We should let ancient history be our guide and let women be our salvation once more.

ACKNOWLEDGMENTS

In many ways this book owes each chapter to the Egyptologists who have devoted large parts of their scholarly lives to particular time periods or certain rulers. For Merneith, I owe debts to Laurel Bestock and Ellen Morris. For Neferusobek, I am grateful for the scholarship of Julia Budka and Gae Callender. Hatshepsut has become near and dear to me since the publication of my own biography on her life in 2014, and while the scholars to whom I am indebted are many, Betsy Bryan and JJ Shirley played particular roles in shaping my understanding of this woman. Nefertiti would have been impossible to write about without the research of Nicholas Reeves, Jim Allen, and Dmitri Laboury. Tawosret's chapter owes debts to Aidan Dodson, Richard Wilkinson, Heather McCarthy, and Pearce Paul Creasman. And, finally, Cleopatra would have been impossible without the work of Julia Sampson, Joyce Tyldesley, and Duane Roller. Women's studies in Egyptology are still only a few decades old, and my own forays into this rich field rely on scholars like Joyce Tyldesley, Ann Macy Roth, Gay Robins, Gae

Callender, and Betsy Bryan. None of these brilliant scholars need to bear the burden of my own idiosyncratic perspectives on women and power; any mistakes or misperceptions in this book are my own.

To the hundreds of students in my many Women and Power in the Ancient World classes at UCLA, I am indebted. Their questions, pushback, confusion, and passion have driven me over the years. This book has also delayed some of my more scholarly contributions, causing some of my colleagues to wait and wait for a number of my unfinished articles. Thank you Alessia Amenta, Rogério Sousa, and Helen Strudwick for your patience with my tardiness. I'll get to that coffins monograph now, I promise.

My UCLA graduate students have been ever so tolerant with my interests in ancient Egyptian women in power. Danielle Candelora and Rose Campbell pulled articles and filled up my Dropbox with research, also reading drafts of the book and making helpful comments. Special thanks to (Drs.) Carrie Arbuckle McCleod and Marissa Stevens, who had to wait longer than they should have for dissertation revisions from me. And I am ever so grateful to Isamara Ramirez, always en pointe, who continued to keep a close watch over my schedule and strategy while I acted as chair of the Department of Near Eastern Languages and Cultures at UCLA. There is indeed no possible way I could have written this book if Isamara hadn't had my back. None. Zero.

Thank you, Rebecca Peabody, for being the best solo writing group partner one could ever have, even though we hardly ever get to meet up anymore now that we have kids and careers and writing careers. You are my best sounding board in everything publishing and strategic, you clever girl. And that reminds me: We haven't seen each other in way too long, so come over this next weekend and bring the girls.

My literary agent, Marc Gerald, somehow never gave up on me, and ended up finding the absolutely perfect new place for me with National Geographic Books. I don't know what he sees in me, but I'm thrilled that he found me and continues to support my little Egyptological ventures in popular nonfiction.

At National Geographic Books, the guidance and passion of Lisa Thomas, Hilary Black, and Allyson Johnson remind me of why women should have power and how they wield it differently. I thank them (and my own overburdened schedule) for setting me up with Linda Carbone, who worked with me—tirelessly and nonjudgmentally—on line after line, note after note, chapter after chapter. Make no mistake, Linda whipped me into shape, and thank the gods for it. And blessed be that Nat Geo machine of NG Live!, glossy yellow magazines, and extraordinary outreach. It's astonishing to be a new member of this venerable family.

My research assistant, Amber Myers Wells, jumped onto this project with both feet, helping me with research, endnotes, images, editing, and, most important, keeping me on task and making sure my graduate students always got their letters of recommendation submitted on time. I always said to Amber when she saved me again and again, "Oh my god, I love you, Amber, and I want to have your babies," at which point she would always say that she had enough babies, thank you very much.

Miquelle McCarthy, my nanny and so much more, stood by me when custody and court overwhelmed my soul and psyche. She did not blink at coming by for a few hours on a given Sunday to let me write or to walk into the horror of Los Angeles County Dependency Court to watch my boy while I faced deep uncertainty and doubt in that horrible courtroom. Miquelle, you have been a rock of solace and comfort in a very stormy sea. No one should be able to write a book in the midst of such personal craziness, and yet, I did—because I knew my son was not only safe with you, but energized, embraced, challenged, and adored.

Finally, I owe so very much to my family. I went through a deep crisis between my last book and this one, testing my belief in human goodness and truth. When the person in whom I had placed my trust and love turned out to be the opposite of human kindness, I had to reevaluate and reframe my own understanding of good and bad; right and wrong. To my family who saved me from emotional and financial ruin, to my mother and father who waited for me to return to them, to my siblings who never gave up on me, to my sister who forgave me, bless you all.

To my beautiful son, Julian, who teaches me the meaning of real life, with all his nuance, grit, human will, stubbornness, joy, often demanding my submission, often surprising me with his wisdom, you teach me more than you can ever know. To my new stepson and stepdaughter, Branden and Kimberly, who show me such true and loving affection, thank you for entering my life.

And to my unexpected, punched-in-the-gut true love, my new husband, Remy, of ramen and whiskey, of painting and pottery, of satellites and mountains, who possesses a breathtaking eye that forces me to stop and examine details of humanity and environment in a way I never have before, who agrees with my mother on just about everything, who brings me coffee every morning, who accepts me in all my loud, interrupting, tall-woman fervor, who treasures me as no one ever has, my heart is yours—in this lifetime and all the rest—I am eternally grateful.

INTRODUCTION: WHY WOMEN DON'T RULE THE WORLD

1   These examples of female kingship occurred over a span of about 3,000 years. This might cause some to caution against seeing it as something of a norm, as presented here, and that other cultures, empires, and modern states might also contain six female heads of state in such a long time span. First, I have yet to find any place on the planet that rivals Egypt in its allowance of female rule. In the rest of the world, female power continues to be an isolated circumstance; the odd woman president or prime minister is voted into power, while a few other women find their way to political rule through assassinations, civil wars, or outside threats on their menfolk. Second, I would argue that the 3,000-year time span, in and of itself, shows that female rule was a regularized feature of Egyptian authoritative systems. Third, I would counter that female rule didn't just appear at the highest political level, as king, but also showed itself in other, still significant, positions, as influential queen, princess, priestess, or matriarch.

2   The instances of women openly taking on the highest political and military rule in the ancient world are few and far
between—a few in Mesopotamia, the Levant, Anatolia,
Persia, and China rose to the head of state, but not all were
formally named as such. In ancient Mesopotamia, Queen
Kubaba of Kish ruled as king during the 26th century B.C.
In the ancient Levant, where kingship was viewed with
suspicion by a nascent but powerful ideological power,
Jezebel and her daughter Athalia of the ninth century B.C.
were condemned to horrific deaths at the hands of Yahweh
priests when they attempted to shore up their family lineages behind the scenes, as regent or just as queen. (Jezebel
was thrown out of a window to be eaten by dogs. Athalia
was executed.) In ancient Assyria, Sammuramat of the ninth
century is remembered as the duplicitous, sexually liberated,
and lover-murdering Semiramis of later Greek texts; she
acted as regent to her young son Adadnirari III. In the fifth
century B.C., Artemisia of Caria, in Anatolia, was the queen
of the Greek city of Halicarnassus who raised a navy for
Persia's Xerxes I in his unsuccessful bid to conquer Greece.
In second-century B.C. China, the extraordinary Empress
Lü Zhi rose to power, first as empress to a weaker husband
she could control, then really coming into her own as
dowager-empress ruling over a young son who was an easily
cowed and terrorized king. After the death of her son,
Emperor Hui, she pulled all the strings when her grandsons
occupied the throne. She ruled 16 years altogether, and is
the best comparison to women like Hatshepsut and Cleo-

patra. After her, Empress Wu of medieval China would carry the torch of female rule. These women who led armies and engaged in political conflict were brilliant exceptions to the patriarchal rule. There simply were not that many of them.

3 For a recent news article summarizing such sociological studies on the evaluation bias against women in the workplace, see Kieran Snyder, "The Abrasiveness Trap: High-Achieving Men and Women Are Described Differently in Reviews," *Fortune,* April 26, 2014, http://fortune.com/2014/08/26/performance-review-gender-bias/. For a news report discussing studies of bias in academic student evaluations, see Laura Bates, "Female Academics Face Huge Sexist Bias—No Wonder There Are So Few of Them," *The Guardian,* February 13, 2015, https://www.theguardian.com/lifeandstyle/womens-blog/2015/feb/13/female-academics-huge-sexist-bias-students.

CHAPTER 1: MERNEITH

1 The Egyptian priest-historian Manetho organized Egyptian history into 30 dynasties, spanning from around 3000 to 300 B.C. For more, see W. G. Waddell, *Manetho* (London: W. Heinemann Ltd., 1940).

2 For sources on human sacrifice, see *Sacred Killing: The Archaeology of Sacrifice in the Ancient Near East,* edited by Anne M. Porter and Glenn M. Schwartz (Winona Lake, Ind.: Eisenbrauns, 2012); *Violence and Civilization: Studies of Social Violence in History and Prehistory,* edited by Roderick Campbell, Joukowsky Institute Publication 4 (Oxford, UK: Oxbow

Books, 2014); *Material Harm: Archaeological Studies of War and Violence,* edited by John Carman (Glasgow, Scotland: Cruithne Press, 1997).

3   The practice of placing sacrificial victims in the king's tomb began with Merneith's grandfather, King Aha, or at least this is when it began on any kind of scale that archaeology can document. More than 50 people lost their lives to accompany the first king of Dynasty I into death. Along with them were also sacrificed donkeys as beasts of burden and transportation and even seven young male lions, representative of kingly strength and prowess. The people who accompanied King Aha to his grave were not enemy combatants. W. M. Flinders Petrie, *The Royal Tombs of the First Dynasty,* Part I (London: Gilbert & Rivington, 1900); W. M. Flinders Petrie, *Tombs of the Courtiers and Oxyrhynkhos* (London: British School of Archaeology in Egypt, 1925).

4   For the analysis of age and sex at death of these hundreds of sacrificial victims, see Laurel Bestock, *The Development of Royal Funerary Cult at Abydos: Two Funerary Enclosures from the Reign of King Aha* (Wiesbaden, Germany: Harrassowitz Verlag, 2009), and Ellen Morris, "Sacrifice for the State: First Dynasty Royal Funerals and the Rites at Macramallah's Rectangle," in *Performing Death: Social Analyses of Funerary Traditions in the Ancient Near East and Mediterranean,* edited by Nicola Laneri (Chicago: University of Chicago Press, 2007), 15–38, and "(Un)Dying Loyalty: Meditations on Retainer Sacrifice in Ancient Egypt and Elsewhere," in *Violence and Civilization: Studies of Social Violence in History and Prehistory,* Campbell, ed., 61–93. No one has

collated the numbers yet, but one of our UCLA graduate students, Roselyn Campbell, is writing on precisely this subject, forthcoming in 2020. While many have disputed or even denied the practice of human sacrifice in ancient Egypt, the presence of hundreds of subsidiary grave sites surrounding the tombs of the earliest kings of a unified Egyptian state suggests otherwise. By and large, the occupants of these graves are relatively healthy and middle-aged (and often male), and each king appears to have buried his retainers in a single event. Campbell's dissertation explores the identity of these individuals and how they came to be buried with their ruler. It has not been proven that these sacrificial victims were certainly family members, in particular the brothers, of the deceased king, but the evidence for high nutrition suggests elite status, while the murder of young men suggests, circumstantially and comparatively, that they were potential rivals to the new king's position.

5   Many historians apply European ideas of primogeniture to Egyptian dynastic succession uncritically. Later records indicate no hard-and-fast rules about primogeniture, much to our dismay. How the Egyptians chose their next king is a question Egyptology has yet to conclusively answer. For more on the Royal Family and the choice of next king, see Aidan Dodson and Dyan Hilton, *The Complete Royal Families of Ancient Egypt* (London and New York: Thames & Hudson, 2004).

6   There has been fierce dispute about where the "real" tombs of the Dynasty 1 kings were located: Abydos or Saqqara. Most Egyptologists assume Abydos was home to the only true royal

tombs and that the Saqqara mastabas were only for high elites. The size and interment of sacrificial grave sites at the Saqqara mastabas, however, suggest to me that both were royal installations of some kind and that we simply do not understand the nature and function of these tombs yet. For summaries of the disagreement about the nature of the Saqqara tombs and whether they were royal or not, see V. Callender, *In Hathor's Image: The Wives and Mothers of Egyptian Kings from Dynasties I–IV* (Prague: Czech Institute of Egyptology, 2011), 34. Also see Ellen Morris, "On the Ownership of the Saqqara Mastabas and the Allotment of Political and Ideological Power at the Dawn of the State," in *The Archaeology and Art of Ancient Egypt: Essays in Honor of David O'Connor*, edited by Zahi Hawass and Janet Richards (Cairo: American University in Cairo Press, 2007).

7   Grave 537 contained a skeleton whose heels were tied to his hips (according to Petrie, *Tombs of the Courtiers and Oxyrhynkhos*), and the body was then thrown into the tomb face-down over a large boulder. The position is so unusual that Petrie suggested the individual might have been buried alive, and the raised head with hand in front of the mouth was an attempt to continue breathing. I am grateful to Roselyn Campbell for her personal communication on this subject.

8   Matthew Adams has proposed the idea that cyanide dispatched these people, although further archaeological investigation is needed. John Galvin, "New Evidence Shows That Human Sacrifice Helped Populate the Royal City of the Dead," *National Geographic* (April 2005), http://ngm.national geographic.com/ngm/0504/feature7/.

9   See Petrie, *Royal Tombs of the First Dynasty*, Part I.

10 Bestock, *Development of Royal Funerary Cult at Abydos*, 49.

11 Ibid., 34.

12 Émile Amélineau, *Les Nouvelles Fouilles d'Abydos*, vol. 3, no. 1 (Paris: Leroux, 1904), 58, 104. Bestock, *Development of Royal Funerary Cult at Abydos*, 34.

13 Bestock, *Development of Royal Funerary Cult at Abydos*, 56.

14 For this object, see the Louvre website, https://www.louvre .fr/en/oeuvre-notices/stele-serpent-king.

15 Merneith's inclusion in the Palermo Stone is still debated. See Shih-Wei Hsu, "The Palermo Stone: The Earliest Royal Inscription from Ancient Egypt," *Altorientalische Forschungen* 37, no. 1 (2010), http://dx.doi.org/10.1524/aofo.2010.0006.

16 Morris, "(Un)Dying Loyalty," 85. The majority of the bodies around the funerary enclosures appear to be male, while the reverse is true of the retainers buried around the tombs. Morris, "Sacrifice for the State," 19. And see these Abydos numbers for each king, culled by Roselyn Campbell (personal communication).

	TOMB	ENCLOSURE	TOTAL
Hor-aha (Aha)	35	12	47
Djer	318	269	587
Djet	174	154	328
Queen Merneith	41?	79	120
Den	135	?	135

17 Morris, "(Un)Dying Loyalty," 85.

18 Walter B. Emery, *Excavations at Saqqara: Great Tombs of the First Dynasty* (Oxford, UK: Oxford University Press, 1954).

19 Emery, *Excavations at Saqqara,* 108.

20 The names of the sacrificed dead were written on small stelae placed into the tomb or in red paint on the interior walls of the tomb. The collection of stelae in the Petrie publication—with their roughly written names and signs at the end of the name, signifying if a man or woman is identified—is a poignant reminder of the lost lives. The dead were placed into these tombs in a fetal position, as was done in prehistoric graves, placed in square wooden boxes pegged together. The interior of the coffins contained white sand, sifted into the graves after deposition, thus surrounding each dead body with purity, almost as an atonement for the demanded sacrifice. Petrie, *Royal Tombs of the First Dynasty,* Part I, plates XXI–XXXVI.

21 Petrie, *Royal Tombs of the First Dynasty,* Part I, plate IV.

22 Hsu, "The Palermo Stone."

23 The stela was first published in Petrie, *Royal Tombs of the First Dynasty,* Part I, 11.

24 Petrie, *Tombs of the Courtiers and Oxyrhynkhos;* T. E. Peet, *Cemeteries of Abydos 2* (London: Egypt Exploration Fund, 1914), 31–32; Bestock, *Development of Royal Funerary Cult at Abydos,* 48.

25 The mastaba tomb in question is numbered Saqqara 3503 by Emery; Emery, *Excavations at Saqqara,* 139–158.

26 Bestock, *Development of Royal Funerary Cult at Abydos,* 39.

27 For this analysis, see Joyce A. Tyldesley, *Chronicle of the Queens of Egypt: From Early Dynastic Times to the Death of Cleopatra,* The Chronicles Series (London: Thames & Hudson, 2006), 26–29. For new discoveries about Neithhotep, see Owen Jarus,

"5,000-Year-Old Hieroglyphs Discovered in Sinai Desert," http://www.livescience.com/53405-wadi-ameyra-photos.html.

28 Silke Roth, *Die Königsmutter des Alten Ägypten von der Frühzeit Bis zum Ende des 12. Dynastie,* volume 46: Ägypten und Altes Testaments: Studien zur Geschichte, Kultur und Religion Ägyptens und des Alten Testaments (Wiesbaden, Germany: Harrassowitz Verlag, 2001), 377.

29 This is on the so-called MacGregor Label. R. B. Parkinson et al., *Cracking Codes: The Rosetta Stone and Decipherment* (New York: California Press, 1999), 74; A. J. Spencer, *Early Dynastic Objects, Catalogue of the Egyptian Antiquities in the British Museum* (London: British Museum Press, 1980), 65, object no. 460.

30 Pierre Tallet, *Zone Minière Pharaonique du Sud Sinaï I, Catalogue Complémentaire des Inscriptions du Sinaï* (Cairo: Institut français d'archéologie orientale du Caire, 2012), 16–18, nos. 1–3.

31 The Palermo Stone gives Den 42 years. See Wolfgang Helck, *Untersuchungen zur Thinitenzeit,* volume 35: Ägyptologische Abhandlungen (Wiesbaden, Germany: Harrassowitz Verlag, 1987). See also Hsu, "The Palermo Stone."

32 Bestock, *Development of Royal Funerary Cult at Abydos,* 38.

CHAPTER 2: NEFERUSOBEK

1 In the third century B.C., Eratosthenes wrote that Nitocris was the 22nd ruler of Thebes, that she was a queen whose name meant "Athena Is Victorious," which is close, given it means "Neith Is Excellent," and that she ruled for six years. Most compellingly, Nitocris seems to appear in the Turin king list, the name set within a cartouche like all the other leaders,

and she is called King of Upper and Lower Egypt. The Turin Canon says the king in question ruled for "two years, one month, and one day." This king list papyrus is in pieces, unfortunately, and Egyptologists have spilled much ink determining which fragments go where. See Kim Ryholt, "The Turin King-List," *Ägypten und Levante* 14 (2004): 135–155.

2   Indeed, as we will see, sometimes the strong men did have their way, including Amenemhat I at the beginning of Dynasty 12, Horemheb at the end of Dynasty 18, and Ramses I at the beginning of Dynasty 19. Ironically, one of these, Horemheb, seems to have been unable to continue his own dynasty, strong and able though he was militarily and politically. It was Ramses I who started a new family of rulers after him.

3   Although some scholars doubt the existence of such an institution in the early dynasties (see V. Callender, *In Hathor's Image: The Wives and Mothers of Egyptian Kings from Dynasties I–IV* [Prague: Czech Institute of Egyptology, 2011]), the king certainly had many wives who were documented in burial or in temple reliefs. The "harem" as an institution or structure is certainly a very controversial thing, as it brings with it the judgment of those who think women should not be compelled to serve one man. Although I do not disavow the inequality such a structure promotes, I do see the advantages it might provide to a hereditary kingship. We historians discount such advantages at our peril. I do not suggest that the ancient Egyptians had a harem like the Turks or the Chinese, but they provided their king with strategies to procreate, i.e., a collection of many young and fruitful women for his reproduction into the next generation.

4   We have no preserved harems for the Old and Middle Kingdoms, only references in texts of officials connected to such an institution, but it is possible to speak of a harem palace in the Fayum called Medinet Gurob for the New Kingdom. Ian Shaw, "The Gurob Harem Palace Project, Spring 2012," *Journal of Egyptian Archaeology* 98 (2013): 43–54.

5   Elfriede Haslauer, "Harem," in *Oxford Encyclopedia of Ancient Egypt,* edited by Donald Redford (Oxford, UK: Oxford University Press, 2000). See also Silke Roth, "Harem," in *UCLA Encyclopedia of Egyptology* (Los Angeles: UCLA, 2012), http://escholarship.org/uc/item/1k3663r3?query=harem.

6   For a popular article on this subject, see Eliza Lenz, "Ten Incendiary Facts about Incest," *ListVerse* (May 24, 2014), https://listverse.com/2014/05/22/10-incendiary-facts-about-incest/.

7   For some rare demographic analysis of ancient Egyptian human remains during pharaonic times, see Eike-Meinrad Winkler and Harald Wilfing, *Tell El-Dab'a VI, Anthropologische Untersuchungen an den Skelettresten der Kampagnen 1966–69, 1975–80, 1985* (Vienna: Verlag der Österreichischen Akademie der Wissenschaften, 1991). For an online summary and discussion of the Egyptian people and life expectancy, see http://www.reshafim.org.il/ad/egypt/people/index.html.

8   Zahi Hawass, Yehia Z. Gad, and Somaia Ismail, "Ancestry and Pathology in King Tutankhamun's Family," *Journal of the American Medical Association* 303, no. 7 (2010): 638–647.

9   The first mention of eunuchs is very late, post-pharaonic certainly, in Horapollon's *Hieroglyphica*. Diodorus of Sicily also mentions castration (*Bibliotheca Historica,* Book I). In the

New Kingdom "Tale of Two Brothers," the god Bata does cut off his penis (not his testicles), but this has a religious meaning, rather than being used as a method of real-world social control. For more on Bata's self-mutilation, see the literary story in Miriam Lichtheim, *Ancient Egyptian Literature, Volume II: The New Kingdom* (Berkeley, Los Angeles, and London: University of California Press, 1976), 203–211.

10 I would argue instead that Hetepti's lack of a King's Wife title doesn't mean she wasn't a wife; it means that she was either a younger, lesser wife or that she found it more advantageous to use a title connecting her to the reigning king than to the dead king, something we should expect. For the argument that Amenemhat IV was not a King's Son, see Kim Ryholt, *The Political Situation in Egypt During the Second Intermediate Period, c. 1800–1550 B.C.*, Carsten Niebuhr Institute Publications (Copenhagen: Museum Tusculanum Press, 1997), 209–213.

11 Three life-size basalt statues of Neferusobek were found in Tell el Da'ba, the later Hyksos stronghold—two picture her seated and one shows her kneeling with arms outstretched holding round jars. See Labib Habachi, "Khatâ'na-Qantîr: Importance," *Annales du Service des Antiquités de l'Égypte* 52 (1954): 443–559.

12 Another statuette in the Metropolitan Museum of Art (MMA 65.59.1), a small, green graywacke piece, is said by Callender to belong to Neferusobek and to show her wearing a *heb sed* cloak with a unique wig and vulture-cobra headdress. This statue has not been definitively identified with Neferusobek, and indeed Metropolitan Museum curator Isabel

Stuenkel (personal communication, 2017) disagrees with the identification as Neferusobek, choosing to think it another 12th Dynasty queen. The piece has the same high cheekbones and large ears of the Berlin statue, so perhaps they belong to the same person. The vulture and cobra headdress is certainly connected to the ruling family, but whether as female king or queen is debatable. If this statue is a representation of Neferusobek, Callender believes that this headdress was a new and unique invention of the female king to highlight her reign, a creative spirit that Nefertiti would later bring to Dynasty 18 when she ruled alongside Akhenaten as co-regent, wearing a strange flat-topped blue crown never seen before.

13 The torso matches the lower part of a statue with enthroned feminine legs and feet now in the Boston Museum of Art, and thus Egyptologists believe it might have belonged to Neferusobek, because the side of that throne is marked with the *sema tawy* motif, the plants of Upper and Lower Egypt tied together in a union that only the king could bring about. See V. G. Callender, "Materials for the Reign of Sebekneferu," in *Proceedings of the Seventh International Congress of Egyptologists, Cambridge, 3–9 September 1995*, edited by C. J. Eyre, Orientalia Lovaniensia Analecta (Leuven, Belgium: Peeters, 1998), 227–236.

14 Roland J. Leprohon, "The Programmatic Use of the Royal Titulary in the Twelfth Dynasty," *Journal of the American Research Center in Egypt* 33 (1996): 165–171.

15 Julia Budka, "Amen-Em-Hat IV, Neferu-Sobek und das Ende des Mittleren Reiches," *Kemet* 9, no. 3 (2000): 17.

16 Callender, "Materials for the Reign of Sobekneferu," 234,

figure 2; Budka, "Amen-Em-Hat IV, Neferu-Sobek und das Ende des Mittleren Reiches," 17.

17 Indeed, there has been much Egyptological discussion about whether she was really sister to King Amenemhat IV at all because she never uses the title "King's Sister," but only "King's Daughter," raising suspicion among some that Amenemhat IV might have been from outside the dynasty and married to Neferusobek only to legitimize the kingship and succession. This theory misses the important fact that no female king could ever lay strong foundations for her rule on her dead husband, but only on her dead father. But see Ryholt, *The Political Situation in Egypt During the Second Intermediate Period, c. 1800–1550 B.C.*

18 Callender, "Materials for the Reign of Sebekneferu."

19 W. M. Flinders Petrie, *Kahun, Gurob, and Hawara* (London: Kegan Paul, Trench, Trübner, 1890), 8.

20 Callender, "Materials for the Reign of Sobekneferu," 228; Sydney Aufrere, "Remarques sur la Transmission des Noms Royaux par les Traditions Orale et Écrite," *Bulletin de l'Institut Français d'Archéologie Orientale* 89 (1989): 12–13.

21 In fact, her choice of Sobek of the Fayum was calculated. Callender compares it to Hatshepsut linking her kingship to the god Amun of Thebes. Neferusobek was linking it to Sobek of the Fayum for economic and ideological reasons. Callender, "Materials for the Reign of Sobekneferu," 236.

22 Ibid., 232; Thierry De Putter, "Les Inscriptions de Semna et Koumma (Nubie): Niveaux de Crues Exceptionnelles ou d'un Lac de Retenue Artificiel du Moyen Empire?," *Studien zur Altägyptischen Kultur* 20 (1993): 255–288.

23 A. H. Gardiner, *Egypt of the Pharaohs: An Introduction* (Oxford, UK: Clarendon Press, 1961); N. Grimal, *A History of Ancient Egypt* (Oxford, UK, and Cambridge, Mass.: Blackwell, 1992), 171. For a refutation of outdated theories related to the reign of Neferusobek, see Callender, "Materials for the Reign of Sebekneferu," 229.

24 W. M. Flinders Petrie, G. A. Wainwright, and E. Mackay, *The Labyrinth Gerzeh and Mazghuneh* (London: School of Archaeology in Egypt, University College, 1912), 54. Callender notes that while the sarcophagi are later in style than 12th Dynasty, this could have been a reuse of the pyramids. Callender, "Materials for the Reign of Sobekneferu," 229.

25 Christoffer Theis, "Die Pyramiden der 13. Dynastie," *Studien zur Altägyptischen Kultur* 38 (2009): 318–319.

26 Ibid., 318; the stela in question is in Marseille (no. 223).

27 R. Engelbach, *Harageh* (London: British School of Archaeology in Egypt, University College, 1923).

CHAPTER 3: HATSHEPSUT

1 As usual, there is scholarly disagreement about the genealogy of this Royal Family. See Ann Macy Roth, "Models of Authority: Hatshepsut's Predecessors in Power," in *Hatshepsut: From Queen to Pharaoh*, edited by Catherine H. Roehrig (New Haven and London: Yale University Press, 2006).

2 Anne K. Capel and Glenn E. Markoe, eds., *Mistress of the House; Mistress of Heaven: Women in Ancient Egypt* (New York: Hudson Hills Press, 1996).

3   Mariam F. Ayad, *God's Wife, God's Servant: The God's Wife of Amun* (London and New York: Routledge, 2009).

4   The mechanisms of this rebirth are mysterious, to be sure, but the God's Wife of Amun was there to make sure that Amun of Thebes had the sexual excitement he needed to be reborn every day, in the manner of the sun god. Other high priestesses ostensibly did this at other temples throughout Egypt, but Thebes was an important center of religious power as the home to Amun's temple institution. For comparisons to other divinities of creation, Atum especially, see J. P. Allen, *Genesis in Egypt: The Philosophy of Ancient Egyptian Creation Accounts,* Yale Egyptological Studies (San Antonio, Texas: Van Siclen Books for Yale Egyptological Seminar, Yale University, 1988).

5   For an overview of temples, rituals, and priests, see B. E. Shafer, "Temples, Priests, and Rituals: An Overview," in *Temples of Ancient Egypt,* edited by B. E. Shafer (Ithaca, N.Y.: Cornell University Press, 1997).

6   G. Lecuyot and A. M. Loyrette, "La Chapelle de Ouadjmès: Rapport Préliminaire I," *Memnonia* 6 (1995): 85–93; G. Lecuyot and A. M. Loyrette, "La Chapelle de Ouadjmès: Rapport Préliminaire II," *Memnonia* 7 (1996): 111–122.

7   G. Elliot Smith, *The Royal Mummies, Catalogue Général des Antiquités Égyptiennes du Musée du Caire Nos. 61051–61100* (Cairo: Institut Français d'Archéologie Orientale, 1912).

8   Kim Ryholt, "The Turin King-List," *Ägypten und Levant* 14 (2004): 135–155.

9   For the oracle marking Thutmose III as king, also known as the Texte de la Jeunesse, see Kurt Sethe, *Urkunden Der 18.*

Dynastie, Band I, Urkunden des Ägyptischen Altertums IV (Leipzig, Germany: J. C. Hinrichsche Buchhandlung, 1906), 155–176; Piotr Laskowski, "Monumental Architecture and the Royal Building Program of Thutmose III," in David O'Connor, *Thutmose III: A New Biography,* edited by Eric H. Cline and David O'Connor (Ann Arbor: University of Michigan Press, 2006), 184.

10 See Andreas Nerlich and Albert Zink, "Leben und Krankheit im Alten Ägypten," *Bayerisches Ärzteblatt* 8 (2001): 373–376. For details on childbirth and childhood in ancient Egypt, see J. J. Janssen and Rosalind Janssen, *Growing Up in Ancient Egypt* (London: Rubicon Press, 1990).

11 For the tale of Horus and Seth, see Miriam Lichtheim, *Ancient Egyptian Literature,* Volume II: *The New Kingdom* (Berkeley, Los Angeles, and London: University of California Press, 1976).

12 This translation follows James Henry Breasted, *Ancient Records of Egypt,* volume 2 of 5 volumes (Chicago: University of Chicago Press, 1906).

13 For an overview of the men who built all these new monuments, see Betsy Bryan, "Administration in the Reign of Thutmose III," in Cline and O'Connor, eds., *Thutmose III.*

14 For discussions of Hatshepsut's regency, see Peter F. Dorman, "The Early Reign of Thutmose III: An Unorthodox Mantle of Coregency," in Cline and O'Connor, eds., *Thutmose III;* A. C. Keller, "The Joint Reign of Hatshepsut and Thutmose III," in Roehrig, ed., *Hatshepsut: From Queen to Pharaoh.*

15 David. A. Warburton, *Architecture, Power and Religion: Hatshepsut, Amun & Karnak in Context* (Zurich: LIT Verlag, 2012).

16 Roehrig, ed., *Hatshepsut: From Queen to Pharaoh,* 88.

17 For Thebes, see Luc Gabolde, "Hatshepsut at Karnak: A Woman under God's Commands," in *Creativity and Innovation in the Reign of Hatshepsut,* edited by José Galán, Betsy M. Bryan, and Peter F. Dorman, volume 69: *Studies in Ancient Oriental Civilization* (Chicago: The Oriental Institute of the University of Chicago, 2014), 33–48.

18 For this inscription, see Labib Habachi, "Two Graffiti at Sehēl from the Reign of Queen Hatshepsut," *Journal of Near Eastern Studies* 16, no. 2 (1957): 88–104. The translation follows his.

19 See the drawing by Deborah Shieh of the block discovered by Henri Chevrier at Karnak Temple in 1933, now in the Luxor Museum, in Kara Cooney, *The Woman Who Would Be King: Hatshepsut's Rise to Power in Ancient Egypt* (New York: Crown Publishing Group, 2014).

20 For discussions of Hatshepsut and her monuments, see Vanessa Davies, "Hatshepsut's Use of Tuthmosis III in Her Program of Legitimation," *Journal of the American Research Center in Egypt* 41 (2004): 55–66; Cathleen A. Keller, "The Statuary of Hatshepsut," in Roehrig, ed., *Hatshepsut: From Queen to Pharaoh,* 158–172; Christina Gil Paneque, "The Official Image of Hatshepsut during the Regency: A Political Approximation to the Office of God's Wife," *Trabajos de Egiptologa* 2 (2003): 83–98; Roehrig, ed., *Hatshepsut: From Queen to Pharaoh;* Zbigniew E. Szafranski, "Deir El-Bahari: Temple of Hatshepsut," *Polish Archaeology in the Mediterranean* 16 (2004): 223–237.

21 Dorman, "The Early Reign of Thutmose III"; Peter F. Dorman, "Hatshepsut: Princess to Queen to Co-Ruler," in

Roehrig, ed., *Hatshepsut: From Queen to Pharaoh*, 87–90; Keller, "The Statuary of Hatshepsut," 158–172

22 This text appears on Hatshepsut's Red Chapel and is in reference to the coronation. The translation is based on Warburton, *Architecture, Power and Religion*, 229. See also *La Chapelle Rouge: Le Sanctuaire de Barque D'hatshepsout,* volume I (Paris: Éditions Recherche sur les Civilisations, 2006). Her coronation is also depicted at her Deir el-Bahri Temple of Millions of Years as well as at Buhen Temple (now reconstructed at the National Museum of Sudan in Khartoum) since the creation of Lake Nasser.

23 Warburton, *Architecture, Power and Religion*, 229–230.

24 J. P. Allen, "The Role of Amun," in Roehrig, ed., *Hatshepsut: From Queen to Pharaoh*.

25 David Loades, *Elizabeth I: The Golden Reign of Gloriana* (London: The National Archives, 2003), 36–37.

26 Rory McCarthy, "I Never Asked for Power," *The Guardian,* August 14, 2002, https://www.theguardian.com/world/2002/aug/15/gender.pakistan.

27 Johnathan Van Meter, "Her Brilliant Career," *Vogue,* December 2009.

28 The translation is based on Lichtheim, *Ancient Egyptian Literature,* Volume II, 28.

29 Translation follows Allen, "The Role of Amun," 84.

30 Roehrig, ed., *Hatshepsut: From Queen to Pharaoh*, 99.

31 Only scraps of this building activity remain, but this motivation is suggested in Luc Gabolde, *Monuments Décorés en Bas Relief, aux Noms de Thoutmosis II et Hatchepsout à Karnak* (Le Caire,

France: Institute français d'archéologie orientale, 2005).

32 Sethe, *Urkunden Der 18. Dynastie.*

33 For all the theories surrounding the enigmatic figure of Senenmut, see Peter F. Dorman, *The Monuments of Senenmut: Problems in Historical Methodology* (New York: Kegan Paul International, 1988).

34 Cooney, *Woman Who Would Be King*, 176–179.

35 Lana Troy, *Patterns of Queenship in Ancient Egyptian Myth and History* (Uppsala, Sweden: Acta Universitatis Upsaliensis, 1986).

36 For discussions of the Middle Kingdom model that Neferusobek provided to Hatshepsut, see Julia Budka, "Amen-Em-Hat IV, Neferu-Sobek und das Ende des Mittleren Reiches," *Kemet* 9, no. 3 (2000): 16–19; Dimitri Laboury, "How and Why Did Hatshepsut Invent the Image of Her Royal Power?," in *Creativity and Innovation in the Reign of Hatshepsut*, Studies in Ancient Oriental Civilization (Chicago: Oriental Institute/ University of Chicago, 2014), 49–92.

37 See, in particular, Betsy M. Bryan, "Administration in the Reign of Thutmose III," in *Thutmose III: A New Biography*, edited by Eric H. Cline and David O'Connor (Ann Arbor: University of Michigan Press, 2006), 101–107; Anthony Spalinger, "Covetous Eyes South: The Background to Egypt's Domination in Nubia by the Reign of Thutmose III," in Cline and O'Connor, eds., *Thutmose III*, 344–369.

38 Warburton, *Architecture, Power and Religion*; Alexandra V. Mironova, "The Relationship between Space and Scenery of an Egyptian Temple: Scenes of the Opet Festival and the Festival of Hathor at Karnak and Deir El-Bahari under

Hatshepsut and Thutmose III," *MOSAIK*, no. 1 (2010): 279–330.

39 Z. Wysocki, "The Upper Court Colonnade of Hatshepsut's Temple at Deir El-Bahari," *Journal of Egyptian Archaeology* 66 (1980): 54–69.

40 Howard Carter, "A Tomb Prepared for Queen Hatshepsut and Other Recent Discoveries at Thebes," *Journal of Egyptian Archaeology* 4, nos. 2/3 (1917): 107–118.

41 Christian E. Loeben, *Beobachtungen zu Kontext und Funktion Königlicher Statuen im Amun-Tempel von Karnak* (Leipzig, Germany: Wodtke und Stegbauer, 2001). Also see the colossal statues at the eighth pylon, at the website of Karl H. Leser, "Maat-ka-Ra Hatshepsut," http://maat-ka-ra.de/.

42 Ann Macy Roth, "Erasing a Reign," in Roehrig, ed., *Hatshepsut: From Queen to Pharaoh*, 277–284.

43 Tim Murphy and Tasneem Raja, "Ladies Last: 8 Inventions by Women That Dudes Got Credit For," *Mother Jones* (October 2013), http://motherjones.com/media/2013/10/ada-lovelace-eight-inventions-women-erasure-credit.

CHAPTER 4: NEFERTITI

1 There is fierce debate about the length of the co-regency of Amenhotep III, some arguing it lasted just a few years (William J. Murnane, *Ancient Egyptian Coregencies* [Chicago: The Oriental Institute of the University of Chicago, 1977], 123–169; 231–233), some contending that it lasted at least seven years (James Allen, "Further Evidence for the Coregency of Amenhotep III and IV?" *Göttinger Miszellen* 140

[1994]: 7–8), and still others claiming it extended for as long as 12 years, into the shift of his capital city (Ray Johnson, "Images of Amenhotep III in Thebes: Styles and Intentions," in *The Art of Amenhotep III: Art Historical Analysis,* edited by L. M. Berman [Cleveland: Cleveland Museum of Art; University of Indiana Press, 1990], 26–46). For a fuller roundtable discussion on the topic, see James Allen, William Murnane, and Jacobus van Dijk, "Further Evidence for the Coregency of Amenhotep III and IV: Three Views on a Graffito Found at Dahshur," *Amarna Letters* 3 (1994): 26–31. Most Egyptologists side with a short to medium co-regency. For the purposes of this chapter, I am sidelining any discussion of this controversial topic. In many ways, any length of co-regency would work for the arguments about Nefertiti I have set forth here.

2 Betsy M. Bryan, "The Statue Program for the Mortuary Temple of Amenhotep III," in *The Temple in Ancient Egypt,* edited by Stephen Quirke (London: British Museum Press, 1997), 57–81.

3 See Dimitri Laboury, *Akhenaton and Ancient Egypt in the Amarna Era* (Cambridge, UK: Cambridge University Press, 2017), 224.

4 See Claude Traunecker, "Nefertiti, la Reine sans Nom," in *Akhenaton et l'Epoque Amarnienne,* edited by Thierry-Louise Bergerot (Paris: Khéops; Centre d'égyptologie, 2005), 135–144.

5 For this extraordinary idea, see Laboury, *Akhenaton and Ancient Egypt in the Amarna Era,* 232.

6 Cyril Aldred suggested that Akhenaten suffered from Froehlich's syndrome (*Akhenaten, King of Egypt* [London: Thames &

Hudson, 1988]). Alwyn L. Burridge suggested Marfan's syndrome ("Did Akhenaten Suffer from Marfan's Syndrome?" in *Akhenaten Temple Project Newsletter* no. 3 [September 1995]: 3-4). Dominic Montserrat suggests that none of his depicted deformities are to be read literally but rather metaphorically, as a being who is both male and female. (See his *Akhenaten: History, Fantasy and Ancient Egypt* [London and New York: Routledge, 2001].) For a distillation of these medical-Egyptological theories, see Megaera Lorenz, "The Mystery of Akhenaten: Genetics or Aesthetics?," http://www.heptune.com/Marfans.html.

7   Zahi Hawass, Yehia Z. Gad, and Somaia Ismail, "Ancestry and Pathology in King Tutankhamun's Family," *Journal of the American Medical Association* 303, no. 7 (2010): 638–645.

8   Dorothea Arnold, J. P. Allen, and L. Green, *The Royal Women of Amarna: Images of Beauty from Ancient Egypt* (New York: Metropolitan Museum of Art, distributed by Harry N. Abrams, 1996).

9   To be clear, I suggest that Amenhotep IV's body and face distortion were meant to communicate a body shaped by bright light on display to his elite populace, probably within a window of appearance. Amenhotep IV even commissioned an entire series of bizarre new colossal statues that mimicked how the king and queen would have appeared in just such a window of appearance, as the sun rose behind them. Nefertiti may have been depicted as one of these colossal figures, in which form she seems to stand naked, holding the crook and flail, covered with the Aten's cartouche names on her chest and arms. The crown of this statue is now broken, but if the piece were whole, it might have represented Nefertiti as the

Egyptian goddess Tefnut, wearing the double crown like the goddess Mut of Karnak. Nicholas Reeves, *Akhenaten: Egypt's False Prophet* (London: Thames & Hudson, 2001), 165–166. John R. Harris originally suggested the female depiction hypothesis. See J. R. Harris, "Akhenaten or Nefertiti?," *Acta Orientalia* 38 (1977): 5–10. For similar ideas that Akhenaten's artistic imagery is suffused with light and movement, see Montserrat, *Akhenaten: History, Fantasy and Ancient Egypt*, 48, and Erik Hornung's *Akhenaten and the Religion of Light* (Ithaca, N.Y.: Cornell University Press, 1999), 44.

10 None of this dissent was written by elites; it must, however, have been verbally communicated to their king because he vaguely records his reaction to "bad" or "offensive" words in his earliest boundary stelae, now quite broken: "If I heard a report in the mouth of an official, in the mouth of . . . , in the mouth of . . . , in the mouth of a Nubian, in the mouth of any people . . . against [my] fath[er] to . . . , [they] were offensive . . ." He also goes on about how no one will tell him where to put his capital city except according to the will of his father, the Aten. He states, "Now it is the Aten, my father, who advised me concerning it, [namely] Akhet-Aten. No official had ever advised me concerning it, to tell me [a plan] for making Akhet-Aten in this distant place . . ." And he continues, "Nor shall the King's Chief Wife say to me, 'Look, there's a nice place for Akhet-Aten someplace else,' nor shall I listen to her. Nor shall any officials in my presence—be they officials of favor or officials of the outside, or the chamberlains, or any people of the entire land—say to me, 'Look, there's a nice

place for Akhet-Aten someplace else,' nor shall I listen to them . . ." These boundary stelae were written largely in the king's own first person voice. He proceeds to record that people spoke against him in Year 4, in Year 3, even before that, and even, he tells us, in the reigns of his predecessors, Thutmose III and Thutmose IV. He seems to be speaking against priestly intervention or the false advising of court functionaries, implying that this kind of overreach was suffered by his kingly ancestors as well. It seems important for Amenhotep IV to point out that he was not alone in dealing with recalcitrant advisers. All this dissent, described in the stelae as "bad words" probably emanated from the strongholds of the old gods. In the end, these expressions of doubt, these "bad words," were enough to make the king abandon all the time and work he had put into his new Aten complexes, and move on. For these translations of the boundary stelae, see William J. Murnane, *Texts from the Amarna Period in Egypt*, Writings from the Ancient World Series (Atlanta: Society of Biblical Literature, 1995), 73–81.

11 See, however, Jacquelyn Williamson, who considers this depiction of the queen alone as lacking in power, compared to what would come later. Jacquelyn Williamson, "Alone before the God: Gender, Status and Nefertiti's Image," *Journal of the American Research Center in Egypt* 51 (2015): 179–192.

12 For instance, see Jan Assmann, "Semiosis and Interpretation in Ancient Egyptian Ritual," in S. Biderman and B. Scharfstein, *Interpretation in Religion* (Leiden, New York, and Cologne: Brill, 1992), 87–109.

13   Thutmose III recorded an account of the battle at Megiddo
     and his other Asiatic campaigns on two walls at the Temple
     of Karnak behind pylon VI. In his account he tells how he
     asked his advisers which road they should take to meet the
     enemy—a narrow road, leading straight to the enemy, or a
     road that would allow them to avoid meeting the enemy
     head-on in close quarters. His advisers fearfully advise him
     not to take the narrow road, but the king rejects their advice
     and boldly declares that he will not only meet the enemy on
     this narrow road, he will lead the army into the battle him-
     self. For a translation of Thutmose III's account of the
     battle at Megiddo, see Miriam Lichtheim, *Ancient Egyptian
     Literature,* Volume II: *The New Kingdom* (Berkeley, Los Ange-
     les, and London: University of California Press, 1976),
     29–35.

14   Most of what we know about the timing of Akhenaten's
     move to his new city comes from his many boundary stelae,
     the first of which was written in regnal Year 5 and the last
     in Year 8, giving a range for scholars to debate whether the
     king moved into the city immediately with the identification
     of the site and subsequent carving of the first stela or if he
     waited until more of the city was built. See Murnane, *Texts
     from the Amarna Period in Egypt,* 73–87. For the city as a whole,
     see Barry Kemp, *The City of Akhenaten and Nefertiti: Amarna and
     Its People* (New York: Thames & Hudson, 2012).

15   For some recent reports on archaeological work at the cem-
     eteries of Amarna, see Anna Stevens, Gretchen Dabbs, and
     Jerome Rose, "Akhenaten's People: Excavating the Lost

Cemeteries of Amarna," *Current World Archaeology*, no. 78 (2016); Anna Stevens, Mary Shepperson, and Anders Bettum, "The Cemeteries of Amarna," *Journal of Egyptian Archaeology* 101 (2015): 17–34.

16 For the Amarna letters, see William L. Moran, *The Amarna Letters* (Baltimore: Johns Hopkins University Press, 1992) and Anson F. Rainey, *The El-Amarna Correspondence: A New Edition of the Cuneiform Letters from the Site of El-Amarna Based on Collations of All Extant Tablets*, edited by William M. Schniedewind and Zipora Cochavi-Rainey. Handbook of Oriental Studies, section 1: "The Near and Middle East," Volume 110 (Leiden and Boston: Brill, 2014).

17 Made by a military officer named Paser. For more, see Reeves, *Akhenaten: Egypt's False Prophet*, 167–168. The erroneous idea that Akhenaten was homosexual was corrected by J. R. Harris, in "Nefertiti Rediviva," *Acta Orientalia* 35 (1973): 5–13.

18 For more on this "pharaohcentrism," see Dmitri Laboury, *Akhenaton* (Paris: Pygmalion 2010), 236.

19 For the idea that the marriage bed was a place of sacred ritual for Akhenaten, see Laboury, *Akhenaton*, 232.

20 Stevens, Dabbs, and Rose, "Akhenaten's People."

21 The spaces for his courtiers were not formally organized, and it seems he let them do as they liked, allowing an organic sprawl of houses and workshops that developed as time went on. See Kemp, *The City of Akhenaten and Nefertiti*. Nonetheless, Amarna has been characterized as more of a Versailles than a Paris, according to Laboury, *Akhenaton*, 265.

22 Reeves, *Akhenaten: Egypt's False Prophet,* 160.

23 There is a debate about whether the title of Great Royal Wife, as attached to Akhenaten's daughters, implies a sexual relationship. Some Egyptologists (for instance, Gay Robins, *Women in Ancient Egypt* [London: British Museum Press, 1993], 21–27) indicate this was in name only and in no way actually practiced. I, however, am of the opinion that Egyptian marriage was not a religious rite of passage, but a sexual one. For the Royal Family, marriage between male and female implied sexual congress for reproductive purposes.

24 For instance, see Marc Gabolde, *D'Akhenaton à Toutânkhamon* (Lyon, France: Université Lumière-Lyon 2, Institut d'Archéologie et d'Histoire de l'Antiquité, 1998), 171.

25 Nicholas Reeves points out it was Henri Gauthier in 1912 who first made this connection, abandoned by most Egyptologists, then proved by John R. Harris in 1973. Reeves, *Akhenaten: Egypt's False Prophet,* 170. J. R. Harris, "Neferneferuaten," *Göttinger Miszellen* 4 (1973): 15–17.

26 Reeves, *Akhenaten: Egypt's False Prophet,* 172–173.

27 For this stela in the Petrie Museum at University College London, numbered UC 410, see James P. Allen. "The Amarna Succession," in *Causing His Name to Live: Studies in Egyptian Epigraphy and History in Memory of William J. Murnane,* edited by P. Brand (Leiden, Netherlands: Brill, 2009), 9–20.

28 Arielle Kozloff, "Bubonic Plague in the Reign of Amenhotep III?," *KMT* (2006): 36–46.

29 Laboury, *Akhenaton,* 325.

30 As Nicholas Reeves puts it, "Fearful of being found in

possession of such seditious items, the owners themselves gouged or ground out the three offending signs which artic-ulated the god Amun's name, even in tiny cartouches con-taining the old king's birth name. Such displays of frightened self-censorship and toadying loyalty are ominous indicators of the paranoia which was beginning to grip the country." *Akhenaten: Egypt's False Prophet,* 154.

31 Ibid., 155. W. G. Waddell, *Manetho* (London: W. Heinemann Ltd., 1940), 131.

32 There is evidence that, as co-king, Nefertiti split her time between Akhetaten and the old strongholds, including Thebes. One text, a graffito at the tomb of Pawah (Theban Tomb 139) in western Thebes, dated to Year 3 of King Neferneferuaten, indicates that worship of Amun was allowed at Thebes again at a certain point, either in Year 3 of her co-regency, or later, in Year 3 of her sole reign, since she appears in this text alone. The graffito in question includes a hymn to the god Amun, the Hidden One of Karnak Temple, recording the grief that had been inflicted on the Egyptian people. A selection reads: "Come back to us, O lord of con-tinuity. You were here before anything had come into being, and you will be here when they are gone. As you have caused me to see the darkness that is yours to give, make light for me so that I can see you. As your Ka endures and as your handsome, beloved face endures, you shall come from afar and cause this servant, the scribe Pawah, to see you." This text almost certainly refers to the eclipse occurring in 1338 B.C., during the last years of Akhenaten's reign, and underscores

that the Theban god Amun, the god of Hiddenness, was the one who blotted out the sun. Akhenaten witnessed an open challenge to his religion, not from his people but from the heavenly bodies themselves. It seems he could not recover. For this translation, see Murnane, *Texts from the Amarna Period in Egypt*, 207–208.

33 For this estimate of the ages of the Royal Family, see Laboury, *Akhenaton*, 329.

34 Akhenaten's burial is scattered now, and the king was almost certainly moved from Tell el Amarna to Thebes, with many Akhenaten funerary objects found in KV 55, in particular (see M. R. Bell, "An Armchair Excavation of KV 55," *Journal of the American Research Center in Egypt* 27 [1990]: 97–137). It is even possible that the body of Akhenaten was found in KV 55; it has been so identified by Zahi Hawass. See Hawass, Gad, and Ismail, "Ancestry and Pathology in King Tutankhamun's Family."

35 The American school is dominated by James P. Allen ("The Amarna Succession," in Brand, ed., *Causing His Name to Live*). The British school is currently led by Nicholas Reeves (*Akhenaten: Egypt's False Prophet*), but Aidan Dodson follows a different understanding of Amarna history and succession from Reeves (see his *Amarna Sunrise* [Cairo: The American University in Cairo Press, 2014] and *Amarna Sunset* [Cairo: The American University in Cairo Press, 2009]). The French school is now headed by Dmitri Laboury (*Akhenaton*), much of which is influenced by Marc Gabolde (*D'Akhenaton à Toutânkhamon*).

36 There are few Egyptologists who connect Smenkhkare with

Nefertiti, but Nicholas Reeves is a notable exception. Most Egyptologists, including James Allen ("Amarna Succession") and Aidan Dodson (*Amarna Sunset*), see Smenkhkare and Neferneferuaten as two separate people. However, for Smenkhkare not to have been Nefertiti, there had to have been two kings with the same throne name, Ankhkheperure, as well as two different kings who shared the Great Royal Wife Meritaten.

There is also a huge amount of disagreement over the order of Neferneferuaten and Smenkhkare, with Dodson assuming that Neferneferuaten *followed* Smenkhkare, not the other way around. The biggest argument in favor of Neferneferuaten coming first in kingly order, however, is Reeves's argument that Tutankhamun was buried in objects reused from Neferneferuaten, indicating, from his perspective, that when Neferneferuaten became Smenkhkare, she abandoned her burial equipment in favor of something better, something that hasn't been found yet, because this tomb has still not been located by archaeologists. See Reeves, "The Burial of Nefertiti?" *Amarna Royal Tombs Project, Occasional Paper No. 1* (2015), and Reeves, "Tutankhamun's Mask Reconsidered," *Bulletin of the Egyptological Seminar* 19 (2015): 511–526. The results of a third radar examination of Tutankhamun's tomb by an Italian team led by Francesco Porcelli were announced in May 2018 as categorically disproving Reeves's theory of further chambers. This conclusion was based on the inability of Porcelli's radar to detect any voids during a spring 2017 survey of the site employing electrical resistivity tomography

(ERT). Significantly, an English team, as part of the third radar investigation and employing very different, more powerful long wave technology, has at the time of writing (July 2018) yet to report. The jury on Reeves's proposal must be considered still very much out.

37 See Norman de Garis Davies, *The Rock Tombs of el Amarna* (London: Egypt Exploration Fund, 1903). The tomb was built between Years 12 and 15, but decorations could, of course, have been added later or changed. Most Egyptologists doubt any new building or decoration at Tell el Amarna after Year 15, or at least there is not any evidence of it. If, however, the tomb of Meryre II was altered in Year 17, when Neferneferuaten became Smenkhkare, an updated relief would fit with the above argument. Otherwise, this image of the female Smenkhkare puts this king's reign during the Amarna habitation and during the reign of Akhenaten, which is problematic for the argument above.

38 New analysis of Tutankhamun's many statues or those of Ay or Horemheb may show they were originally commissioned by Smenkhkare or some other earlier king, in the same way that recent analysis has shown that the burial equipment of Tutankhamun was originally made for an earlier king. Indeed, I suggest that the colossal Cairo statue (JE 59869), thought to be Tutankhamun or Ay, was originally an Amenhotep III statue, recarved by Nefertiti as king, probably as Smenkhkare. There is dark-red lip color on this piece, as on Nefertiti's Berlin bust. The nose has been redone, also similar to her Berlin bust. This statue bears the cartouche of Horem-

heb, but has been dated to Tutankhamun based on style.

39 However, see Hawass, Gad, and Ismail, "Ancestry and Pathology in King Tutankhamun's Family," in which Nefertiti is identified with the mummy called the Younger Lady, matched to Tutankhamun through DNA evidence.

40 There is even some evidence from the tomb of Tutankhamun for a close relationship with Neferneferuaten and Smenkhkare, including a globular vase (JE 62172) inscribed with the double names of Akhenaten and Smenkhkare, perhaps highlighting Tutankhamun's (grand)mother and father (Horst Beinlich and Mohamed Saleh, *Corpus der Hieroglyphischen Inschriften aus dem Grab des Tutanchamun* [Oxford, UK: Griffith Institute, 1989]). Many other objects—including coffins, mask, and organ coffinettes—indicate they were reused from Ankhkheperure Neferneferuaten. The golden throne of Tutankhamun also provides a kind of archaeological stratigraphy from the last part of Akhenaten's reign forward, as each occupier of it changed its decoration to fit his or her needs. Nicholas Reeves proved these reuses in a lecture called "The Gold Throne of Tutankhamun," presented at New York University for the American Research Center in Egypt on June 19, 2014. Reeves argues that the throne was originally made for Akhenaten's wife, Nefertiti Neferneferure. It was then altered to fit her as co-regent, Ankhkheperure Neferneferure, then changed to fit the next king, Ankhkheperure Smenkhkare, presumably when she served as sole king, and then finally altered again to be used as throne for the boy-king, Nebkheperure Tutankhaten,

soon to have his name changed to Nebkheperure Tutankhamun. Confusing, to say the least, but it's the most convincing
proof of Nefertiti's changing roles through time—from
queen, to co-king, and then to king on her own. This throne
was always hers until it was given to Tutankhamun.

41 The amount of ink spilled trying to connect this Hittite history with Egyptian history is great. The queen's dead king-
husband is called Niphururiya in the Hittite text, which could
link up with Nebkheperure Tutankhamun. Nicholas Reeves
sees Nefertiti as the candidate for the queen (see *Akhenaten:
Egypt's False Prophet,* 176–177). But others find it more likely
that the story refers to Ankhesenamun, the wife of Tutankhamun, because she had to marry her "servant," presumably the
nonroyal man Ay. Neither Nefertiti nor Meritaten married a
servant, as far as we know (Aldred, *Akhenaten, King of Egypt,*
297). Another theory is that Akhenaten's daughter Meritaten
is the queen of the whole affair, who after the death of her
father-husband Akhenaten did not want to tie herself to her
younger brother, the supposed "servant." According to this
theory, Zananza did indeed show up in Egypt, only to become
the mysterious and short-lived Smenkhkare (Gabolde,
D'Akhenaton à Toutânkhamon, 187–191). The many permutations
into which this particular evidence can be twisted is confusing
indeed.

42 The third-century B.C. priest-historian Manetho remains
the most famous keeper of a historically accurate king list—
warts, heretics, and all—passed down to us today only in the
quotes of later classical authors. Manetho tells us about a

certain Amenophis who ruled for 30 years, 10 months, whom we can conjecture was Amenhotep III. The next king in Manetho's list is a certain Orus who ruled for 36 years, five months, probably Amenhotep IV, soon to become Akhenaten. The next king in Manetho's list is "his daughter Acencheres," who ruled for 12 years, one month, followed by her brother Rathotis, who ruled for nine years. If this "daughter" Acencheres was Nefertiti (especially given her throne name Ankhkheperure), Rathotis could be identified as Tutankhamun. The kings after Rathotis are two male kings, named Acencheres I and II, who might actually be Ay and Horemheb. The female power preserved in Manetho's history fits very well with what we know of the Amarna time period. See Waddell, *Manetho,* 102–103.

43 Indeed, the only other place I have seen a cobra and vulture on the forehead of a monarch is on a queen, particularly that of 19th Dynasty Nefertari at her Abu Simbel Small Temple (C. Desroches-Noblecourt and C. Kuentz, *Le Petit Temple d'Abou Simbel,* 2 volumes. [Cairo: Ministère de la Culture/ Centre de documentation et d'étude sur l'ancienne Égypte, 1968]); Marco Zecchi, *Abu Simbel: Aswan and the Nubian Temples* (Cairo: The American University in Cairo Press, 2004).

44 Here Nicholas Reeves and I disagree. He believes the face plate was removed and reinstalled with the portrait of the boy-king Tutankhamun. I suggest that the mask was buried with Nefertiti's face. It matches all the other coffins in the coffin set. All the other coffins show evidence of reuse, ostensibly for Tutankhamun, as they were taken from Nefertiti's assemblage

prepared for her as co-king. Thus, if portraits match from coffins to mask to coffinettes, I suggest all were made for Nefertiti as co-king and then adapted for Tutankhamun in name inscriptions—without adaptations to the face plates of any piece. Also, note that Ray Johnson and Marc Gabolde agree with Nicholas Reeves on the traces of the original inscription for Neferneferuaten, beneath the hieroglyphs of Tutankhamun's name. The Tutankhamun mask was clearly reused from this previous ruler. See Reeves, "Tutankhamun's Mask Reconsidered."

Chapter 5: Tawosret

1. It's astounding that we can even talk about the many sons of Ramses II at all, when previous 18th Dynasty kings only named their heir. Merneptah succeeded his father, Ramses II, but he is named as the 13th son in most temple depictions, farther down the line than one would expect. For Merneptah's place among Ramses II's many other sons, all ostensibly in competition (overt or hidden) with one another during their father's long reign, see Kenneth A. Kitchen, *Pharaoh Triumphant: The Life and Times of Ramesses II, King of Egypt* (London: Warminster, 1983), 97–124.

2. Aidan Dodson, *Poisoned Legacy: The Fall of the Nineteenth Egyptian Dynasty* (Cairo: The American University in Cairo Press, 2016), 9.

3. Ramses II did marry one of his sisters, a certain Hentmire, but she is little mentioned and had no position of power. See Kitchen, *Pharaoh Triumphant*, 98.

4. See, for instance, the reconstructions for Dynasty 19 posited

by Aidan Dodson and Dyan Hilton in their *Complete Royal Families of Ancient Egypt* (London: Thames & Hudson, 2004), 158–183.

5   For more on the Bronze Age Collapse, see Eric Cline, *1177 B.C.: The Year Civilization Collapsed* (Princeton, N.J.: Princeton University Press, 2014).

6   For more on the Sea Peoples, see Eric Cline and David O'Connor, *Mysterious Lands* (London: University College London Press, 2003); R. D'Amato and A. Salimbeti, *The Sea Peoples of the Mediterranean Bronze Age 1450–1100 B.C.* (London: Osprey, 2015).

7   For a translation of this stela, see Miriam Lichtheim, *Ancient Egyptian Literature,* Volume II: *The New Kingdom* (Berkeley: University of California Press, 1976), 73–78.

8   For a summary discussion of ancient Egypt and the Exodus, see Kent R. Weeks, *The Lost Tomb* (New York: William Morrow, 1998), 275–279.

9   Dodson, *Poisoned Legacy,* 31–46.

10   A tomb in the Valley of the Kings may not seem like such a big deal, but in this age of anti-women-in-power it was an unprecedented funerary honor given to a Great Royal Wife. It is hard to account for it. One Egyptologist has even suggested that Tawosret must have been older than Seti II, providing her with a position almost like that of a co-ruler, thus explaining this tomb, so strange was this gift of final resting place among kings (C. H. Roehrig, "Forgotten Treasures: Tausret as Seen in Her Monuments," in *Tausret: Forgotten Queen and Pharaoh of Egypt,* edited by Richard H.

Wilkinson [Oxford, UK: Oxford University Press, 2012],
50–51). However, for Roehrig's reconstruction of history
to work, Seti II would not have been an established man
when he took the throne but rather a boy-king, one of the
last sons Merneptah was able to produce in his harem. This
is not the historical reconstruction taken in this narrative,
but it provides an indication of how contested this history
remains.

11 The royal names Amunmesses took upon his accession to
the throne were all Theban, including "Great of Might Who
Makes Thebes Great for the One Who Created Him" or
"Amunmesses Ruler of Thebes." See Jürgen von Beckerath,
Handbuch der Ägyptischen Königsnamen (Mainz, Germany: Philipp
von Zabern, 1999), 158–159. Amunmesses was not a man to
tell half truths, apparently; he claimed only what he had won:
the South. He likely planned his assault of the North, ready
to change his throne names later to reflect his expanding rule
over all of Egypt when he took the Delta, too.

12 The texts from Deir el Medina, the village that housed the
workmen who actually built and decorated all those royal
Theban tombs, named the rival king "Mese" or "Mose," probably a shortened version of Amunmesses. Why this familiarity
and lack of formality was used is unclear, but they certainly did
what the man ordered, usurper or not. Indeed, the similarity
to the name Moses of the biblical narrative has been enough
to elicit scholarly attention to other similar details, such as a
revolt against the king (R. Krauss, *Moïse le Pharaon* [Monaco:
Editions du Rocher, 2000]). Still, Amunmesses' base of sup-

port was southern, Nubian, not Levantine or Canaanite. It would be Seti II and Tawosret who would connect themselves to Canaanite mercenary forces and administrative aid, not Amunmesses. Maybe Mose wasn't Amunmesses at all, but someone else. See Dodson, *Poisoned Legacy,* 58–67.

13 Dodson, *Poisoned Legacy,* figure 72.

14 No matter how xenophobic it was, Egypt had always been a place where Egyptianization was possible. It was the degree of foreign look and cultural manner that was the problem, not whether one was light- or dark-skinned. It was about how one dressed, behaved, and spoke. But proper Egyptianization demanded time. It seems that either Bay had not been in Egypt long enough or he still held firm to his non-Egyptian cultural ways. For examples of this process in the Levant, see Carolyn R. Higginbotham, *Egyptianization and Elite Emulation in Ramesside Palestine* (Leiden, Boston, and Cologne: Brill, 2000).

15 And this is the part of the story where we wonder if Siptah was Seti II's son at all. Let's go through the facts. King lists and reign lengths provide a reign of less than six years for Seti II, only enough time to produce a five-year-old with his newly established harem, if there was a wish to circum-vent Seti II's established sons. Siptah's mummy shows a man of around 15 or 16 years of age; since Seti II ruled for just six years, Siptah's mummy would show only a 10- or 11-year-old child if he was from Seti II's new harem. Was Siptah from Seti II's wife from his earlier life? Seti II's sons with that wife, Takhat, were potentially all adults with established positions, and Takhat was potentially beyond

childbearing years, even before Seti II took the throne. Given the conflict between Seti II and Amunmesses and recent and dramatic shifts in loyalty, Seti II's older sons may have been either dead in battle or passed over by their father, demanding that a younger son be chosen as the next king, a much younger son. Some Egyptologists even see Siptah as a son of Amunmesses, thus a grandson of Seti II, and a compromise as king, a kind of fresh start between the warring factions engaged in so much civil discord. Dodson, *Poisoned Legacy*, 93.

16 Some suggest that Siptah's mother was called Sutijya and have used the name to argue that she originated in Syria, too, having been brought into the Egyptian harem as a girl (Thomas Schneider, "Siptah und Beja: Neubeurteilung einer Historischen Konstellation," *Zeitschrift der Ägyptischen Sprache* 130 [2003]: 134–146); Callender, "Queen Tausret and the End of Dynasty 19," *Studien zur Altägyptischen Kultur* 32 [2004]: 81–104).

17 Dodson, *Poisoned Legacy*, 88, figure 84.

18 Bay even set himself up as the power broker in diplomatic relations. A cuneiform text found at the great Syrian city of Ugarit called him the "Chief of the Bodyguards of the Great King of the Land of Egypt, Baya." See J. Freu, "La Tablette RS86.2230 et la Phase Finale du Royaume d'Ugarit," *Syria* 65 (1988): 395–398; Dodson, *Poisoned Legacy*, 102–103. In another text (part of a relief at Deir el Bahari at the podium of the 11th Dynasty funerary complex of Mentuhotep II), Bay told King Siptah that he "put my eye on you when you were alone," Dodson, *Poisoned Legacy*, 88; Kenneth A. Kitchen,

Ramesside Inscriptions: Historical and Biographical, volume IV (Oxford, UK: Blackwell, 1968–1990), 370.

19 According to Dodson (*Poisoned Legacy,* 100), "The nature of the relationship between Tawosret and Bay cannot be other than a matter of speculation, but the parallelism seen at Amada and implicitly in the Valley of the Kings, clearly echoes that of royal consorts. There is, of course, a temptation to declare the two lovers, or even spouses, given that the queen was a widow, and Bay without a known wife: it can only be emphasized that such conclusions cannot be any more than speculation or even historical fiction."

20 See Hartwig Altenmüller, "Tausret und Sethnacht," *Journal of Egyptian Archaeology* 68 (1982): 107–115; Altenmüller, "The Tomb of Tauber and Setnakht," in *The Treasures of the Valley of the Kings,* edited by Kent Weeks (Cairo: American University in Cairo Press, 2001), 222–231; Roehrig, "Forgotten Treasures," in Wilkinson, ed., *Tausret.*

21 Pierre Grandet, "L'Execution du Chancelier Bay. O. IFAO 1864," *Bulletin de l'Institut Français d'Archéologie Orientale* 100 (2000): 339–356.

22 See Pierre Grandet, *Le Papyrus Harris I (BM 9999)* (Cairo: Institut Français d'Archéologie Orientale, 1994), plate 76. Translation after Dodson, *Poisoned Legacy,* 90.

23 For the archaeological report on Tawosret's tomb, see Hartwig Altenmüller, "Das Grab der Königin Tausret im Tal der Könige von Theben. Erster Vorbericht über die Arbeiten des Archäologischen Instituts der Universität Hamburg im Winter 1982/83," *Studien zur Altägyptischen Kultur* 10

(1983): 1–24. For Siptah's burial, see Altenmüller, "Das Verspätete Begräbnis des Siptah," *Göttinger Miszellen* 145 (1995): 29–36; and Altenmüller "Das Präsumtive Begräbnis des Siptah," *Studien zur Altägyptischen Kultur* 23 (1996): 1–9.

24 For more on this statue, see Roehrig, "Forgotten Treasures," in Wilkinson, ed., *Tausret*, 55–58.

25 The timing is debated. See Dodson, *Poisoned Legacy*, 116–117, and Wilkinson, ed., *Tausret*, 97.

26 See Dino Bidoli, "Stele des Konig Setnacht," *Mitteilungen des Deutschen Archäologischen Instituts, Abteilung Kairo* 28 (1972): 193–200; Rosemarie Drenkhahn, *Die Elephantine-Stele des Sethnacht und ihr historischer Hintegrund* (Wiesbaden, Germany: Harrassowitz Verlag, 1980), 44–45. Translation after Dodson, *Poisoned Legacy*, 119.

27 The text in Dodson, *Poisoned Legacy*, 120, reads: "[T]he gods then inclined themselves to peace, so as to put the land in its proper state in accordance with its normal condition, and they established their son, who came forth from their flesh, as ruler of every land, upon their great throne, Userkhaure-setepenre Meryamun, son of Re Setnakht Meryre Meryamen. He was Khepri Seth when he was enraged; he set in order the entire land that had been rebellious; he killed the rebels who were in the land of Egypt. He cleansed the great throne of Egypt, being the ruler of the Two Lands on the throne of Atum."

28 For this ostracon, see Wilkinson, ed., *Tausret*, 45.

29 Susan Redford, *The Harem Conspiracy* (DeKalb, Ill.: Northern Illinois University Press, 2002); Zahi Hawass, Somaia

Ismail, Ashraf Selim, Sahar N. Saleem, Dina Fathalla, Sally Wasef, Ahmed Z. Gad, Rama Saad, Suzan Fares, Hany Amer, Paul Gostner, Yehia Z. Gad, Carsten M. Pusch, Albert R. Zink, "Revisiting the Harem Conspiracy and Death of Ramesses III: Anthropological, Forensic, Radiological, and Genetic Study," *British Medical Journal* (December 17, 2012); Pascal Vernus, *Affairs and Scandals in Ancient Egypt* (Ithaca, N.Y.: Cornell University Press, 2003), 109–120.

30 The Epigraphic Survey, *Medinet Habu,* VIII: *The Eastern High Gate* (OIP 94) (Chicago: University of Chicago Press, 1970), https://oi.uchicago.edu/research/publications/oip/medinet-habu-vol-viii-eastern-high-gate-translations-texts.

Chapter 6: Cleopatra

1 Most Greco-Roman sources for Cleopatra can be found in the handy Prudence J. Jones, *Cleopatra: A Sourcebook* (Norman: University of Oklahoma Press, 2006).

2 For more on the history and politics of the Ptolemaic period, see J. G. Manning, *The Last Pharaohs: Egypt under the Ptolomies, 305–30 BC* (Princeton, N.J.: Princeton University Press, 2009); Günther Hölbl, *A History of the Ptolemaic Empire* (London: Routledge, 2001).

3 Some might argue that Tell el-Da'ba, Tanis, and Pi-Ramses were positioned to look out of Egypt, too, and this is indeed true, from a riverine and a Levantine perspective. But these cities were nonetheless positioned well within Egypt proper, with easy access to both the urban strongholds of Memphis and the Upper Egyptian Nile Valley (see *The Archaeology,*

Geography, and History of the Egyptian Delta during the Pharaonic Period, edited by A. Nibbi [Oxford, UK: DE Publications, 1986]). Alexandria was the first Egyptian city with an outside view to the larger Mediterranean (see P. M. Fraser, *Ptolemaic Alexandria* I–III [Oxford, UK: Clarendon, 1972]).

4 For more on fiscal decisions and taxation, see chapter 5, "Creating a New Economic Order," in Joseph Manning's *The Last Pharaohs,* 117–164.

5 See, for example, L. Colliers and F. P. Retief, "Poisons, Poisoning and the Drug Trade in Ancient Rome," *Akroterion* 45 (2000): 88–100.

6 See Sheila L. Anger, "The Power of Excess: Royal Incest and the Ptolemaic Dynasty," *Anthropologica* 48, no. 2 (2006): 165–186.

7 Some maintain that Cleopatra V was Cleopatra VII's mother, but this is nowhere explicitly stated. Given the dearth of information, most choose to see Cleopatra's maternal lineage as purposefully veiled. However, Duane Roller (*Cleopatra: A Biography* [Oxford, UK: Oxford University Press, 2011], 15) boldly states, "The identity of her mother is uncertain, but she probably was a member of the Egyptian priestly family of Ptah, yet also with some Macedonian ancestry herself," himself citing Waldemar Heckel, *Who's Who in the Age of Alexander the Great: Prosopography of Alexander's Empire* (London: Blackwell, 2006), 165–166. For the first mention of this theory that Cleopatra was part Egyptian, see Werner Huß, "Die Herkunft der Kleopatra Philopator," *Aegyptus* 70 (1990): 191–203.

8   Given the uncertainty swirling around Cleopatra's mother, the queen's ethnicity is, of course, also hotly debated. Multiple ancient authors note her ability to speak Egyptian, a circumstantial piece of evidence that many scholars believe implies an Egyptian (half or full) mother, or at least exposure to Egyptian culture for some other undisclosed reason. Duane Roller (*Cleopatra*, 15) states that Cleopatra was "perhaps three-quarters Macedonian and one-quarter Egyptian, and it was probably her half-Egyptian mother who instilled in her the knowledge and respect for Egyptian culture and civilization." See also Duane Roller, "Cleopatra's True Racial Background (and Does It Really Matter?)," *Oxford University Press Blog* (December 2010), http://blog.oup.com/2010/12/cleopatra-2/.

9   Joyce Tyldesley, "Foremost of Women: The Female Pharaohs of Ancient Egypt," in *Tausret: Forgotten Queen and Pharaoh of Egypt,* edited by Richard H. Wilkinson (Oxford, UK: Oxford University Press, 2012), 22.

10   See *Ptolemy II Philadelphus and His World,* edited by P. McKechnie and P. Guillaume (Leiden, Netherlands: Brill, 2008).

11   For this confusing history from Ptolemy VI to VIII, see Hölbl, *A History of the Ptolemaic Empire,* 181–194.

12   M. Aldhouse-Green, *Boudica Britannia: Rebel, War-Leader and Queen* (Harlow, UK: Pearson Education, 2006).

13   Prudence J. Jones, "The Life of Antony," in *Cleopatra: A Sourcebook,* 101–102.

14   See Jones, *Cleopatra: A Sourcebook,* and Earnest Cary's (Loeb Classical Library) translation of Cassius Dio, book 42, from

The Roman History, http://penelope.uchicago.edu/Thayer/e/
roman/texts/cassius_dio/42*.html.

15 We only hear about how "the Romans" rejected her, but
there were many kinds of Romans. Indeed, the life force of
the growing Isis cult in the Roman Empire speaks to a
groundswell of support among non-elite Romans for Cleopatra and what she represented. Interestingly, Arab
recollections of Cleopatra elevated her to scholar, scientist,
philosopher, and freedom fighter against Roman aggression
(see Okasha El-Daly's *Egyptology: The Missing Millennium* [Lon-
don: UCL Press, 2005].

16 See Jones, *Cleopatra: A Sourcebook,* for Plutarch's account of
Antony's life, book LXII, 99–100.

17 Michel Chauveau, *Cleopatra: Beyond the Myth* (Ithaca, N.Y.:
Cornell University Press, 2002), 60.

18 See references to Plutarch's "Life of Antony," in Jones, *Cleopatra: A Sourcebook,* 36, 55, 58–59, 140.

19 See Mary Boatwright, *The Romans from Village to Empire*
(Oxford, UK: Oxford University Press, 2004), 269–271.

20 Duane W. Roller, *Cleopatra: A Biography* (Oxford, UK: Oxford
University Press, 2011), 99.

21 See Cassius Dio, *Roman History* 50.4.3–6 in Jones, *Cleopatra: A
Sourcebook,* 147–149: "[Antony] seemed to have been put
under her spell, for she so bewitched and captivated not only
him but also all his advisors that she hoped to rule the Romans
... they voted to declare war on Cleopatra, but they declared
no such thing against Antony, as they knew that he would
become an enemy on his own (for he was not about to betray

Cleopatra and take Octavian's side). They also wished to hold the following against him: that he of his own accord went to war against his own country on the Egyptian queen's account, although his countrymen had not provoked him at all."

22 For ancient texts from the Battle of Actium, see Jones, *Cleopatra: A Sourcebook*, 147–179.

23 For the accounts of Cleopatra's supposed suicide by Florus and Cassius Dio, see Jones, *Cleopatra: A Sourcebook*, 190.

24 The death of Cleopatra is treated in Jones, *Cleopatra: A Sourcebook*, 180–201.

25 Plutarch says that Cleopatra died at age 39 in "Life of Antony," 85–86. See also Jones, *Cleopatra: A Sourcebook*, 194.

26 Read Suetonius's account of this event from *The Divine Augustus,* 17.3–18 in Jones, *Cleopatra: A Sourcebook*, 201.

27 Cassius Dio, *Roman History,* 25.1, suggested Ptolemy was assassinated because Caligula was jealous of his wealth, while Suetonius in his history, *Caligula,* 35.2, pointed to a theater crowd's admiration of Ptolemy's purple cloak as the inspiration for Caligula's ire. Later historians, such as Anthony A. Barrett, indicate that Ptolemy's assassination might have been politically motivated. See Cassius Dio, *Roman History,* Volume VII: Books 56–60, trans. Carey; Suetonius, *The Lives of the Twelve Caesars,* translated by John Carew Rolfe (Loeb Classical Library); and Barrett, *Caligula: The Abuse of Power* (London: Routledge, 2015), 159–160.

28 For more on the life of Zenobia, see Patricia Southern, *Empress Zenobia: Palmyra's Rebel Queen* (New York: Continuum, 2008); Patricia Southern, *The Roman Empire from Severus to*

Constantine (London: Routledge, 2001); and Richard Stoneman, *Palmyra and Its Empire: Zenobia's Revolt Against Rome* (Ann Arbor: University of Michigan, 1994).

29 Hugh Bowden, *Mystery Cults of the Ancient World* (Princeton. N.J.: Princeton University Press, 2010); Kathrin Kleibl, *Iseion: Raumgestaltung und Kultpraxis in den Heiligtümern Gräco-Ägyptischer Götter im Mittelmeerraum* (Worms, Germany: Wernersche Verlagsgesellschaft, 2009).

EPILOGUE

1 See R. J. Simon and S. Baxter, "Gender and Violent Crime," in *Violent Crime; Violent Criminals,* edited by N. A. Weiner and M. E. Wolfgang (Newbury Park, Calif.: Sage, 1989), 171–197; Anne Campbell, *A Mind of Her Own: The Evolutionary Psychology of Women,* 2nd ed. (Oxford, UK: Oxford University Press, 2013), particularly chapter 3 on women and their aggression in comparison with men. For recent press about such studies, see Dorian Furtuna, "Homo Aggressivus. Male Aggression: Why Are Men More Violent?," *Psychology Today* (September 22, 2014), https://www.psychologytoday.com/blog/homo -aggressivus/201409/male-aggression; and Ian Hughes, "Why Are Men More Likely to Be Violent Than Women?," *TheJournal.ie* (February 26, 2015), http://www.thejournal.ie/ readme/violence-against-women-1959171-Feb2015/.

2 Roger D. Masters and Frans B. M. De Waal, "Gender and Political Cognition: Integrating Evolutionary Biology and Political Science," *Politics and the Life Sciences* 8, no. 1 (1989): 3–39.

3   The obvious example here is Sheryl Sandberg, *Lean In: Women, Work, and the Will to Lead* (New York: Random House, 2013).

4   See Mari Ruti, *The Age of Scientific Sexism: How Evolutionary Psychology Promotes Gender Profiling and Fans the Battle of the Sexes* (New York and London: Bloomsbury Publishing, 2015).

FURTHER READING AND ESSENTIAL RESOURCES

All of Egypt's female leaders bear the burden of disputed histories. I have included notes in the text only when those disputes are an essential part of my narrative or where further elucidation of the evidence is necessary to understanding my text. Otherwise, I have collected all the resources used to write this book into the following list. Most sources are in English, but I have included essential German and French sources as well. Many are available online. Journal articles can be accessed through online databases, such as JSTOR, available at most research libraries.

GENERAL HISTORICAL RESOURCES—EGYPT AND BEYOND

Kuhrt, Amélie. *The Ancient Near East: c. 3000–330 B.C.* London: Routledge, 1995.

Mann, Michael. *The Sources of Social Power.* Volume 1: *A History of Power from the Beginning to A.D. 1760.* Cambridge, UK: Cambridge University Press, 1986.

Shaw, Ian. *The Oxford History of Ancient Egypt.* Oxford, UK: Oxford University Press, 2003.

Waddell, W. G. *Manetho*. London: W. Heinemann Ltd., 1940.

Wilkinson, R. H., *The Complete Temples of Ancient Egypt*. London: Thames & Hudson, 2000.

———. *The Complete Gods and Goddesses of Ancient Egypt*. London: Thames & Hudson, 2003.

GENDER STUDIES AND WOMEN'S STUDIES

Beard, Mary. *Women and Power: A Manifesto*. London: Profile Books, 2017.

Budin, Stephanie Lynn. *Women in Antiquity: Real Women Across the Ancient World*. New York: Routledge, 2016.

Capel, Anne K. *Mistress of the House, Mistress of Heaven: Women in Ancient Egypt*. New York: Hudson Hills Press with Cincinnati Art Museum, 1996.

DePaulo, Bella. "The Age of Scientific Sexism: How Evolutionary Psychology Promotes Gender Profiling and Fans the Battle of the Sexes," 2015 Review, Psych Central, https://psychcentral.com/lib/the-age-of-scientific-sexism-how-evolutionary-psychology-promotes-gender-profiling-fans-the-battle-of-the-sexes/.

Diamond, Jared. *The World until Yesterday: What Can We Learn from Traditional Societies?* New York: Penguin Books, 2013.

Friedl, Ernestine. "Society and Sex Roles." *Human Nature* (April 1978): 100–104.

Graves-Brown, Carolyn. *Sex and Gender in Ancient Egypt: "Don Your Wig for a Joyful Hour."* Swansea: Classical Press of Wales, 2008.

Holland, Julie. *Moody Bitches: The Truth about the Drugs You're Taking, the Sleep You're Missing, the Sex You're Not Having, and What's Really Making You Crazy*. New York: Penguin Books, 2016.

Ingalhalikar, Madhura, Alex Smith, Drew Parker, Theodore D. Satterthwaite, Mark A. Elliott, Kosha Ruparel, Hakon Hakonarson, Raquel E. Gur, Ruben C. Gur, and Ragini Verma. "Sex Differences in the Structural Connectome of the Human Brain." *Proceedings of the National Academy of Sciences* 111, no. 2 (2014): 823–828.

Masters, Roger D., and Frans B. M. de Waal, "Gender and Political Cognition: Integrating Evolutionary Biology and Political Science." *Politics and the Life Sciences* 8, no. 1 (1989): 3–39.

Nelson, Sarah Milledge, editor. *Women in Antiquity: Theoretical Approaches to Gender and Archaeology*. Lanham, Md.: AltaMira Press, 2007.

Pomeroy, Sarah B. *Goddesses, Whores, Wives, and Slaves: Women in Classical Antiquity*. New York: Schocken Books, 1995.

Robins, Gay. *Women in Ancient Egypt*. Cambridge, Mass.: Harvard University Press, 1993.

Roth, Ann Macy. "Father Earth, Mother Sky: Ancient Egyptian Beliefs about Conception and Fertility." In *Reading the Body: Representations and Remains in the Archaeological Record*, edited by Alison Rautmann, 187–201. Philadelphia: University of Pennsylvania Press, 2000.

Tyldesley, Joyce. *Chronicle of the Queens of Egypt: From Early Dynastic Times to the Death of Cleopatra*. London: Thames & Hudson, 2006.

Vivante, Bella. *Women's Roles in Ancient Civilizations: A Reference Guide*. Westport, Conn.: Greenwood, 1999.

Ziegler, Christine. *Queens of Egypt: Hetepheres to Cleopatra*. Paris: Somogy Art Publishers, 2008.

Egyptian Literature in English Translation

Breasted, James Henry. *Ancient Records of Egypt,* volumes 1–5. Chicago: University of Chicago Press, 1906. https://archive .org/details/BreastedJ.H.AncientRecordsEgyptAll5Vols1906.

Lichtheim, Miriam. *Ancient Egyptian Literature.* Volume I: *The Old and Middle Kingdoms.* Berkeley: University of California Press, 1975.

———. *Ancient Egyptian Literature.* Volume II: *The New Kingdom.* Berkeley: University of California Press, 1976.

———. *Ancient Egyptian Literature.* Volume III: *The Late Period.* Berkeley: University of California Press, 1980.

Parkinson, R. B. *The Tale of Sinuhe and Other Ancient Egyptian Poems, 1940–1640 BC.* Oxford, UK: Oxford University Press, 1997.

Merneith

Albert, Jean-Pierre. *Le Sacrifice Humain, en Egypte Ancienne et Ailleurs.* Paris: Soleb, 2005.

Campbell, Roderick, editor. *Violence and Civilization: Studies of Social Violence in History and Prehistory.* Joukowsky Institute Publication. Oxford, UK: Oxbow Books, 2014.

Emery, Walter B. *Excavations at Saqqara: Great Tombs of the First Dynasty.* Oxford, UK: Oxford University Press, 1954.

Kaiser, Werner. "Zur Südausdehnung der Vorgeschichtilchen Deltakulturen und zur Frühen Entwicklungbin Oberägypten." *Mitteilungen des Deutschen Archäologischen Instituts Abteilung Kairo 41* (1985): 61–87.

Keita, S. O. Y., and A. J. Boyce. "Variation in Porotic Hyperostosis in the Royal Cemetery Complex at Abydos, Upper Egypt: A Social Interpretation," *Antiquity* 80, no. 307 (2015): 64–73.

Morris, Ellen. "On the Ownership of the Saqqara Mastabas and the Allotment of Political and Ideological Power at the Dawn of the State." In *The Archaeology and Art of Ancient Egypt: Essays in Honor of David O'Connor*, edited by Zahi Hawass and Janet Richards, 171–190. Cairo: American University in Cairo Press, 2007.

———. "Sacrifice for the State: First Dynasty Royal Funerals and the Rites at Macramallah's Rectangle." In *Performing Death: Social Analyses of Funerary Traditions in the Ancient Near East and Mediterranean*, edited by Nicola Laneri, 15–38. Chicago: University of Chicago Press, 2007.

———. "(Un)Dying Loyalty: Meditations on Retainer Sacrifice in Ancient Egypt and Elsewhere." In *Violence and Civilization: Studies of Social Violence in History and Prehistory*, edited by Roderick Campbell, 61–93. Joukowsky Institute Publication. Oxford, UK: Oxbow Books, 2014.

Pätznick, Jean-Pierre. "Meret-Neith: In the Footsteps of the First Woman Pharaoh in History." In *Egypt 2015: Proceedings of the Seventh European Conference of Egyptologists (2nd-7th June 2015, Zagreb, Croatia)*, edited by Mladen Tomorad and Joanna Popielska-Grzybowska, 289–306. Oxford, UK: Archeopress Egyptology, 2017.

Petrie, W. M. Flinders. *The Royal Tombs of the First Dynasty, Part I*. London: Gilbert & Rivington, 1900.

———. *The Royal Tombs of the Earliest Dynasties, Part 2*. London: The Egypt Exploration Fund, 1901.

Porter, Anne M., and Glenn M. Schwartz, editors. *Sacred Killing: The Archaeology of Sacrifice in the Ancient Near East*. Winona Lake, Ind.: Eisenbrauns, 2012.

Raffaele, Francesco. "Late Predynastic and Early Dynastic Egypt." Last modified 2017. http://www.xoomer.alice.it/francescoraf/index.htm.

Spencer, A. J. *Early Egypt: The Rise of Civilisation in the Nile Valley.* London: British Museum Press, 1993.

Teeter, Emily, editor. *Before the Pyramids: The Origins of Egyptian Civilization.* Chicago: Oriental Institute of the University of Chicago, 2011.

Van Dijk, Jacobus. "Retainer Sacrifice in Egypt and Nubia." In *The Strange World of Human Sacrifice,* edited by Jan N. Bremmer, 135–155. Leuven, Belgium: Peeters, 2007.

Wilkinson, Toby A. H. *Early Dynastic Egypt.* London: Routledge, 1990.

Neferusobek

Aufrere, Sydney. "Remarques sur la Transmission des Noms Royaux par les Traditions Orale et Écrite." *Bulletin de l'Institut Français d'Archéologie Orientale* 89 (1989): 1–14.

Budka, Julia. "Amen-Em-Hat IV, Neferu-Sobek und das Ende des Mittleren Reiches." *Kemet* 9, no. 3 (2000): 16–19.

Callender, V. *In Hathor's Image: The Wives and Mothers of Egyptian Kings from Dynasties I–IV.* Prague: Czech Institute of Egyptology, 2011.

Callender, V. G. "Materials for the Reign of Sebekneferu." In *Proceedings of the Seventh International Congress of Egyptologists, Cambridge, 3–9 September 1995,* edited by C. J. Eyre. Leuven, Belgium: Peeters, 1998.

De Putter, Thierry. "Les Inscriptions de Semna et Koumma (Nubie): Niveaux de Crues Exceptionnelles ou d'un Lac de

Retenue Artificiel du Moyen Empire?" *Studien zur Altägyptischen Kultur* 20 (1993): 255–288.

Fay, Biri, Rita E. Freed, Thomas Schelper, and Friederike Seyfried. *Neferusobek Project: Part I.* Volume I: *The World of Middle Kingdom Egypt (2000–1550 BC)*, edited by Gianluca Miniaci and Wolfram Grajetzki. London: Golden House Publications, 2015.

Habachi, Labib. "Khatâ'na-Qantîr: Importance." *Annales du Service des Antiquités de l'Égypte* 52 (1954): 443–559.

Laboury, Dimitrí. "Citations et Usages de l'Art du Moyen Empire à l'Époque Thoutmoside." In *Vergangenheit und Zukunft: Studien zum historischen Bewusstsein in der Thutmosidenzeit*, edited by Susanne Bickel, 11–28. Basel, Switzerland: Schwabe Verlag Basel, 2013.

Leprohon, Roland J. "The Programmatic Use of the Royal Titulary in the Twelfth Dynasty." *Journal of the American Research Center in Egypt* 33 (1996): 165–171.

Murnane, William J. "Ancient Egyptian Coregencies." *Studies in Ancient Oriental Civilization* 40 (1977).

Petrie, W. M. Flinders, G. A. Wainwright, and E. Mackay. *The Labyrinth Gerzeh and Mazghuneh*. London: School of Archaeology in Egypt, University College, 1912.

Ryholt, Kim. *The Political Situation in Egypt during the Second Intermediate Period, c. 1800–1550 B.C.* Carsten Niebuhr Institute Publications. Copenhagen: Museum Tusculanum Press, 1997.

———. "The Late Old Kingdom in the Turin King-List and the Identity of Nitocris." *Zeitschrift für Ägyptische Sprache und Altertumskunde* 127 (2000): 87–100.

———. "The Turin King-List." *Ägypten und Levante* 14 (2004): 135–155.

Shaw, Ian. "The Gurob Harem Palace Project, Spring 2012." *Journal of Egyptian Archaeology* 98 (2013): 43–54.

Theis, Christoffer. "Die Pyramiden Der 13. Dynastie." *Studien zur Altägyptischen Kultur* 38 (2009): 311–342.

Weinstein, J. M. "A Statuette of the Princess Sobekneferu at Tell Gezer." *Bulletin of the American Schools of Oriental Research* 213 (1973): 49–57.

HATSHEPSUT

Ayad, Mariam F. *God's Wife, God's Servant: The God's Wife of Amun.* London and New York: Routledge, 2009.

Carter, Howard. "A Tomb Prepared for Queen Hatshepsut and Other Recent Discoveries at Thebes." *Journal of Egyptian Archaeology* 4, nos. 2/3 (1917): 107–118.

Cline, Eric, and David O'Connor, eds. *Thutmose III: A New Biography.* Ann Arbor: University of Michigan Press. 2006.

Cooney, Kara. *The Woman Who Would Be King: Hatshepsut's Rise to Power in Ancient Egypt.* New York: Broadway Books, 2015.

Davies, Vanessa. "Hatshepsut's Use of Tuthmosis III in Her Program of Legitimation." *Journal of the American Research Center in Egypt* 41 (2004): 55–66.

Dorman, Peter F. *The Monuments of Senenmut.* London: Kegan Paul International, 1988.

Galán, José M., Betsy M. Bryan, and Peter F. Dorman, editors. *Creativity and Innovation in the Reign of Hatshepsut.* Papers from the Theban Workshop 2010. *Studies in Ancient Oriental Civilization* 69 (2014): Chicago: The Oriental Institute.

Leser, Karl H. "Maat-ka-re Hatshepsut." Last modified 2013. http://www.maat-ka-ra.de/english/start_e.htm.

Mironova, Alexandra V. "The Relationship between Space and Scenery of an Egyptian Temple: Scenes of the Opet Festival and the Festival of Hathor at Karnak and Deir El-Bahari under Hatshepsut and Thutmose III." *MOSAIK,* no. 1 (2010): 279–330.

Paneque, Christina Gil. "The Official Image of Hatshepsut during the Regency: A Political Approximation to the Office of God's Wife." *Trabajos de Egiptologa* 2 (2003): 83–98.

Pinkowski, Jennifer. "Egypt's Ageless Goddess." *Archaeology* 59, no. 5, https://archive.archaeology.org/0609/abstracts/mut.html.

Roehrig, Catharine H., editor. *Hatshepsut: From Queen to Pharaoh.* New Haven, Conn.: Yale University Press, 2006.

Ryholt, Kim. "The Turin King-List." *Ägypten und Levante* 14 (2004): 135–155.

Szafranski, Zbigniew E. "Deir El-Bahari: Temple of Hatshepsut." *Polish Archaeology in the Mediterranean* 16 (2005): 93–104.

Warburton, David A. *Architecture, Power and Religion: Hatshepsut, Amun & Karnak in Context.* Zurich: LIT Verlag, 2012.

Wysocki, Z. "The Upper Court Colonnade of Hatshepsut's Temple at Deir El-Bahari." *Journal of Egyptian Archaeology* 66 (1980): 54–69.

NEFERTITI

Allen, James P. "Causing His Name to Live: Studies in Egyptian Epigraphy and History in Memory of William J. Murnane." In *Culture and History of the Ancient Near East,* edited by Peter J. Brand and Louise Cooper, 9–20. Leiden, Netherlands: Brill, 2009.

Arnold, Dorothea, J. P. Allen, and L. Green. *The Royal Women of*

Amarna: Images of Beauty from Ancient Egypt. New York: Metropolitan Museum of Art, distributed by Harry N. Abrams, 1996.

Bryan, Betsy M. "The Statue Program for the Mortuary Temple of Amenhotep III." In *The Temple in Ancient Egypt,* edited by Stephen Quirke, 57–81. London: British Museum Press, 1997.

Dodson, A. *Amarna Sunset: Nefertiti, Tutankhamun, Ay, Horemheb, and the Egyptian Counter-Reformation.* Cairo and New York: The American University in Cairo Press, 2009.

Harris, J. R. "Nefernerferuaten." *Göttinger Miszellen* 4 (1973): 15–17.

———. "Nefertiti Rediviva." *Acta Orientalia* 35 (1973): 5–13.

———. "Akhenaten or Nefertiti?" *Acta Orientalia* 38 (1977): 5–10.

Hawass, Zahi, Yehia Z. Gad, and Somaia Ismail, "Ancestry and Pathology in King Tutankhamun's Family." *Journal of the American Medical Association* 303, no. 7 (2010): 638–647.

Laboury, Dimitri. *Akhenaton and Ancient Egypt in the Amarna Era.* Cambridge, UK: Cambridge University Press, 2017.

Moran, W. L. *The Amarna Letters.* Baltimore: Johns Hopkins University Press, 1992.

Murnane, William J. *Texts from the Amarna Period in Egypt.* Writings from the Ancient World Series, edited by Edmund S. Meltzer. Atlanta: Society of Biblical Literature, 1995.

Reeves, Nicholas. *Akhenaten: Egypt's False Prophet.* London: Thames & Hudson, 2001.

———. *The Burial of Nefertiti?* Amarna Royal Tombs Project. Valley of the Kings Occasional Paper No. 1. Tucson: University of Arizona Egyptian Expedition, 2015. http://www.factum-arte.com/resources/files/ff/publications_PDF/The_Burial_of_Nefertiti_2015.pdf.

Stevens, A. *The Archaeology of Amarna*. Oxford, UK: Oxford Handbooks, 2015.

Stevens, Anna, Gretchen Dabbs, and Jerome Rose. "Akhenaten's People: Excavating the Lost Cemeteries of Amarna." *Current World Archaeology*, no. 78 (2016): 14–21.

Stevens, Anna, Mary Shepperson, and Anders Bettum. "The Cemeteries of Amarna." *Journal of Egyptian Archaeology* 101 (2015): 17–35.

Tyldesley, Joyce. *Nefertiti's Face: The Creation of an Icon*. Cambridge, Mass.: Harvard University Press, 2018.

Williamson, Jacquelyn. "Alone Before the God: Gender, Status and Nefertiti's Image." *Journal of the American Research Center in Egypt* 51 (2015): 179–192.

TAWOSRET

Altenmüller, Hartwig. "Tausret und Sethnacht." *Journal of Egyptian Archaeology* 68 (1982): 107–115.

———. "Das Präsumptive Begräbnis des Siptah." *Studien zur Altägyptischen Kulture*, 23 (1996): 1–9.

———. "The Tomb of Tausert and Setnakht." In *Valley of the Kings*, edited by Kent R. Weeks, 222–231. New York: Friedman/Fairfax Publishers, 2001.

———. "Tausrets Weg zum Königtum: Metamorphosen einer Königin." *Das Königtum der Ramessidenzeit, Akten des 3. Symposiums zur Ägyptischen Königsideologie in Bonn, 7–9.6.2001. Ägypten und Altes Testament*, 36, 3 (2003): 109–128.

———. "Das Bekenntnis der Großen Königlichen Gemahlin Tausret zu Sethos II. Noch einmal zu den Sarkophagen des

Amunherchopeschef und des Mentuherchopeschef aus KV 13." In *Weitergabe: Festschrift für Ursula Rößler-Köhler zum 65. Geburtstag*, edited by Ludwig D. Morenz and Amr El Hawary, 15–26. Wiesbaden, Germany: Harrassowitz Verlag, 2015.

Bakry, Hassan S. K. "The Discovery of a Statue of Queen Twosre (1202–1194? B.C.) at Madinet Nasr, Cairo." *Rivista degli Studi Orientali* 46, nos. 1/2 (1971): 17–26.

Beckerath, J. von. "Queen Twosre as Guardian of Siptah." *Journal of Egyptian Archaeology* 48 (1962): 70–74.

Callender, Vivienne G. "Queen Tausret and the End of Dynasty 19." *Studien zur Altägyptischen Kultur* 32 (2004): 81–104.

———. "The Cripple, the Queen and the Man from the North." *KMT* 17, no. 1 (2006): 52.

Cline, Eric. *1177 B.C.: The Year Civilization Collapsed*. Princeton, N.J.: Princeton University Press, 2014.

Cline, Eric, and David O'Connor, editors. *Mysterious Lands*. London: University College London Press, 2003.

Creasman, Pearce Paul. *Archaeological Research in the Valley of the Kings and Ancient Thebes: Papers Presented in Honor of Richard H. Wilkinson*. Tucson: University of Arizona Egyptian Expedition, 2013.

———. "Excavations at Pharaoh-Queen Tausret's Temple of Millions of Years: 2012 Season." *Journal of the Society for the Study of Egyptian Antiquities* XXXIX (2013).

Creasman, Pearce Paul, Rebecca Caroli, Tori Finlayson, and Bethany Becktell. "The Tausret Temple Project: 2014 Season." *Ostracon* 25 (2014): 3–13.

Creasman, Pearce Paul, W. Raymond Johnson, J. Brett McClain, and Richard H. Wilkinson. "Foundation or Completion? The

Status of Pharaoh Queen Tausret's Temple of Millions of Years." *Near Eastern Archaeology* 77, no. 4 (2014): 274–283.

D'Amato, R., and A. Salimbeti. *The Sea Peoples of the Mediterranean Bronze Age 1450–1100 B.C.* London: Osprey, 2015.

Dodson, Aidan. "Messuy, Amada, and Amenmesse." *Journal of the American Research Center in Egypt* 34 (1997): 41–48.

———. "The Decorative Phases of the Tomb of Sethos II and Their Historical Implications." *Journal of Egyptian Archaeology* 85 (1999): 131–142.

———. *Poisoned Legacy: The Fall of the Nineteenth Egyptian Dynasty.* Cairo: The American University in Cairo Press, 2016.

Drenkhahn, R. *Die Elephantine-Stele des Sethnacht und ihr historischer Hintegrund.* Volume 36: Ägyptologische Abhandlungen. Wiesbaden, Germany: Harrassowitz Verlag, 1980.

Freu, Jacques. "La Tablette RS 86.2230 et la Phase Finale du Royaume d'Ugarit." *Syria* 65, nos. 3/4 (1988): 395–398.

Gilmour, Garth, and Kenneth A. Kitchen. "Pharaoh Sety II and Egyptian Political Relations with Canaan at the End of the Late Bronze Age." *Israel Exploration Journal* 62, no. 1 (2012): 1–21.

Grandet, Pierre. "L'Execution du Chancelier Bay. O. IFAO 1864." *Bulletin de L'Institut Français d'Archéologie Orientale* 100 (2000): 339–345.

Kitchen, K. A. *Pharaoh Triumphant: The Life and Times of Ramesses II.* Warminster, UK: Aris & Phillips Classical Texts, 1983.

Lesko, Leonard H. "A Little More Evidence for the End of the Nineteenth Dynasty." *Journal of the American Research Center in Egypt* 5 (1966): 29–32.

McCarthy, Heather Lee. "Rules of Decorum and Expressions of

Gender Fluidity in Tawosret's Tomb." In *Sex and Gender in Ancient Egypt: "Don Your Wig for a Joyful Hour,"* edited by Carolyn Graves-Brown, 83–113. Swansea: Classical Press of Wales, 2008.

Simon-Boidot, Claire. "Canon et Étalon dans la Tombe de Taousret." *Chronique d'Égypte* LXXV, 149 (2000): 30–46.

Wilkinson, Richard H., ed. *Temple of Tausret: The University of Arizona Egyptian Expedition Tausret Temple Project, 2004–2011.* Tucson: University of Arizona Egyptian Expedition, 2011.

———. *Tausret: Forgotten Queen and Pharaoh of Egypt.* New York: Oxford University Press, 2012.

Yurco, Frank J. "Was Amenmesse the Viceroy of Kush, Messuwy?" *Journal of the American Research Center in Egypt* 34 (1997): 49–56.

CLEOPATRA

Ager, Sheila L. "The Power of Excess: Royal Incest and the Ptolemaic Dynasty." *Anthropologica* 48, no. 2 (2006): 165–186.

———. "Marriage or Mirage? The Phantom Wedding of Cleopatra and Antony." *Classical Philology* 108, no. 2 (2013): 139–155.

Ashton, Sally Ann. *Cleopatra and Egypt.* Oxford, UK: Wiley-Blackwell, 2008.

Brown, Pat. *The Murder of Cleopatra: History's Greatest Cold Case.* New York: Prometheus Books, 2013.

Burstein, Stanley M. *The Reign of Cleopatra.* Westport, Conn.: Greenwood Press, 2004.

Chauveau, Michel. *Cleopatra: Beyond the Myth.* Ithaca, N.Y.: Cornell University Press, 2002.

Goldsworthy, Adrian. *Antony and Cleopatra.* London: Weidenfeld & Nicholson, 2010.

Hölbl, Günther. *A History of the Ptolemaic Empire*. London: Routledge, 2001.

Jones, Prudence J. *Cleopatra: A Sourcebook*. London: Haus Publishing, 2006.

Kleiner, Diana E. E. *Cleopatra and Rome*. Cambridge, Mass.: Belknap Press of Harvard University Press, 2005.

Lange, Carsten Hjort. "The Battle of Actium: A Reconsideration." *Classical Quarterly* 61, no. 2 (December 2011): 608–623.

MacLachlan, Bonnie. *Women in Ancient Rome: A Sourcebook*. London: Bloomsbury Academic, 2013.

Manning, J. G. *The Last Pharaohs: Egypt under the Ptolemies, 305–30 BC*. Princeton, N.J.: Princeton University Press, 2009.

Miller, Ron, and Sommer Browning. *Cleopatra*. New York: Chelsea House Publishers, 2008.

Plutarch. "The Life of Antony." In *The Parallel Lives*. Cambridge, Mass.: Loeb Classical Library Edition. 1920.

Pomeroy, Sarah B. *Women in Hellenistic Egypt: From Alexander to Cleopatra*. New York: Schocken Books, 1984.

Roller, Duane W. *Cleopatra: A Biography*. New York: Oxford University Press, 2011.

Royster, Francesca T. *Becoming Cleopatra: The Shifting Image of an Icon*. New York and London: Palgrave Macmillan, 2003.

Schiff, Stacy. *Cleopatra: A Life*. New York: Little, Brown and Company, 2011.

Sheppard, Si. *Actium 31 BC: Downfall of Antony and Cleopatra*. Oxford, UK: Ilios Publishing, 2009.

Tyldesley, Joyce. *Cleopatra: Last Queen of Egypt*. London: Profile Books, 2008.

INDEX

ABOUT THE AUTHOR

Kara Cooney is a professor of Egyptology at UCLA. Specializing in social history, gender studies, and economies in the ancient world, she received her PhD in Egyptology from Johns Hopkins University. In 2005, she was co-curator of *Tutankhamun and the Golden Age of the Pharaohs* at the Los Angeles County Museum of Art. Cooney produced a comparative archaeology television series, titled *Out of Egypt*, which aired in 2009 on the Discovery Channel and is available online via YouTube and Amazon.

The Woman Who Would Be King: Hatshepsut's Rise to Power in Ancient Egypt, Cooney's first trade book, was released in 2014 and draws on her expert perspective on Egypt's ancient history to craft an illuminating biography of its least well-known female king.

Cooney's current research in coffin reuse, primarily focusing on the Bronze Age Collapse during Egypt's 20th and 21st Dynasties, is ongoing. Her research provides an up-close look at the socioeconomic and political turmoil that affected even funerary and burial practices in ancient Egypt. This project has taken her around the world over the span of 10 years to study and document nearly 300 coffins in various collections, including those in Cairo, London, Paris, Turin, Berlin, Brussels, New York, Vienna, Florence, and Vatican City. Her book *Recycling For Death* will be published in 2021.